# ALSO BY DAVID J. SILBEY

*A War of Frontier and Empire:*

*The Philippine-American War, 1899–1902*

# THE
# BOXER REBELLION
## AND THE
# GREAT GAME IN CHINA

# THE
# BOXER REBELLION
## AND THE
# GREAT GAME IN CHINA

## DAVID J. SILBEY

🅗 HILL AND WANG
A DIVISION OF FARRAR, STRAUS AND GIROUX
NEW YORK

Hill and Wang
A division of Farrar, Straus and Giroux
18 West 18th Street, New York 10011

A portion of this book originally appeared, in somewhat
different form, in *MHQ: The Quarterly Journal of Military History*.

Library of Congress Cataloging-in-Publication Data
Silbey, David.
    The Boxer Rebellion and the great game in China / David J. Silbey.
       p.   cm.
    ISBN 978-0-8090-9477-6 (cloth : alk. paper)  1. China—History—
Boxer Rebellion, 1899–1901.  2. Europeans—China—History.
3. Americans—China—History.    I. Title.

DS771.S55 2012
951'.035—dc23

                                                    2011036619


Designed by Jonathan D. Lippincott

www.fsgbooks.com

1   3   5   7   9   10   8   6   4   2

# FOR MARI

# CONTENTS

# THE
# BOXER REBELLION
## AND THE
# GREAT GAME IN CHINA

# INTRODUCTION: A MORNING WALK

In early summer 1900, Roger Keyes went for a walk. He was a lieutenant commander of the Royal Navy and, by grace of Queen Victoria and God, the captain of Her Majesty's ship *Fame*. He was in China, around the globe from his home country, and it was a beautifully warm day. There seemed little reason why he, and thirty-two of his sailors, might not go for a stroll along the riverfront near Dagu.

If, Keyes thought, he and his heavily armed men happened upon the Chinese arsenal that he had earlier discovered, well, it would be simple good luck. There was no way that his admiral, James A. T. Bruce, could criticize him for such an encounter. After all, he was, as the admiral had ordered, keeping his ship well back from danger. He had carefully moored it just over a mile away, exactly Bruce's prescription. He and the admiral's post-captain, George Warrender of the HMS *Barfleur*, had scouted the arsenal the previous day. Keyes had been cautious with the post-captain to make sure that "Warrender should not see the fort itself," as it looked "unpleasantly formidable with its modern 6-inch guns."[1] Keyes kept that to himself, and Warrender approved the suggestion that Keyes come back by himself to reconnoiter further the next day.

The arsenal controlled the river between Dagu and Tianjin, a supply line absolutely critical to the British and the multitude of other nations whose ships currently sat in the Bohai Sea, off the China coastline. That fleet had just successfully captured the forts protecting the Dagu River mouth, and now it was the only thing preventing them from reestablishing contact with the besieged foreign enclaves inland at Tianjin, saving a mixed Western force that had gotten hopelessly bogged down north of that city, and ultimately relieving the Western legations in Beijing itself, under attack by not only the army of the throne of China but also the countless numbers of a mystical Chinese sect called the Boxers.

So, Roger Keyes went for a walk. He headed directly toward the arsenal that had "tormented" him for days. Local Chinese had insisted that it was unoccupied, and Keyes, whatever he confessed to Warrender or Bruce or later in his memoirs, intended to try to take it. It was a breathtaking bit of audacity from the twenty-seven-year-old lieutenant commander. Even more breathtaking, it worked.

As Keyes and his men approached, there was no reaction from the fort, and no one seemed to be occupying the walls. Even better, the front gate stood open. Keyes led his men at a trot through the gate and discovered that the fort had been abandoned. Suddenly, much to the young officer's surprise, he found himself the owner of one slightly used Chinese fortress. Two things confounded him at that moment. First, he did not have enough men to hold the fort, and leaving it to gather more risked giving the Chinese time to reoccupy. Second, and worse, was how to explain to the admiral that his innocent walk had turned into a full-scale assault.

Keyes was undaunted. If the British could not have the fort, then neither could the Chinese. He quickly set his men to spiking the guns they found, and he himself put together a fuse leading into the magazine of the arsenal, heavy with gunpowder and shot. Guns crippled, he sent his men out and then lit the fuse, leaving the fort at a dead sprint to beat the explosion. That explosion was, Keyes would write later, "very severe."[2] This was something of an understatement, as the sound of the blast reached to the fleet sitting offshore and sent a black plume of smoke into the sky that could be seen for miles.

Getting back to the *Fame*, Keyes wrote his report to Admiral Bruce. "Acting in accordance with your order . . . to reconnoiter, and if possible destroy all munitions of war in the Hsin Chieng fort," Keyes started, and then explained the day's events.[3] Bruce, upon reading this, may well have choked on his coffee, as he had distinctly not given any such order to Keyes, most especially the latter part. But he could hardly punish success, and so the admiral, showing a remarkable tolerance for the headstrong officer, merely forwarded Keyes's report to the British Admiralty with his own note that the "fort commanded the river, and it is most important that it should have been destroyed."[4]

And he was right, for Keyes had opened up the route to Tianjin and beyond. It was the kind of imperial buccaneering that marked the entire summer of 1900, representatives of the various empires taking it upon themselves to act aggressively and on their own initiative. Empire creating itself on the scene, and to the surprise of the mother country. This book is the story of that larger conflict of 1900, one in which the government and people of China took on the assembled forces of the world's empires, young and old. The war was called different names: the Boxer Revolution, by many in the West; the Boxer Uprising, by Mao Zedong; or the Third China War, by the British. Whatever its name, it was a global event, a war of ancient powers and a war of modern ones, a war of people and a war of governments, a war of religion and a war of conquest. It was the last war of an ancient Chinese dynasty and, in fact, the last war of any Chinese dynasty. It was a familiar kind of war to the British and an unfamiliar type to the Americans. It was an important war then, and an important war for any time marked by distant conflicts in places with unfamiliar names.

## 1900

The year 1900 was both beginning and end. It was the end of the nineteenth century and the beginning of the twentieth. It was a year, it seemed to many Americans and Europeans, for looking to the continued march of progress. The Western world had become modern, scientific, and governed by rationality, a smoothly running machine, oiled gears meshing easily to propel it ever forward and upward. Progress was a watchword, not so much sought as assumed.

The truth was not that simple. Chaos was not uncommon in the world of 1900. The final year of the nineteenth century was witness to the rumblings of the tidal shifts that would flood the world and remake it. The old empires—Britain, France, Russia, Austria-Hungary—watched the certainties that had carried them to dominance erode away. The new empires—the United States, Germany, and Japan—fought to gain their rightful places at the imperial table. Even within those empires, conquered peoples were showing a worrying disposition not to remain conquered. In German East Africa, the Germans were fighting a genocidal war against the Hehe. In South Africa, the British were losing a war against the Boers. In the Philippines, the United States was struggling to suppress a Filipino insurgency.

Worse, people at home in these countries were also proving uncooperative. Russia was struggling with a widespread anarchists' movement, a movement that successfully assassinated Czar Alexander II back in 1881. In Britain, waves of industrial unrest unsettled society, and the slow fading of Queen Victoria signaled the end of an era. The United States was still emerging from the aftershocks of the worst depression in its history, which started in 1893 and lasted most of the decade, and struggled with its own unrest, unrest that saw the assassination of three presidents in thirty-six years. In Germany, the passing from the political scene of Otto von Bismarck, the unifier of Germany, created confusion both within Germany and without. The new kaiser, Wilhelm II, built an imperial navy to rival the British, who were not pleased. In France, the Dreyfus affair still split the nation between those who supported the young captain of artillery and those who believed him a spy.

In the Far East, China slipped into chaos in the summer of 1900. Tens of thousands of adherents of a rebellious cult marched on Beijing. The Boxers, as they were dismissively known by the members of the Western embassies in the capital city, wore red sashes and practiced devotions that combined spiritual and physical elements. They believed themselves impervious to physical harm, up to and including bullets. As they moved from town to town, they set up training fields in the public squares and put on recruiting exhibitions for the locals. They usually succeeded in getting a significant number to join, most particularly the young and disaffected. Everywhere they went, they preached ardently against the West, whether it be the Christian missionaries everywhere in China, the Chinese Christian converts, or the Western businessmen who had bankrupted entire sectors of the Chinese economy. They were all foreign, and all enemies.

So, even as in China tradition warred with modernity, at the other end of the globe in Paris tradition and modernity cooperated. The second staging of a revived Olympic Games took place in the summer of 1900, reaching back to renew Europe's links to its historical ancestors. The Olympics took place as part of the 1900 World's Fair, the Exposition Universelle, which was dedicated to showing off the greatest technological and social wonders of 1900. Thus was the ancient and the modern mixed together, with Art Nouveau standing alongside the marathon. The distinction between ancient and modern may have been as much imagined as real—the marathon had not existed in ancient Greece, and "New Art" had deep roots in previous generations—but the world perceived a difference.

That difference, fairly or unfairly, came to dominate understandings of the war in China. It was ancient against modern, barbaric against civilized, decadent against vigorous. That perception was true, but not enough. The Boxer Rebellion was all of those things and more and less. Let us understand how.

# 1

# AN IMPERIAL WORLD, AN IMPERIAL CHINA

Progress came with responsibilities. Western governments and the main share of their people believed firmly that a mandate and requirement of their modernity was to shepherd the more benighted and uncivilized folks into the light of a Christian and scientific world. Rudyard Kipling may have written the poem "The White Man's Burden" to encourage the United States to take the Philippines, but he could have penned it for any Western power. Conquest was for the benefit of the subjugated. They were children to be reared by the benevolent paternalism of their rulers, a "burden" but a loving one, supposedly. There was little to distinguish between benighted peoples, and even the language used about them could be transferred from one imperial holding to another, unaltered. A German play from 1899 about the German base in China started with the line "Here among these Kaffirs," importing whole and without irony the racist language used in South Africa to describe Africans.[1]

The avatar of this rule, sixty-three years on the throne in 1900, was Queen Victoria of Britain. Unmaternal in the black weeds of mourning, worn since the death of her husband, Prince Albert, Queen Victoria was the face of traditional empire, underpinned by the modern strivings of the British state and economy. She was empress of a British dominion that circled the globe. The British bragged aggressively and truthfully that the sun always shone on some part of their imperium.

The beneficence of British sovereignty brought with it the rewards of commerce, technology, law, and good common sense. They did not often inquire of their subjects whether this was actually true, but it was a comforting tale to tell themselves and required only a little blurring of the memories of the uncomfortableness with the American colonists in the previous century. But a rude shock came nearly a century after Yorktown. In 1857, a massive revolt erupted in India. It was of Indian soldiers and civilians alike, and threatened British control of the colony they referred to as the "Jewel in the Crown" of the empire.

Both sides fought the revolt with great brutality. Most notable on the Indian side was the Cawnpore Massacre, at which hundreds of British were slaughtered after surrendering and being promised safe passage. The British matched that brutality on their side in a range of ways, the most remembered of which was the blowing of mutineers from the ends of cannon. In the end, the British successfully suppressed the revolt, though not before thousands had died.

The Indians would come to call this the Great Uprising and identify it as an early upsurge of Indian nationalism, a violent precursor to Gandhi and the Indian National Congress. The British always referred to it as the Sepoy Mutiny, and that sense of an illegitimate resistance to settled and accepted rules stayed with them for the rest of the nineteenth century. The Indians, the British believed, had been junior partners in this great empire, partners with specific rules and responsibilities. Rudyard Kipling's "Gunga Din" epitomized the earlier British sense of a valiant partnership between colonizer and colonized:

Now in Injia's sunny clime,
Where I used to spend my time

A-servin' of 'Er Majesty the Queen,
Of all them black-faced crew
The finest man I knew
Was our regimental bhisti, Gunga Din.[2]

The famous last line of the poem—"You're a better man than I am, Gunga Din!"—spoke of that alliance.

But now the Indians had violated those rules and abrogated those responsibilities by revolting, and the British were shocked by the betrayal. Representative of this vision was the rebellious sepoy, the Indian soldier who, having taken the imperial salt, had slaughtered British women and children. In a sense "The White Man's Burden" espoused the post-mutiny feeling, less of partnership than a stern stewardship of barbaric races:

Take up the White Man's burden—
Send forth the best ye breed—
Go bind your sons to exile
To serve your captives' need;
To wait in heavy harness
On fluttered folk and wild—
Your new-caught, sullen peoples,
Half-devil and half-child.[3]

The difference between "the finest man I knew" of "Gunga Din" and the "Half-devil and half-child" of "The White Man's Burden" was the difference pre- and post-mutiny. Of course, this was the British perception, and what the colonized, the "subalterns," thought of all of this was rarely considered. Amar Singh was a Rajput nobleman and officer in one of the units of the princely states. He spoke of how the British acted: "The Indians are looked upon as inferiors in the scale of humanity . . . however young or junior a British officer may be he always looks down upon the other as an ignorant fellow."[4]

## OTHER EMPIRES

The British had the largest empire, but they were not alone. Other European nations, like France, Russia, and the Netherlands, had sizable empires and enormous captive populations at their beck and call. They, like the British, ruled these lands through a thin skim of their own people living and ruling abroad. These colonial administrators, military and civilian alike, lived their lives abroad, often only rarely coming home to the imperial motherland. "East of Suez," as the British referred to it, was where they grew up, married, raised their children, and controlled the destiny of millions of lives. Despite the barriers of nation, such imperial administrators, whether French, Russian, British, or Dutch, knew one another well. They served together as ambassadors and consuls and liaisons in the cities of empire. They traveled together. They fought together. They shared drinks and dinners in harbors in the Pacific and the Indian Ocean and the Atlantic and the Mediterranean. They spoke one another's languages. Sometimes they slept with one another's wives, or husbands. In many cases they were more familiar with one another than they were with their own relatives back in their home countries.[5]

It is interesting to note that despite such fundamental unfamiliarity with their homelands, they assiduously resisted the impetus to go native, insisting instead on their foundational Britishness, or Frenchness, or Russianness and importing or creating a society in that image wherever they might go. If they could not go to Britain or France or Russia, then Britain or France or Russia would come to them.

But that is too simple. It is not that most pined for the motherland and were prevented from going. Most did not want to go to Britain, or France, or Russia, or any of the other imperial homelands. Their homes were in the empire, and even in retirement that is where they remained. The homeland was never a dream to be sought by these cadres of empire, it was an allegiance of culture and nation, which gave them both shield against the colonized and justification for the colonization. They remained British or French or Dutch even when it might have been decades since they saw Britain or France or the Netherlands.

But again that is too simple. We should not fall prey to the vision of the oblivious colonial administrator, resolutely refusing to understand the people he ruled, unable to speak their language, and insisting on the markers of his own home to the exclusion of all else: roast beef in a land where cows were sacred, to choose a British example. The administrators were smarter than that; they learned the local languages, frequently a number of them. They understood the cultures of their subordinates—sometimes incompletely or not well but often with impressive subtlety. They lived their lives in those cultures, lived their lives with the colonized groups, separated in many ways but intermingled in many others: "intermixture, borrowing, fusion, and appropriation . . . over the course of centuries," as scholars put it.[6] Campaigning in the field did not allow British officers to segregate themselves from their Indian soldiers all that effectively. The distance between British officer and Indian soldier was no wider than that between British officer and British soldier: the distance of command, not incomprehension. "Such a sahib" was a common term of approval, not just from Indian soldier to British officer, but from British officer to British officer.[7] Most important, they lived their lives distant from those making decisions in London, or Paris, or St. Petersburg, and they grew used to measuring the world on the ground and reacting accordingly. That autonomy was, in a sense, what Roger Keyes understood that day in the summer of 1900.

## NEW POWERS

Conspicuously excluded from this imperial adventure were the Germans. Only lately reunified, Germany came to power after much of the world had already been captured, claimed, or otherwise allocated. The Germans certainly aimed to make up for lost time, especially after the fall of Otto von Bismarck, the man most responsible for German unification. Kaiser Wilhelm II, the man who had pushed Bismarck out, lusted for the international respectability that an extensive empire would bring, and lusted too for the navy that would service such an empire. Wilhelm II, striving to live up to the example of his predecessor and with a crippled left arm he felt keenly, strove for respect. That desire had brought him and his country into conflict with the more established powers.

The buildup of the German navy that Wilhelm began in the 1890s badly frightened the British. Their navy, the world's most powerful, was the foundation of their imperial and military power, and also something of a cultural touchstone. The British, always somewhat worried about their power, placed a messianic faith in their Senior Service. Trafalgar Square in the center of London, completed in the 1840s, was the church of that faith, commemorating a battle at which dominion of the seas—or so it seemed—had been won. Admiral Horatio Nelson, alone on his high column, was its Christ. When the Germans began building their own navy, and one that seemed aimed at first equaling and then surpassing the Royal Navy, the British thus felt the threat at a personal and emotional level.

In many ways, this was a familial squabble. By descent, Queen Victoria and her children were more German than they were English, and even the Anglo-Saxons were Germanic in their heritage. Family fights, however, are often the more intense for the blood ties. England and Germany became enemies quickly, and previous enemies became friends. Overcome were generations of British enmity toward France, sidelined were decades of worry about the aggressive Russian bear on the border of British holdings in India. The British began to move closer to those two traditional enemies as a way of counterbalancing the Germans.

Germany was not alone in rudely thrusting itself into the international fray. Two other nations had begun to establish themselves as global powers, one expected, one not. The expected power was the United States. By the middle of the nineteenth century, it was already one of the world's largest economies and on a rapid ascent to global power. The American Civil War interrupted that rise temporarily. It also revealed the potential of American power: by 1865, the American army was the largest and most experienced in the world, one that could intimidate the French into abandoning their machinations in Mexico and force them to leave their puppet emperor Maximilian to be deposed by popular uprising and shot by firing squad. By 1865, the American navy was the most modern and, by sheer count of ships, the largest in the world. It did not have the globe-spanning capabilities of the British, nor the concentration of large ships of the line, but it was enough to make the lords of the British Admiralty look nervously across the Atlantic.

The military power, however, was short-lived. The United States demobilized rapidly after the Civil War, and by the 1870s and 1880s the American army had been reduced to under thirty thousand men and spread in forts throughout the west of the continent. The navy was a shadow of its former self, unable to rival even South American navies, let alone the British. The United States did not particularly care to concern itself with worldly rivalries, focusing instead on recovering from the Civil War, conquering the American West, and surviving wave after wave of industrial revolution. By 1891, the United States was so weak even in its own hemisphere that, humiliatingly, it had to back down in a naval confrontation with Chile.

Even before that climbdown, however, things had begun to shift. The writings of Alfred Thayer Mahan, an American naval officer, had emphasized the way in which a strong navy was critical to being a strong nation. Mahan's views perfectly encapsulated what leaders around the world were coming to believe, and so he became the spokesman for a generation of strategists who insisted on the preeminence of naval power. It is not so much that Mahan created a new way of thinking as that he already crystallized what the leaders and strategists were thinking. Reading Mahan, for them, brought the spark of recognition more than the flash of insight.[8]

One of those who so believed was Kaiser Wilhelm II of Germany, who had Mahan's magnum opus, *The Influence of Sea Power upon History, 1660–1783*, translated into German and stocked his navy's wardrooms with copies. Other believers included many within the U.S. strategic community, like Theodore Roosevelt, who wrote admiring letters to Mahan. The result in the United States (as it was in Germany) was the beginnings of a substantial naval building program, as the United States attempted to take its place among the global powers. Though somewhat interrupted by the massive economic crash of 1893, the United States put together a substantial fleet, the precursor of the navy that would dominate the globe in the twentieth century.

The United States announced its new presence by rudely handling Spain in the Spanish-American War of 1898. Spain was on a long decline from the glories of the sixteenth century, but no one expected America to defeat it with such brutal ease. Suddenly American power had to be taken seriously. Add to that the American acquisition of the Philippines as part of the peace treaty with Spain, and not only was the United States asserting itself in its own hemisphere, but it was projecting power thousands of miles away. Holding the Philippines and, most critically, the deep waters of Manila Bay gave the United States an extremely useful naval base close to one of the last arenas of imperial contention, the as-yet-unconquered Chinese Empire. This was Mahanian power projection at its finest.

The other new power was already close to China. Japan had lately shown itself to be, at the least, a regional power of some import. Brought rudely out of a self-imposed shell by the application of American and British pressure in the 1850s, Commodore Perry's ultimatum from the waters of Tokyo Bay only the most famous example, the Japanese had decided that they did not wish to be dominated by the West. After more than a decade of chaotic political maneuvering and a civil war, the Meiji Restoration of the late 1860s put into place a program of calculated modernization that the ruling class hoped would enable Japan to remain independent of outside domination. In this, many of the Japanese ruling elite patterned themselves on the rise of Bismarckian Germany. The Meiji Constitution was explicitly modeled on the German constitution, with substantial input from a number of German thinkers.[9]

By the 1890s, that plan had essentially succeeded. The coming-out party for the Japanese, as the Spanish-American War was for the Americans, was a surprise victory over the Chinese in the Sino-Japanese War of 1895. The Japanese navy wiped out the Chinese Northern Fleet at the Battle of Yalu on September 17, 1894, much to the shock of everyone, including the Japanese themselves.[10] They ended up winning the war handily and imposing terms on the Chinese. The victory made the Japanese an equal player in the game of empire, the Japanese foreign minister, Mutsu Munemitsu, insisted:

> Victory would enable us to raise the position of our country in the eyes of the nations of the world. The Western Powers would now be compelled to amend

their ill-disposed view that our civilization was merely a skin-deep imitation. With this victory, Japan could no longer be regarded as a mere Far Eastern park known only for its beautiful mountains and rivers; she should now be reckoned with as a definite world power.[11]

The Western powers did not entirely agree. In the racial calculations of the day, driven by a belief in the scientific superiority of Europeans (and even within Europe, of northern Europeans over southern Europeans), the Japanese did not rank with the white races. Their defeat of China, while impressive, had been, as the Europeans saw it, over another inferior race. The victory over the Russians in the Russo-Japanese War of 1904–1905 still lay in the future. As a result, Japan, while a nation to be considered, was still seen as not quite as important a player as long-established European powers, despite Mutsu's assertions.

The clearest example of this sense came in the aftermath of the Sino-Japanese War. The Japanese had taken Taiwan from the Chinese and gained a controlling interest in Korea, but wanted more. The Treaty of Shimonoseki, which ended the war in April 1895, required the Chinese to hand over the Liaodong Peninsula, which had a lovely deepwater harbor. The Japanese aimed to make that harbor the "Gibraltar of the East."[12] Russia, Germany, and France decided quickly that giving the Japanese such a dominating position at the entry to the Bohai Sea was not acceptable. On April 23, the Russian, German, and French ministers called upon the Japanese foreign minister in Tokyo and handed him a document with some friendly advice. "The possession of the Liaodong Peninsula claimed by Japan would be a constant menace to the capital of China, and would at the same time render illusory the independence of Korea; it would henceforth be a perpetual obstacle to the Far East."[13] The implication—as always with such friendly advice—was that the

Japanese had better rethink their decision to take the peninsula. This they did, knowing that they had little chance of standing against the three great powers simultaneously.

Though the Japanese managed to extract a payment from the Chinese government for the return, it was nonetheless a humiliating reminder of the continuing weakness of their position, even after all the modernization.[14] The shock was so profound and enduring that when Emperor Hirohito surrendered to the Americans in August 1945, he invoked the Triple Intervention as having had a similar level of shame for his ancestor. "The decision I have reached is akin to the one forced upon my Grandfather, the Emperor Meiji, at the time of the Triple Intervention. As he endured the unendurable, so shall I, and so must you."[15] It was a remarkable statement of how deeply the embarrassment of 1895 burned itself into Japanese memory.

The Japanese public, which had been "immersed in the intoxicating mood of victory," was appalled. There were waves of public protests, and several people ritually killed themselves in protest. The popular "Song of Diplomacy" epitomized the Japanese public reaction:

In the West there is England
In the North, Russia.
My countrymen, be careful!
Outwardly, they make treaties,
But you cannot tell
What is at the bottom of their hearts.
There is a Law of Nations, it is true,
But when the moment comes, remember,
The Strong eat up the Weak.[16]

The public identified Russia as the ringleader of the intervention and thus the main target of Japan's growing resentment.[17] In the immediate aftermath of the war and the Triple Intervention, the Japanese continued to modernize and expand their military, until by 1898 the defense budget constituted more than 50 percent of all government spending.[18]

Compared with the Chinese and other Asian races, however, the Japanese did well. They were, to invoke Kipling yet again, further "toward the light." The Japanese were disciplined, tidy, and modern. Japan was no longer "an incompetent Asian nation," one observer wrote, but "a formidable foe and a powerful friend."[19] This image extended even into fiction: "The difference between your people," one author had his Western character explain to a Japanese character, "and the Chinese is that you do not adopt, you adapt . . . The Chinese imitate, but do not grasp the reason of a thing. Give me valor and intelligence against mere force and superiority in numbers."[20] Mahan, who had lived in Japan, agreed, saying that the Japanese were "racially Asiatic . . . adoptively European."[21] Some of this perception was undercut by the Japanese massacre of civilians and surrendered Chinese soldiers in Port Arthur during the Sino-Japanese War, but memories of the slaughter faded relatively quickly.[22] Japan had arrived, if not quite all the way.

There was a difficulty for these new powers, however. The world by the 1890s had been largely apportioned among existing empires. The British was the largest, but the French, Dutch, Ottoman, and Russian Empires were substantial as well. The last great splitting up of land for conquest had been the African continent in the mid-1880s. By the end of the century there were few areas left for exploitation. The alternative to finding new lands to take over was to go after the weaker of the old empires and take their colonies away from them, as the United States had done to Spain in its acquisition of Cuba, Guam, Puerto Rico, and the Philippines. But the weaker empires had been losing lands steadily already, and so the pickings were slim.

## AN IMPERIAL CHINA

There was one area still open for conquest in the European minds. In Asia lurked China, with its hundreds of millions of people, ripe for sales, ripe for exploitation, ripe for conquest. The Chinese—the Westerners thought—were decadent, an age-old people of sagging will and power. If the Japanese victory in the Sino-Japanese War showed their vitality, the Chinese loss showed their weakness. Powerful nations circled the incipient Chinese corpse hungrily. Winning China would win markets, and dominance, either continuing or new. As one American observer put it, "On the decision of the fate of China may, perhaps, hinge the economic supremacy of the next century."[23]

The problem, naturally, was that as they eyed China, those empires also had to keep an eye on one another. China was located in a vulnerable geographic spot, close to a number of the empires. It shared borders with the British, Russian, and French Empires. It was a short distance from Japan and the new American possessions in the Philippines. Even the Germans had enough islands in the Pacific to manage a naval presence off the Chinese coastline. The empires scrambled to acquire hunks of China for themselves while trying to stop the other empires from getting there first. European rivalries traveled around the globe and found a home in Asia.

This was nothing new, of course. The European powers had squabbled over hunks of territory for centuries and brought those enmities back home. On the northwest frontier of India, the British and the Russians had long played the so-called Great Game of intrigue and maneuvering. But the cast of players in China was larger and more frantic. This was one of the last targets for conquest, and when China had been apportioned, it would be something of a closing of the imperial frontier.

The Chinese hoped desperately to avoid that conquest. They, for most of the nineteenth century, had been successful in moderating imperial demands on their land. Long practice at negotiating and compromising with central Asian powers and peoples, even their own, had made the Chinese ruling class adept at finding a way through difficulties both internal and external. Sometimes those ways had been expensive and unpleasant, but they had been largely successful at keeping China together and keeping some semblance of a Chinese government in place.

Until the nineteenth century, China had, in fact, been successful at keeping the European powers at a substantial distance and controlling how many inroads they made. The ruling dynasty in the eighteenth century, the Qing, had used the economic resources of a largely peaceful China to mount military expeditions abroad to places like Burma and Nepal and had actually presented a substantial threat to the growth of European power. Unfortunately for the Qing, that internal peace had not lasted, upset by, among other things, the massive explosion in the population of China, which went from approximately 150 million in 1700 to around 350 million a hundred years later.[24] The impressive fertility of the river valleys of China had enabled such growth, but by the beginning of the nineteenth century even good harvests were producing only just enough food to feed the population, and yet the numbers continued to grow, reaching 430 million by the middle of the nineteenth century.

This made the agricultural infrastructure that produced such harvests even more critical, but the government had spent prodigiously mounting its external expeditions, and the result was an ongoing neglect of the dikes and irrigation channels that tamed the droughts and floods to which much of China was prone. Thus, even as the population continued to grow, the system of food production became more and more vulnerable to catastrophes that would either starve the crops of water or inundate them.

In addition, despite the growth in population, not much more land was brought under cultivation during the same period. That meant that there was little room for stable expansion: the generations born in the nineteenth century frequently found themselves with little hope of acquiring land and becoming solid members of the community. Instead, millions became marginalized, useful only as a source of cheap and disposable labor. Failing that, the only recourse for many was to become migrants, searching for work and frequently indulging in banditry on the side. There was so much of the latter that the Chinese started talking of "bandit season" when "nobody dares to go out . . . unless escorted and well armed."[25] The only communities available to these marginalized groups were the so-called secret societies, organizations with vague religious and political ideas and names like the Big Sword Society and the Society of Heaven and Earth. These acted as social groups, mutual-aid societies, and support for both men and women who had little else.

This was a recipe for internal chaos. There was a long tradition of peasant revolts in Chinese history, revolts well remembered by a suddenly restless population.[26] A substantial number of the ruling dynasties of China had been brought down by such revolts, including the predecessor of the Qing, the Ming dynasty. This too was something the peasants remembered. The result was a century of revolution, both large- and small-scale. Most critical of the early internal breakdowns was the White Lotus Rebellion from 1796 to 1804, in which arose a secret society that fomented revolt in several large provinces. The Chinese military had grown complacent about internal threats after a century of relative peace and proved only marginally able to stop the rebellion. The White Lotus Rebellion thus set a precedent of internal revolts that were suppressed only with great difficulty and effort by the government.

Simultaneously, the Chinese discovered that they could no longer resist the West effectively. Aided by the technological leap of the Industrial Revolution, the economic and social recovery after the Napoleonic Wars, and the beginnings of a disciplined nationalism, Western powers like Britain and Russia began putting heavy pressure on the Chinese to open up to trade and make other concessions. Perhaps the most blatantly aggressive of these came in 1839. British shipping of opium to China, which had the salutary effect (from the British perspective) of keeping Indian and Chinese trade in financial balance, had made the Chinese government understandably nervous about a rapidly growing population of addicts. The attempt to stop the British importation of opium failed miserably, however. The British used the ban as an excuse for war, and in the first of the Opium Wars (1839–1842) the Chinese, to their horror, discovered themselves incapable of matching the British militarily. Defeat after defeat eventually led to the Treaty of Nanjing in 1842, which opened five Chinese cities to British merchants, most important Shanghai in the south, and laid a heavy indemnity on the Qing. Thus, even as China dissolved internally, it discovered to its dismay that its external borders, so long essentially inviolate, were now pregnable.

The contradiction of a civilized power forcing an addictive drug upon a decadent country did not escape everyone. The Board of Foreign Missions of the Presbyterian Church, which had just started its missionary efforts in China in the late 1830s, highlighted the strange morality:

> The contraband trade of *opium*, is at this time the greatest barrier to the Gospel in China . . . What a spectacle is presented here! The government of a nation not possessing the Bible, and unblessed by the light of the

Gospel, laboring to protect their people from a moral pestilence, which is carrying dismay and poverty and wretchedness through the land . . . and the merchants of other governments, nominally Christian, employing ships and capital and bribes to force that very evil upon them.[27]

Though the House of Commons in Britain passed a resolution condemning the opium trade in 1843, it was carefully nonbinding, and thus carried no force of law. The reality was that the British were not particularly worried about the potential hypocrisy, and the opium trade flourished.

## THE TAIPINGS

Things in China went from bad to worse. The 1850s witnessed a series of ever more intense uprisings. Nomadic peasant groups in north-central China revolted, as did the Muslim population of the northwest. But most dangerous of all was the Taiping Rebellion (1850–1864), which mixed a confused Christianity, picked up in a muddled way from Western missionaries, with long-standing Chinese beliefs in utopia to create a doctrine that promised both the end of the world and its perfection, possibly at the same time. This was enough to attract millions to the banners of the Taipings, headed by their messianic leader, Hong Xiuquan. Here, it seemed to many, was an explanation for the struggle and difficulty of Chinese life; here, too, was a solution. The Taipings were successful both socially and, shockingly to the Qing, militarily, defeating a series of government armies and establishing a capital for the Taiping Tianguo (Heavenly Kingdom of Great Peace) in Nanjing. It took fourteen years of hard fighting for the Qing to build an army and defeat the Taipings, an effort that was successful in 1864: successful but exhausting. The devastation was immense. Millions died and entire provinces were laid waste to by the fight.

The rebellion provoked within the Qing a desire to understand and correct their own failings. "Self-strengthening," as government leaders called it, would enable the Qing not only to keep the peace but also potentially to ward off the foreign powers. To this end, the Qing began creating government structures to deal with the world as it was, rather than as they wished it. They created an office, the Zongli Yamen, the job of whose members was to liaison with foreign ministers, merchants, and officers. They began to create foreign-language schools to teach Chinese civil servants the languages of outside nations. They began building arsenals and shipyards to make modern, Western-style weapons for the military forces. On the domestic front, the Qing strove to root out corruption among officials, to rebuild the agricultural infrastructure, and to regularize the harvests. They worked to reestablish the role of strict Confucianism in running the country, so as to give a moral foundation to their governance.

Reform was undercut, however, by the conservative tendencies of China's rulers, and the confused situation at the very top of the government. The Xianfeng emperor, Yizhu, had come to the throne in 1850 at age nineteen and had no time to settle in before the outbreak of the Taiping Rebellion. He was generally competent, but nowhere near what was needed to handle a China in flames.

The situation became worse shortly into his reign when the British used a drummed-up pretext to start the Second Opium War (1856–1860) with the Chinese. On October 8, 1856, a ship, the *Arrow*, was boarded by Chinese authorities in Canton to capture two suspected pirates, and the entire crew was arrested and taken off. The ship was Chinese owned and crewed (with the exception of the master, who was Irish) but had been registered with British authorities in Hong Kong. This, supposedly, gave the *Arrow* immunity from the Chinese maritime authorities, though the registration had actually expired at the end of September. The evidence also suggests that the *Arrow* was not flying the British flag in the harbor, as it was the practice of British ships to haul down the Union Jack upon arrival in port. The Irish master was absent, breakfasting with friends on another ship. Nonetheless, the Chinese authorities risked a great deal in taking the crew off the ship after discovering its British registration (even if expired). Still, though their actions may have constituted an "insult of a very grave character," as the local British consul called them, in reality they were simply an easily correctable error on both sides that could have and should have been quickly resolved.[28]

That they were not and that the *Arrow* incident in fact led to a large-scale war between Britain, France, and China had more to do with the continuing aggressiveness of the imperial powers and the hapless chaos of Chinese politics and society. But war it was to be, with the British authorities in Hong Kong accepting the local consul's assertion that the Chinese had cravenly hauled down the Union Jack flying over the *Arrow* in the process of arresting its crew. Oddly, they began military actions before the reports of the incident had even made it back to London. Lord Palmerston, the British prime minister, found himself in a shooting war before the reason for shooting was known.

That is not to say that that government objected, particularly. The Second Opium War (though it had nothing really to do with opium), the *Arrow* War (though the *Arrow* was much more the aggrieving party than the Chinese), or the Second Anglo-Chinese War (which omitted France's role entirely) lasted until 1860. It was not a great success for the Chinese. Initial defeats led to the signing of a series of treaties much in the favor of the Western nations in 1858. Unfortunately for Yizhu, he made the mistake of listening to some of the more aggressive counselors in his court and attempted to back out of some of the pacts almost immediately. This led to the resumption of hostilities and the eventual march of an Anglo-French force on Beijing itself, which it captured easily in late 1860 and then looted with great gusto and no small amount of destruction. Among the treasures destroyed was the Summer Palace of the Chinese emperors, hundreds of years of history, and untold wealth burned over three days by the British soldiers. "Wretchedly demoralizing work for an Army," wrote Charles Gordon, a young British officer who participated.[29]

## CIXI

The emperor was forced to flee into the interior of China, and the strain and stress proved too much. He died in August 1861, leaving the throne to his five-year-old son, Zaichun, conceived with and born to one of his concubines, and a handpicked group of regents. It was not an ideal arrangement, but it soon gave way to something worse. The mother of Zaichun, Lady Yehenara (the name she had been given upon becoming a concubine) or Noble Lady Yi (her name upon birthing the heir to the throne), proved to have both more ambition and smarts than anyone allowed. Through adroit maneuvering, she sidelined—fatally, for some—her main rivals and managed to make herself the dominant power behind the throne.

The newly titled Empress Dowager Cixi was to dominate the next half century of Chinese governance. She could not stop China's decline or even slow it. It is not clear that anyone could have managed the job. China faced a perfect storm of internal and external problems that might well have been beyond the ablest to handle. Nonetheless, Cixi would essentially oversee the end not only of her own dynasty but of dynastic rule in China altogether.

The obvious parallel to Cixi was Queen Victoria of Britain, who ruled for a longer period of time, but began her reign deep in the nineteenth century and finished it near the turn of the twentieth. When she came to the throne, Britain was the dominant global power; by the time she died, Britain was beset. The two, in fact, had some contact, with Victoria writing a letter to Cixi asking the empress dowager to spare the life of a British merchant sentenced to death in a Chinese court, a request Cixi granted. There is even a rumor that Cixi had a portrait of Victoria hung in her rooms in the Forbidden City.[30] She shared some of the same insight and intelligence that marked Victoria, especially in her later years. A Western woman, Maud Ledyard, met Cixi for the first time in 1900 at a court dinner and "saw quickly what makes her the moving power of China . . . it is more her eyes, however, that impress one—full of expression and keenness."[31] Nor was Cixi inherently conservative, at least on a personal level. Ledyard recalled cigarettes being offered to the ladies after dinner.[32] During the uprising itself, some foreigners would refer to the empress dowager as "the only man in China."[33]

Cixi, however, found herself hamstrung by her position. Clearly, she understood the need for reform. The situation hardly allowed for anything else. But that reform had to be managed in such a way so as not to undercut the power of the ruling classes: the Manchu nobility, the Chinese civil servants, and, most critically, the Qing themselves. Worse, because Cixi's position was never entirely legitimate, she remained vulnerable throughout her reign to internal politicking by her rivals and, indeed, her own family. It was a delicate line to walk, and Cixi strayed a number of times.

The result in the 1870s and 1880s was a combination of policies both conservative and progressive. On one hand, for example, the Chinese began to build Western-style military armies, equipped with modern weapons and subject to the more intense discipline of the industrial age. On the other hand, those armies remained under the control of the traditional Chinese nobility and were often used more as political power bases for those generals than as a deterrent to the foreign powers. China's rulers believed they could meld the values of Confucianism with the modernity of the West. As one official said at the time: "Chinese learning for the fundamentals, Western learning for practical applications."[34]

In addition, the Chinese attempted to control and leverage the building of railroads. They wanted the railroads but hoped to avoid the foreign influence that came with them. The Chinese aimed for balance between using the foreign nations to build railways where the Chinese could not afford to and not allowing them to build in ways that would critically damage Qing power. That was the strategy at least. The reality, unfortunately for the Qing, was much more complicated. Building the railroads was not merely a bilateral exercise between China and the given foreign power. Instead, it brought in all the other powers, concerned that one of their compatriots was getting an advantage. The Great Game lived not only in India.

Contributing to their problems, Chinese cultural elites simply did not believe in their own inferiority, and thus often acted from an assumption of equality that no longer existed. In a cultural, racial, and social sense, they were right, of course, but in a military, economic, and industrial sense China had fallen grievously far behind the West and Japan. They were often thus unwilling to sacrifice the symbols of that cultural superiority to focus on ameliorating the economic and strategic ones. For example, in the years running up to the Sino-Japanese War, the government began building a railway line that stretched to the Russian border in Manchuria. This line would have helped enormously on both military and economic levels against the Russians in Manchuria and the Japanese in Korea, but it was nowhere close to being completed when the war started, largely because nearly half of the allotted funds had been diverted to the rebuilding of the Summer Palace.[35] The symbolism was obvious. The British had destroyed the Summer Palace because, at least partly, it represented the power and the majesty of the Chinese Empire. Now that same Chinese Empire was determined to rebuild it, even though doing so undercut the reestablishment of at least some of that power.

The catastrophe of the loss to Japan was enough to make the Chinese rethink their strategy, and it is instructive to look at that defeat, for it illustrated the way in which China was still a substantial player, but also the way in which modernization became an imperial and international issue all its own. In the aftermath of the loss, the Chinese came to believe that they needed a counterweight to the Japanese. The Triple Intervention offered an instructive lesson in the limits of Japanese power and led the Qing to look to the Russians, the local imperial power, as a potential ally. A Sino-Russian alliance was duly signed the next year, with the Chinese giving the Russians essentially a free hand in northern Manchuria and the rights to build a shortcut for the Trans-Siberian Railway across Manchuria to Vladivostok, cutting hundreds of miles off the route.

That left the Chinese railway line through southern Manchuria in abeyance, especially as the government had decided to focus on a Beijing to Tianjin line. Tianjin, although inland, had become a major foreign enclave and, linked by river and rail to the nearest port at Dagu, would give the Chinese much more effective economic access to the world. The Manchuria line could still serve a useful purpose, however, for the Qing. They had recently rejected a British proposal to build a railway between the city of Hankou and Beijing. To alleviate possible British resentment over that rejection, the Qing offered the British a chance to build the southern Manchuria line. The problem—and there were factions within the court who realized this—was that such an offer looked to the Russians as if the Chinese were giving the British a chunk of *their* area, deliberately so, to counterbalance Russian influence. As a result, the Russian finance minister, Sergei Witte, decided to press his case with the Chinese even more sternly. He urged both the Chinese and the British to back away from the agreement. The British refused, with some hostility, and suddenly the Qing found themselves in the middle of an international crisis. Though the two sides backed away from war, the tension remained an issue for the rest of the decade. What had been an attempt at modernization nearly became an international calamity.[36]

But even the shock of the 1895 loss to Japan was not enough to make Cixi and the nobility reform China's government in any meaningful way. Certainly, they avoided anything that would have substantially reduced their power. Things were somewhat different on the level of the provincial governors and other more local officials. They found themselves dealing with Western merchants, soldiers, and missionaries on a daily basis, and that required a fair amount of flexibility and compromise. But at the national level, the imperial government refused, for the most part, to countenance much in the way of change.

The partial exception to this came in 1898. Cixi's nephew and adopted son, the Guangxu emperor, had come to the throne in the 1870s as a young boy. Cixi was regent and, along with the other main power in court, Prince Gong, ruled for Guangxu. As he got older, Guangxu chafed at both the restrictions and conservatism of Cixi's reign. He had long kept company with a coterie of intellectuals from Canton, who advocated rapid reform. In 1898, Prince Gong died, warning his nephew as he died not to trust the "Cantonese scum."[37] Guangxu ignored the warning and, taking advantage of the political confusion caused by Gong's death, tried to set in motion a burst of reforms while plotting to sideline the empress dowager. In this "Hundred Days Reform," memorandum after memorandum emerged from the emperor's court, rewriting the entire structure of Chinese governance and trying to remake Chinese society on the fly.

Unfortunately for both the Guangxu emperor and his reformer allies, Cixi was not interested in being sidelined, and she had the keen political skills of an experienced survivor. Playing on the nervousness of the conservative Manchu nobility and the unease of the Chinese mandarins, both of whom were seeing familiar structures and traditions crumble around their ears, Cixi engineered a political coup that essentially deposed the Guangxu emperor and confined him to his rooms in the Forbidden City: a gilded cage, but a cage nonetheless.

Cixi quickly undid the reforms and executed as many of the reformers as she could find. The smarter among them, upon sensing which way the wind was blowing, fled to whatever foreign enclave they could find in search of safety. In that way, some saved their lives. She aimed to bump off the emperor himself, it seems, preparing the ground by sending out a memorandum to the provincial governors on how terrible his health was and how there was little likelihood of a recovery. The provincial governors hastily wrote back, saying that they would be tragically undone if the emperor was to die. This seems to have been enough of a warning that Cixi decided against Guangxu's ill health proving fatal. Instead, she rehabilitated him and presented to the world that they were co-rulers, although with her senior. This joint leadership was called the "Two Palaces" by senior Chinese officials, and it at least eased the possible political fallout of the coup.[38]

But whatever the perception, Cixi was solidly in charge after 1898, as much as any Chinese ruler jostling amid the ethnic and political factions of court and country ever could be. Substantial reform seemed dead. Conservative elements, Cixi large among them, dominated the court. Cixi even found the courage to reject an Italian demand for concessions in 1899. But while the empress dowager could handily manage an upstart emperor, she soon found that controlling lowly peasants was much more difficult. Reform, violent and unpredictable, was not, it turned out, the preserve of the nobles and royalty. Instead, ordinary Chinese had their own ideas of what should be done. Those ideas, it came to be clear over the next two years, could be summarized by a slogan that hundreds of thousands, if not millions, found attractive: "Support the Qing, exterminate the foreigners."

## 2

# A POPULAR ERUPTION

The slogan belonged to the Yi-he quan, a secret society whose name translated roughly to "Righteous Fists of Harmony" or "Boxers United in Righteousness." Sometimes they were referred to as the Yi-he tuan, the "Militia United in Righteousness," which emphasized an official connection to the Chinese government. Yi-he quan was more accurate, however, given that the relationship of the insurgents to the dynasty was tenuous at best, with suspicion on both sides.

Westerners labeled them the Boxers, and the name stuck. It was not inappropriate, given the emphasis on unarmed forms of combat and the fact that the word "boxers" had been used for similar earlier secret societies. This, even though they did little that resembled what Westerners thought of as boxing. Certainly, the 9th Marquess of Queensberry, who gave his name to the codified rules of boxing and who died on January 31, 1900, just as the Boxer Rebellion was starting to heat up, would not have recognized what the Yi-he quan did. Their martial arts rituals were much more about display, at least at first, than actual fighting.

The Boxers left behind little in the way of direct evidence. Most of them were illiterate. They did not have an overall leader or leaders, though there were local heads. The structure of the society itself was decentralized, and it built up in the form of a network rather than a hierarchy. They did not communicate with each other except in person for the most part, and sometimes the only things that various Boxer groups shared were a slogan, a style of dress, and a commitment to a variety of physical rituals and beliefs. Sometimes they shared not even that.

All this is to say that the origins, actions, and ideas of the Boxers remain shrouded. There is little in the way of inside evidence about their efforts, and their actions were often the result of individual choices that, replicated across hundreds of thousands of Boxers, ended up being group decisions. The foundation of the movement was two allied beliefs. Boxers thought that through a variety of physical and religious rituals they could gain physical invulnerability to harm. These spiritual martial arts, as they could be called, had to be practiced and repeated, publicly and often. Boxer rituals were about display, whether it was to potential recruits or actual enemies: street theater, of a sort. Allied to this was a belief about who was causing the problems of China. Here the Boxers' slogan was clear: "Support the Qing, exterminate the foreigners." The latter part of that phrase could hardly be simpler. It was the foreigners, from the missionaries and railway workers to the soldiers and diplomats, who were responsible for China's plight. The solution was even simpler. The foreigners had to be wiped out. Those following the beliefs were male, though there was a female auxiliary called the Red Lanterns who were reputed to have mystical powers.

That was largely it. The Boxers had a simple set of principles, allied to a basic set of rituals. They had few leaders, and certainly none that were national. They did not have much of a hierarchy. There were individual Boxer units, but they did not normally come together into larger, organized groups. They were a people's organization, in the most grounded sense.[1]

## SHANDONG

To understand the Boxers, we need to get right down into the day-to-day lives of ordinary Chinese to see their beliefs and motivations. These particular Chinese lived in the Shandong Province of northern China. The western border of the province was due south of Beijing, and it stretched irregularly to the coastline, even intruding into the Yellow Sea in the form of the Shandong Peninsula, which, with the similar Liaodong Peninsula to the north, enclosed the Bohai Sea. This gave access to the coastline nearest Beijing and was thus an area of immense concern to Chinese and Westerners alike.

Both the Yellow River and the Grand Canal crossed the province, bringing water, fertile soil, trade, floods, and corruption with them. Along the banks of the Yellow River was some of the richest soil anywhere, and by the late nineteenth century that soil had become one of the most densely inhabited areas in the world. In fact, in Shandong, the Yellow River ran its course above the level of the land itself and required substantial levees to keep it from flooding. These levees were the responsibility of the local officials, and their reputations rose and fell along with the water level.

The Grand Canal, a spectacular feat of engineering, had been built starting in the fifth century B.C. It linked northern and southern China with an avenue of trade and spanned, at its greatest, over a thousand miles. Along its route lived boatmen, merchants, and other groups. In Shandong, it crossed the Yellow River and so was vulnerable to the river's flooding. A massive flood in 1855 had not only altered the course of the Yellow River but severed the Grand Canal in half. That breach was not fully repaired by 1900, and the symbolism of the capital of China being partially cut off from large sections of the rest of the country is too obvious to ignore. Certainly, the cut had profound economic effects on the local inhabitants, many of whom had been economically dependent on the thousands of grain barges coming through Shandong on their way to Beijing.

Still, even by 1855, the canal was beginning to decline in importance as an economic connector. Large amounts of the agricultural product that had previously gone on the canal had started to be shipped by sea. Even more critically, the building of north-south railways had reduced usage.

The railroad, in fact, was remaking China in 1900, in ways both positive and negative. It had enormous advantages. As Ma Jianzhong, a disciple of Li Hongzhang, put it:

> The sheer convenience of railroad transportation has dispelled worries about the effects of floods, drought and banditry . . . Trains travel as fast as lightning or a whirlwind. They can transport huge amounts of material to distant places and cover thousands of *li* as if it were next door . . . There is no other way to establish the basis for wealth and strength than to build railways.[2]

But it also had two disastrous effects, one national and one local. The national effect came from the enormous cost of building railways. The capital necessary could only be raised by the Qing either by taking out loans from Western banks or by giving Western companies the rights to build and run the railways. Both of those effectively handed over China's transportation network to the imperial powers.[3]

The local effect was less obvious but critical to the formation of the Boxers. The coming of the railways put enormous numbers of Chinese out of business. Boatmen or laborers on the canal were simply no longer relevant. Shandong in particular felt this blow keenly. The intersection of the canal and the Yellow River had given the province enormous economic advantages in the previous centuries, economic advantages that

had disappeared by the end of the nineteenth century. The result was substantial dislocation of both people and industries
and the loss of livelihoods for entire generations of locals. This
effect was not a particularly mysterious one, and even Western
observers picked up on it pretty quickly. Wilbur Chamberlin, a
reporter for the New York *Sun*, laid out the situation while waiting in Shanghai in September 1900 to get a boat up to northern
China:

> Everything in China has been done by hand. All the
> carrying has been so done, as well as all the manufactur-
> ing. Now, the foreigners come in and introduce rail-
> roads. Every pound of freight that these railroads carry
> was formerly carried by the Chinese coolies. One rail-
> road takes the place of a thousand or ten thousand coo-
> lies, who have, like their ancestors for generations, been
> carrying freight for a living. These coolies are thrown
> out of employment. Every railroad is carrying passen-
> gers and every passenger carried had formerly to ride in
> hand-drawn contrivances or was carried by coolies. So
> the railroads drive out of business all the Chinese in the
> passenger or freight-carrying business . . . It is not so
> hard to see the cause of trouble when you hunt for it,
> is it?[4]

Chamberlin's analysis was acute. The railway, modern and efficient, was reshaping the Chinese economy and violently dis-
placing thousands, if not millions, from their livelihoods.

Shandong's other great geographic advantage was proving a
mixed blessing in the nineteenth century. Being on the coastline gave its residents easy access to trade with other parts of
China and Korea and to fishing in the Yellow Sea. Like the Yellow River, however, this geographic advantage turned out to
have drawbacks in an imperialist world. The close location of

the Shandong Peninsula to the Bohai Sea, Tianjin, and by extension Beijing, and its proximity to Korea, to the Russian holding at Port Arthur, and to the Yellow Sea and Japan made it attractive as a base for the imperial powers. The British claimed a spot first in the mid-1890s by forcing the Chinese to concede the port town of Weihai at the far end of the peninsula to them to serve as a naval base. The Germans moved shortly thereafter, grabbing Qingdao on the southern coastline of the peninsula as their own base of operations in northern China. This Scramble for Concessions, as it became known, seemed to be leading to the partition of China.

## MISSIONARIES

There were religious frictions as well. "Take away your opium and your missionaries," Prince Gong reputedly said to Sir Robert Hart, the British head of the Chinese Imperial Maritime Customs Service, "and all will be well!"[5] Both the Catholic Church and a range of Christian denominations had long been active in China, sending thousands of missionaries during the nineteenth century and building large organizations within the country. The missionaries worked to convert the local Chinese to Christianity and to provide humanitarian services that they felt lacking. Thus, in addition to proselytizing, the Catholics and Christians established both schools and hospitals. By 1900, the Presbyterian Church alone was operating ten hospitals, 150 schools, and fifty-one churches in China.[6] In Shandong Province, there were fifty-five Christian schools.[7] The number of Chinese converted to Christianity by the Presbyterians went from five thousand in 1864 to fifty-five thousand in 1889.[8]

The missionaries were a curiosity in the rural Chinese society. They were alien in physical appearance, dress, behavior, religion, and custom. Captain H.T.R. Lloyd of the Royal Marine

Light Infantry summed up the reactions to that alienness: "If you go at all far inland the ponies shy and the dogs bark at Europeans." Eva Jane Price, a missionary from Iowa working in Shanxi Province in central China, wrote, "These people have such strange notions about us. They think our eyes are different so that we have the power to see long distances and even into the very earth itself." Price's window was just above the wall of the compound where the missionaries were staying, and the local Chinese, deeply curious, climbed the wall to peer in at her and "look and look until they are satisfied." Shooing them away did not work, so Price quickly learned to "go on with what I am doing" until they left. More came each day, and Price later wrote, "It surely does require a good deal of heavenly grace to enable one to stand it, and my supply has dwindled very low."[9]

There were, however, some similarities in the cultures. When Mary Lane, the mother of William Lane, arrived in Jining, Shandong, along with her son and his wife, she discovered that she had some recognizable status: "Old women hobble about to get a glimpse of me, remarking of [her son's wife], 'Oh, she is all right, she has her mother-in-law with her.' At last, a refuge has been found for that much-reviled class. In far-off China, they will find appreciation and a work to do. Come on, mothers-in-law!"[10]

The missionaries helped the local Chinese societies in a number of ways, aiding with education and medical care, often for marginalized members of society. For example, in 1894, in Shandong the Baptists established a school for girls, a group that traditionally did not get educated.[11] In addition, the missionaries brought with them contacts with the outside world in a kind of "cultural exchange" that benefited the local Chinese.[12]

On the other hand, however, the missionaries created serious disruptions in the local societies, disruptions that led to resentment on the part of a large number of Chinese. Something as simple as the presence and apparent freedom of Western women proved shocking to the Chinese. In some cases, the Chinese simply refused to believe that the missionary women were indeed women. In Xuzhou, in Jiangsu Province, directly to the south of Shandong, the wives of the missionaries were dogged by the rumor that they were men dressed as women for the purpose of luring small children to some unspecified doom. It was not until Nettie Grier breast-fed her child in front of a local woman that the gossip disappeared.

Second on the list of disruptions, the message of the missionaries was essentially one of Chinese inadequacy. Sir Robert Hart, again:

> As for the missionary class, their devotion, zeal, and good works are recognized by all: and yet, while this is so, their presence has been felt to be a standing insult, for does it not tell the Chinese their conduct is bad and requires change, their cult inadequate and wants addition, their gods despicable and to be cast into the gutter, their forefathers lost and themselves only to be saved by accepting the missionary's teaching?[13]

In a cultural sense, then, the missionaries outlined to the Chinese what the West believed about them: that they were backward and uncivilized. This was hardly a message to endear them to many.

Third, the missionaries themselves were essentially exempt from Chinese law. As part of a number of treaties, foreign nationals came only under the law of their home country. They were essentially immune to the power of the Chinese authorities. In Linyi, Shandong, after a legal fracas, the local official printed a declaration announcing the treaty immunity of the missionaries, framed a copy, and hung it at the entry to the Presbyterian mission in the town. The local missionaries felt this was a "conspicuous testimony for the political and diplomatic honor of the Chinese government," perhaps missing the effects on the locals of having such a promulgation of Chinese powerlessness so immediately available.[14] This made them, whether the missionaries wanted it or not, an alternate power structure in the Chinese communities, a power structure that the locals had to deal with, predict, and otherwise watch.

Such immunity made Christianity attractive to a fair number of Chinese for reasons that had nothing to do with religion. Converting to Christianity gave marginalized groups, including criminals, a level of power that they could find nowhere else. Though the Chinese converts were not themselves exempt from Chinese law, they had a powerful ally in the missionaries who were, and who would likely intervene on their side in the case of legal problems. Thus, a bandit could join the Church and gain a certain amount of protection from prosecution for his crimes. Even better, Chinese Christians could enlist the aid of their Church in dealing with lawsuits, a favored and traditional way in Chinese society of settling disputes. "Relying on foreign strength" was the Chinese catchphrase for such behavior, and it was not looked upon kindly.[15]

The leverage that this gave Chinese Christians caused deep resentment among the local inhabitants. The magistrate of Baoding, west of Tianjin, said, "The people were angered by the interference . . . in their lawsuits. They felt that they could not obtain justice."[16] There is a whiff of class warfare going on here: the traditional powers in local societies were not pleased to find their power undermined. Many of the missionaries were aware of the way they were being used. One Jesuit priest remarked that as a result of conversion, some of the Chinese Catholics had "gone from being the oppressed to the oppressors."[17] In 1896, the governor of Shandong, Li Bingheng, wrote a memorial to the throne outlining the issues: "After the Western religion moved into China, the converts are often bad elements without normal professions. They depend on the missionaries to win court cases, or intend to escape the law after committing crimes."[18]

The locals came to believe that they simply had no way of resisting the local churches except through violence. One early example of the ensuing wave of violence came in the 1870s, in Jinan, Shandong. The Presbyterian Church there purchased a building to use as a chapel. The previous place of worship had been outside in front of the missionary's home, uncomfortable except in the most moderate of seasons. The Reverend Jasper S. McIlvaine thought that the new location, directly on the main market street, would be much superior. Unfortunately, it proved too conspicuous for the local Chinese, who seem to have seen it as an overly familiar assertion of the Christian presence. As a result, the building was attacked and knocked down by a mob, and the local missionary was dragged through the streets, saved only by a friendly policeman. The legal entanglement over this situation lasted until 1885, when the American secretary of the legation in Beijing intervened to speed negotiations. The missionaries were given a different, more out-of-the-way location, compensated monetarily, and allowed to continue their mission. The incident reveals clearly the sometimes torturous relationships between the missionaries and the local populace, the ability of foreigners to intervene in local legal matters, and the general difficulties that the Chinese government had in handling such situations.

The missionary stations, in response, fortified themselves to protect against attack. Heavily armed mission houses were not uncommon. A Jesuit station in northern China built around itself moats fifteen to twenty feet wide and ten to fifteen feet deep. Behind those moats was a wall twenty-five feet high mounted with eleven cannon.[19]

## A RELIGIOUS BLITZKRIEG

The problems with missionaries were particularly acute in Shandong. The American Presbyterian Church had its largest missionary presence there, with nearly thirty-eight hundred converts in 1895. The coastline and the imperial stations there gave the churches easy access to the province and enabled them to spread widely. As a result, Shandong found itself overrun by missionaries in the late nineteenth century, much to the inhabitants' resentment.

Particularly aggressive were the Germans. They had established in the province both a naval presence and a religious one, and both were marked by a deeply pugnacious spirit. The head of the local German missionaries, Johann Baptist von Anzer of the Society of the Divine Word, was willing to use whatever levers he needed to spread the Catholic Church throughout Shandong. He was well connected too, being friends with Kaiser Wilhelm II, who called Anzer his "First Courier of Christianity."[20] Anzer, in addition to being militantly Catholic, was militantly German and pushed Germany's interests as much as he did the Catholic Church's. He draped a "huge German flag" from his church steeple, and over the veranda of his house were the Latin words "Vivat, crescat, floreat Germania," which translated as "May Germany live, flourish, and grow." According to a visitor, nationalist songs were frequently sung "enthusiastically."[21]

At the same time, Anzer was not merely simplistically a German nationalist, nor did he remain resolutely a German abroad, refusing to understand or integrate himself into the local culture. He wore Chinese clothing. He ate Chinese food. He learned and spoke Mandarin. One of his overwhelming goals was to get the Chinese government to anoint him officially as a mandarin, something he achieved in 1902.[22] Anzer was one member of that imperial cadre that had spread around the globe, with all its oblivious and subtle features. In his case, in fact, there was some sense of his using Chinese culture as a lever against German culture. Anzer came from a working-class family in Germany. His father was a butcher. Anzer's cultural status in Germany was thus fairly low. Adopting the exotic role of Chinese mandarin gave him a status abroad that he did not quite have at home, a status which then translated back to Germany.

Anzer's aggressiveness was mirrored by German aggressiveness in his support. The Germans saw the missionaries—at least the German ones—as being arms of German expansion and control and were willing to push hard to advance the causes of both. In one incident in 1890, a newly arrived German consul forced his entry into the city of Yanzhou, where the German missionaries had been denied the right to establish a station, and, when the local crowd proved restive, drew his revolver and threatened to shoot the first Chinese to approach him and die rather than retreat. He did not succeed in getting what he wanted, but came close to provoking a riot in the city. In another, the murder of two German missionaries in 1897 led to the Germans demanding and the Chinese agreeing to a lease on the port at Qingdao. Thus did the missionary and national mission come together. Anzer was doing God's work, and the kaiser's.

There are two critical points here, one obvious and one more subtle. The obvious point is that the missionaries, of all stripes, were not particularly discriminating in either their methods or their recruits. The muscular Christianity of the late nineteenth century worried less about the disruption caused in native societies and more about the sheer conversion of Christians. Proselytization was combat, as A.J.H. Moule put it in a missionary conference in Shanghai in 1890: "Is Christ's Church militant indeed on earth? Are we all bound to fight manfully under His banner against sin, the world and the devil? Has the Son of God indeed gone forth to war?"[23] Needless to say, Moule's answer to the questions was affirmative. China, Moule continued, was an "advanced post in an enemy's country."[24] The missionaries—or many of them at least—were at war, and in war there are attacks and casualties and damage. This was religious imperialism, imposition more than conversion.

The more subtle point is that the ordinary people of China, peasants and city dwellers alike, had an enormous number of direct encounters with foreign representatives, missionaries, and members of the military and government. Foreign relations in China were not, as we might tend to assume, the province only of high officials and diplomats. Instead, they were very much the experience of average folk. Chinese in Shandong, as well as elsewhere, could thus be expected to have substantial opinions about foreign countries thousands of miles away, based on the behavior of their local representatives. They could also be expected to have an opinion on how their own government, both local and national, was doing in handling those foreigners.

## ROBIN HOODS

The local people were not shy about registering their displeasure with both foreigners and local officials. The people of Shandong had the reputation of being "warlike, industrious, and intelligent," as one Western observer put it. Both the Chinese army and the Chinese navy recruited there heavily because of those perceived qualities. This provincial character went along with a long tradition of local resistance to external impositions, whether from the national government or foreign powers. The inhabitants of Shandong frequently met such impositions with protest, anger, and violence. "Quarrels, brawls, and combats are daily occurrences," said one German missionary.[25]

The best example of Shandong's character came from its status as the home of Mount Liang, a small rise (around six hundred feet) that made up for its lack of geographic prominence by its legendary stature. Mount Liang was home for a fictional set of "righteous bandits" who roamed through Shandong and the surrounding provinces righting wrongs and helping the poor and dispossessed. They were similar to the Western mythos surrounding Robin Hood. Mount Liang was their Sherwood Forest. The stories of the bandit adventures were laid out in the fourteenth-century novel *Water Margin*, one of the foundational pieces of fiction in Chinese culture. It was widely read and widely available, converted into plays and traveling shows, updated, remade, and generally familiar to most Chinese. It was translated into Japanese in the eighteenth century and English in the twentieth. Well after the Boxer Rebellion, the stories would become movies, anime, and a number of television series.

The point is that the tales laid out in *Water Margin* had the kind of cultural momentum that informs a society. In a sense, like Robin Hood, *Water Margin* and its bandits were a way for generations to put together their own ideas about the world around them and how that world should and did work. The people of Shandong saw themselves in some senses as inheritors of those bandits, with the responsibility to honor that inheritance by acting against perceived injustice. Living in Shandong made one the descendant, moral if not actual, of a righteous bandit.

There was another inheritance in Shandong, for the province was also the birthplace of one of the most critical of all the Chinese philosophers, Kong Zi. Confucius, as he was known in the West, was born in southern Shandong several thousand years before the Boxer Rebellion but had become the founding

father of Chinese governance. His name and ideas were explicitly invoked in the organization of the Chinese state, the civil
service exams, and the traditions that drove Chinese society.
Shandong had birthed him, and in that sense Shandong at least
partly owned his moral legacy.

The combination is fascinating. Confucianism emphasized
the moral responsibility of the individual and the active development of that moral responsibility. In Shandong, part of that
moral responsibility was to act outside the law, but in a righteous way. The bandits of Mount Liang were not simple criminals; they did what they did to overcome unjust situations that
could not be overcome within the legal system. The model for
the young of Shandong was to look for ways to achieve the right,
even if that meant stepping outside the law to do it.

The critical question, of course, was, how much did the ordinary peasant understand or contemplate such issues? Would
uneducated Chinese constantly on the edge of starvation actually think in these larger ways? It may seem unlikely, but we
should not underestimate the level to which these lessons were
transmitted by means other than literate. Carnivals and fairs
were weekly standards throughout Shandong, as they were
through the rest of China, and part of those carnivals and fairs
was street theater of the most varied kind. That street theater
had both entertainment and religious components. The local
temple gods would be invited to come into the street and provided with front-row seats. The subject matter of that theater
was stories of romantic bandits, of righteous heroes outside the
law, and of the founding father of Chinese culture. They were,
in point of fact, stories that would include the Mount Liang
bandits and Confucius himself, regularly and at great length.
Many of the gods the Boxers spoke of worshipping were lifted
directly from these street operas, making the cultural connection eminently clear.[26]

In particular, the western area of Shandong that ran along

the Grand Canal as its north-south axis and was bisected by the Yellow River was renowned for its restive spirit, frequent banditry, and general surliness. The area was impoverished, with most peasants there living just above starvation level. Typical peasants might have meat once a year if they were lucky. In a year with some sort of natural disaster, there was no meat, and survival itself was at stake. In the south, there was enough wealth to have a moderately substantial landlord class, who owned most of the agricultural land. In the north of this area, there was not enough wealth to manage even that, and the landlords in the northwest of Shandong were poor by the national standards. The normal domination of the wealthy landlords and government officials was here much weaker.

## SECRET SOCIETIES

Things worsened in Shandong in 1898 when the Yellow River flooded, destroying the harvests of hundreds of thousands. The next year, as if to be ironic, a drought started, one that continued into 1900. The combination pushed the already marginal peasant economy over the edge into near disaster, and thousands were either on the edge of starvation or forced off their land.

The result was a steady rise in banditry and crime of all types, and an increase in size of the secret societies that were, in some sense, the last refuge of the dispossessed. One of these secret societies, which resembled the Big Sword Society of southwest Shandong, became the Yi-he quan, the Boxers. They were one of many in Shandong, but the only one to end up shaking not only China but the world.

There is an obvious reason for the rise of the Boxers. The Chinese state was weak and corrupt. Into the vacuum moved a range of unofficial or semiofficial groups who acted to provide what the state could not. The Christian churches were one; the secret societies were another. The conflict between the two could thus be seen not just as between natives and foreigners or traditional values and modern ones or between varying religions but as two rival organizations fighting for influence. It is notable that when the Boxers started their attacks, their first targets were the Chinese Christians. They were the ones getting the illegitimate benefits in local society, and they were the ones assaulted first.

Because of that, though, there was less of a response to the initial Boxer attacks in the summer and fall of 1899 than if the foreign missionaries had been under siege. The warnings were there in the fall of 1899. Letters poured in to the Western ambassadors from missionaries throughout the northeast of China, telling ominous tales of the growing anti-Christian, anti-Western, antimodern sentiment. Reports came to the Chinese government from local governors, telling of the growth of the Boxers and asking the throne what they should do. In both cases, the writers got little in the way of useful response. The Western officials, for the most part, ignored or underplayed the danger. Claude MacDonald, the British consul at Beijing, wrote home to London to notify them of the situation but sent the warning by ship rather than telegraph. The rest of the Western contingent ignored the situation altogether. Sir Robert Hart wrote of why afterward:

> Rebellion was ever on the point of upsetting the dynasty—the Government was always on its last legs—foreigners were to be exterminated on a given date—the powers were about to partition China—etc., etc., etc.: each year—nay, every month, the press or local rumour, Cassandra-like, foretold woe . . . and still life went on unchanged and the cry of Wolf grew more and more meaningless.[27]

In 1900, the missionaries were Cassandra: speaking the truth, but ignored.

The Chinese government reacted not with apathy but with confusion. Suppressing the Boxers would have been a straightforward response, but the cult was clearly popular, and its anti-Western attitudes were not necessarily unpleasant to the empress dowager's ears. Allowing them to grow was another straightforward reaction, but who could say whether the Boxers would limit themselves to Christian and Western targets? The empress dowager received conflicting advice from her courtiers and from the regional governors. Whom she listened to depended on the latest news. Sometimes she referred to the Boxers as "Boxing people" and sometimes as "Boxing bandits."[28] Whether she ever decided on a single policy is not clear, but by the late spring of 1900 her conservative tendencies and the growing sense that here was a movement that could, perhaps, be used against the Western powers edged her toward favoring the Boxers and trying to control their actions. She gave money to the Boxers and publicly signaled her views by beheading a number of anti-Boxer politicians.

Hard on the politicians, but the decision would prove harder on China in the long run. It would, in fact, lead nearly directly to the destruction of the Qing dynasty, the Manchu rulers who had dominated for three hundred years. In her quest to preserve Manchu power, she doomed it. It is hard, however, to criticize Cixi. She was stuck between the ongoing and avaricious pressures of the world's empires and a popular movement that seemed to have no leaders and no organization and yet spread like lava, burning and unstoppable.

# 3

# AN INFORMAL WAR

Abroad, China remained something of a mystery to the world. Contemptuous they might be of the Chinese, but Westerners were also fascinated. China seemed a great but decaying empire, thousands of years old and resolutely stuck in that past. It was ripe for the importation of religion, business, and civilization, but on such an overwhelming scale as to drown the individual. The Scramble for Concessions was one side of this, a naked imperial attempt to grab great hunks of this failing empire. The other side was exemplified by the approach of the American secretary of state, John Hay. Hay saw China as a market to be exploited rather than dismembered. In the Open Door note of September 6, 1899, sent to all the European governments, Hay argued for access to China for all, that "all the great Powers interested in China" should undertake a policy "eminently beneficial to the commercial interests of the whole world." He proposed several principles to that aim and asserted that such a policy would be good for all: "[The policy] would powerfully tend to remove dangerous sources of irritation and possible conflict between the various Powers; it would reestablish confidence and security; and would give great additional weight to the . . . interest of reform in Chinese administration."[1]

Hay's proposal had much less to do with the morality of imperialism and much more to do with the advantage such an open door would give to the booming American economy. Nonetheless, it was greeted as naïveté of the highest order, with the other imperial powers refusing to agree unless the others did as well. If we were to add in the religious perceptions of China, driven by the missionary organizations, we would have a triumvirate of visions, of China as target, as commercial interest, and perhaps as Jewish traveler mugged by the side of the road, helpless until a Samaritan came along.

But it was not just at the highest level that the West viewed China, and it is worth taking a look at some of the coverage of China by *The New York Times* to get a sense of this contradictory perception. The *Times* struggled to comprehend and describe China. It was a country racked by "internal convulsions" and political intrigue, and yet the "greatest potential market of the world." China was mysterious and unknowable, and the paper wrote in a way that made its feeling palpably clear, at one point confessing a basic lack of knowledge about even the royal household of China, whose "members . . . are practically unknown." The uncertainty even came through in the prose of the articles. Stories were full of hedges and wafflings that revealed editorial confusion: it was, the *Times* often intoned, "almost safe to predict" something about China.[2]

One result of this was a combined skepticism and credulity on the part of the paper. The *Times* would often aggressively debunk one rumor while eagerly accepting another. Thus, the *Times* wrote that in 1898 the rumors of the emperor of China's death had been proven "unfounded," but immediately the paper wrote that "it has been stated on good authority that [the emperor] was cruelly used, and even imprisoned and half-starved."[3] There was no apparent realization of the irony of discounting one past rumor while instantaneously propagating another one.

The *Times*'s coverage, confused as it was, treated China on multiple levels. One of those was international, as the paper focused on the aggressive (if not thuggish) maneuverings of the great powers and China's shifting ability to resist them. China was not so much being conquered as it was being organized by the Western powers, if organized by violence, by intimidation, and by edict. Or at least that's the way *The New York Times* presented it. China was not really present in this reporting. Instead, it was a bare playing field on which others warred in sporting matches that went back and forth but were never quite ended. Thus the *Times* declared, on January 17, 1900:

> Any power which chooses may, according to our contention, maltreat the Chinese as much as it choose and carve up their inheritance to suit itself. All that we ask is that we shall hereafter be permitted to trade there, as now, on the footing of the most favored nations, which is to say, on the same footing as the conquering and partitioning power.[4]

A conquered part of China would simply be a "certain tract" that the European power had the "right to police at its own expense." In that sense, China seemed property to be mortgaged and owned and tended. The Chinese themselves were not civilized, and the model for dealing with them was the British one: "It has paid her to subdue savages in quest of new markets."[5]

On a different level, the *Times* did acknowledge that China existed as an international actor, albeit a wily and underhanded one. The empress dowager, the *Times* gravely noted, had published a "secret decree . . . in which she speaks of the danger which threatens the empire from foreign aggression" with "tiger-like voracity." But even here, the paper refused to credit this to the Chinese. Instead, this "stiffening of China's backbone" had to come from an outside source. The paper speculated that the Japanese had reached an "understanding" with the empress that led to her defiance, a speculation reinforced by another article which pointed out that the Japanese were offering to establish a military academy in Beijing staffed with Japanese instructors to educate Chinese officers.[6]

At yet another level, the Chinese did appear in the pages of the paper. In a book review of Arthur Smith's *Village Life in China*, the *Times* spoke of the Chinese as "that wonderful people . . . this great race." The "great race," the *Times* continued, had fallen on hard times because of the "many disabilities" of Chinese society, which had "retard[ed its] advancement in modern civilization." Christianity, the paper announced, was the only solution.[7] Even more individually, on January 17, 1900, the *Times* wrote of Li Hongzhang, a Chinese statesman already well-known in the West. The article was particularly interesting because it was written from the perspective of Li himself. He had been "withdrawn from the Tsung Li Yamen [Zongli Yamen] in 1898 at the demand of Great Britain but he was not degraded." He was a "favorite" of the empress dowager and was thus given a range of jobs, including a survey of the Yellow River, a "very trying tour," the paper wrote. Following that, the empress sent him to Canton to be "Viceroy of the Kwantung [Guangdong] and Kwangse [Guangxi] Provinces." The tone of the article continued in this personal vein: as viceroy, "Li has on his hands the vexatious situation due to the aggression of the French . . . [He] steps into a nest upholstered with bayonets."

The article finished with this contemplative, almost familial line: "The Canton Viceroyalty is one of the most lucrative in China, but to contend successfully with the Chinese factions, with his enemies at Peking, and with the French will puzzle the old statesman." The article was remarkable in focusing on a single Chinese, and focusing with great intimacy. It was the foreigners here who were anonymous, and Li Hongzhang who was the familiar character. It was the goals, worries, and challenges of Li that dominated the story to the exclusion of all else. A hint of why came in the second paragraph, where the article mentioned that Li was accompanied in his work by "N. J. Pettrick, formerly United States Vice Consul at Tientsin, [Li's] private secretary." Pettrick was either the source or the author of the article, and so represented Li's viewpoints back to the West. In a strange way, thus, China existed as property and as playground, as other and as a real, live person who could be vexed or puzzled or degraded.[8]

## FLOWERING

What the paper, the Chinese court, and much of the rest of the world largely missed was how much the crisis was blooming in the summer and fall of 1899. It was in winter that this finally began to come to the attention of the foreign powers, and then only because of the reports of Western missionaries actually on the ground in Shandong. On December 7, 1899, Edwin H. Conger, the American ambassador to China, wrote to the secretary of state, John Hay, about a "very critical state of affairs among the missionaries and their converts" in Shandong. The minister explained: "The season has been a poor one, crops have failed on account of the drought; great poverty and want prevail. An unusual amount of looting is a result, and naturally, the foreigners or their followers come in for the larger share of grief." Conger went on to note the actions of the Boxers, who were "doing much damage to the Christian converts, extorting money from them, threatening the missions, and giving ample cause for serious alarm."[9]

The murder of the Reverend Sidney Brooks broke through the inattention. Over the New Year, Rev. Brooks, a missionary, was captured in Shandong and then beheaded and mutilated. His death was reported globally, and the blame was laid at the feet of the Boxers. *The New York Times* wrote that Brooks was "killed by members of the seditious society known as 'Boxers,' who had been very active in destroying villages and slaughtering native Christians."[10] The *Times* felt it necessary to introduce the Boxers to their readers, and they portrayed the society as one that, until that time, had targeted "native Christians." Brooks's murder, rightly or wrongly, was seen as the moment when the Boxers crossed over into targeting foreigners, and thus being worthy of attention.

The British minister, Sir Claude MacDonald, demanded a response from the Chinese government. On January 11, the Chinese issued an imperial decree. The Qing tried to tread carefully between several competing ideas. The situation, the decree started off by noting, was much more complicated than it seemed:

> When worthless vagabonds form themselves into bands and sworn conspiracies, and relying on their numbers, create disturbances, the law can show absolutely no leniency to them. On the other hand, when peaceful and law-abiding people practice their skill in mechanical arts for the self-preservation of themselves and their families, or when they combine in village communities for the mutual protection of the rural populations, this is in accordance with the public spirited principles of keeping mutual watch and giving mutual help.[11]

In other words, many of the secret societies were simply the acts of local Chinese defending themselves. The decree went on to single out the legal issues that surrounded the missionaries, and admonished local officials not to treat either side favorably: "When litigation arises between converts and people, it should be dealt with according to justice, without the slightest particularity for either side."[12] The solution to all this?

As for our common people, let them give thought to the
protection and security of their native places, their per-
sons, and their homes. Let them not give ear to those
who would unsettle their minds and so bring upon
themselves calamities and military operations. Nor let
them on the other hand presume upon influence and
authority to oppress their fellow villagers.[13]

Needless to say, this was not what MacDonald, the other foreign ministers, or the missionary organizations wanted to hear.
It seemed rather to them that the throne was trying to lay the
blame for the disruption upon the missionaries and their converts and say that the local Chinese were simply trying to defend their interests. More, it chastised the local officials for not
backing the "common people" up to a greater degree. The implications seemed obvious to MacDonald. The Chinese throne
was not interested in dealing with the Brooks murder in a way
the British minister found just. Instead, it was, in essence, cri-
tiquing the missionaries for bringing danger on themselves. Nor
was MacDonald alone in his evaluation. Edwin H. Conger
wrote a stiff note to the Zongli Yamen, stating that "these secret societies, such as the Boxers and Big Knife, actually believe that they have the secret sympathy and endorsement of
the Throne; and, unhappily, many sinologues insist that the
Imperial Decree of the 11th instant in large measure justifies
this belief."[14] This was to become a common theme: the sense
on the part of the Western nations that the Qing were either
controlling or condoning the Boxers.

Even when the Chinese offered compensation and tried,
convicted, and executed (one by decapitation, one by strangulation) two men for the murder of Brooks, the international
community remained unconvinced of the government's true
intentions. Rumors abounded that the men executed had not
been the real killers, who were being hidden by the Chinese, or

that the real killers had been allowed to buy their way out of execution by paying $600 to a "dissolute opium smoker who wished to provide for his family." With the kind of ornate detail that baseless rumors often have, the man sentenced to die by strangulation "had to pay only $400 for his substitute." The rumor did not make clear whether that was because strangulation was seen as a less horrible way to die or if the opium smoker had proven a better negotiator.[15]

As the situation in Shandong became of international concern, the issue was then subject to all the regular imperial rivalries. When Conger joined with the French, German, and British ambassadors to protest the actions of the Boxers, he received a rebuke (albeit gentle) from John Hay:

> While the Department finds no objection to the general terms of this paper, it would have preferred if you had made separate representation on the question instead of the mode adopted, as the position of the United States in relation to China makes it expedient that, while circumstances may sometimes require that it act on lines similar to those other treaty powers follow, it should do so singly and without the cooperation of other powers.[16]

The Boxers became part of the great imperial game, subject to all the delicate rules that governed that game. This maneuvering would continue throughout the crisis and long after.

Nonetheless, the reports received by the foreign consuls made the Brooks murder seem part of a larger and more serious breakdown. No one quite knew what was going on, but "the wildest rumors are prevalent," wrote one missionary to W. R. Carles, the British consul in Tianjin, "in regard to the intention of those desperadoes, the Boxers, to pay us a visit and make us feel the power of their wrath."[17] The "natives [were] drilling in nearly every village around," wrote another.[18] There was a sense that the Boxers, unexplainable and hostile, were spreading faster than they could be contained, faster than they could be understood.

Though perhaps overstated, the reports correctly identified a substantial expansion by the Boxers. The spring that year had seen a continuation of the drought, putting an increased burden on the shoulders of the local peasants, but at the same time, oddly enough, freeing many of them from their labors. The impossibility of harvesting a nonexistent winter crop or planting new seeds in the dry ground meant for many Chinese an enforced and hungry leisure. "The rain has not been sufficient to set the people to work," a missionary wrote in mid-April.[19] The peasants, perhaps most critically the young peasants, had time for other activities like joining the Boxers. Charles Davis Jameson, an American mining engineer, was traveling along the Grand Canal in May 1900:

> The country was barren and burnt brown; crops that should have been ready for the market were only a few inches above the ground and shrivelled by the heat of the sun and the lack of water. God knows, the people looked poor enough in this part of the country at any time, but they now seemed absolutely poverty stricken and on the verge of starvation.[20]

George Morrison, a British reporter in China, wrote in his diary on April 17, "The danger of the Boxers is increasing. The danger is *scarcity of rain* which is attributed to the disturbance of the *feng shui* by foreigners. If rains come, the Boxers will soon disappear."[21]

Morrison was correct, and the Boxer movement spread rapidly across northern China. The pattern was usually the arrival in a virgin town or village of a few experienced Boxers, who would set up shop in a public area like a square or a marketplace or an open yard. There they would display their physical prowess and lecture to anyone who would listen on the tenets of their group. None of these were terribly complicated or written, making them easy to transport from place to place and easy to learn. People would be invited to join in the Boxer drills. Before long, the town would have a thriving band that was made up of both locals and outsiders. This could happen quite quickly, and a number of missionaries talked about how a Boxer group seemed to "spring up very suddenly."[22]

## RIOT

The Boxers also grew more and more aggressive as the spring developed, each step a progressive ramping up of the crisis. Brooks's murder was not repeated immediately. Instead, the Boxers at first usually limited their actions to the putting up of "vile" and "calumnious" placards outside Christian communities.[23] Some of the placards explained, quite clearly, the Boxers' grievances:

> There are many Christian converts
> Who have lost all their senses.
> They deceive our Emperor,
> Destroy the gods we worship,
> Pull down temples and altars,
> Permit neither joss-sticks nor candles,
> Cast away tracts on ethics
> And ignore reason.
> Did you not know that
> Their aim was to engulf the whole country?
> There are no talented people [in sight]

But dirt and garbage.
They undermine the very root of the Empire
And open its door wide.
We have divine power at our disposal
To arouse our people and display an array of weapons
In order to protect the realm from decay.
Our pleasure is to see the Son of Heaven unharmed.
Let the officials perish
But the people remain invincible.
Bring your own provisions,
Come and do away with the scourge of the country.[24]

And, indeed, they soon turned to doing away with the "scourge of the country," beating Chinese Christians when they caught them in public. Their goal at first seemed to be to get the Chinese Christians to recant. In one case, they kidnapped a Chinese Christian and "set about torturing him to make him burn incense and worship their images." Failing that, they "tied [him] up to a tree by his thumbs in order to make him recant."[25] Chinese Christian churches were burned, though at first this tended to happen at night, when no one was present.

There was a sense here of people working themselves up to more and more extreme actions, of the slow-motion development of a riot, albeit one spread across the hundreds of miles of northern China. As Conger put it in early March: "They are insolent, abusive, and threatening to both missionaries and native Christians, but making no recent actual attacks."[26]

Soon, however, murder superseded torture and arson. If they could not reconvert the Chinese Christians, then the Boxers would eliminate them. Thus, in April and May, the Boxers started murdering Chinese Christians, often in ritualistic ways, by tying them to trees, cutting off their arms, and then disemboweling them.

In essence, what broke out was a war between the Chinese Christians and the Boxers. The Boxers were attacking the Christians, it seems, not particularly for religious reasons (though that is what got remembered) but because of their privileged position in the local societies. This was a local conflict writ large, as two power groups within villages, towns, and cities went after each other. Since the Chinese Christians gained their status through association with the Western missionaries, it should not be a shock the Boxers next went after those missionaries.

This the Boxers did. They started by threatening the foreign missionaries and spreading a range of hostile rumors. In one example, the missionaries were poisoning Chinese wells. The rumors were believed, and local businesses did brisk sales in "remedies against the . . . poisoning . . . and the evil spells said to be used by [foreigners]."[27] Threats followed the rumors, and by May many missionaries were afraid to leave their compounds, in fear of their lives "as Boxers are everywhere and use all sorts of threats."[28] On June 1, the Reverends H. V. Norman and C. Robinson were ambushed and captured by a group of Boxers. Norman was murdered straightaway, while Robinson was held captive, tortured, and murdered a few days later. If the murder of Brooks had been the moment the world started taking notice, the murders of Norman and Robinson were, for the Westerners on the ground in China, the start of the war.

But the Boxers did not limit themselves to the missionaries. The other foreign targets were the railway workers and merchants traveling the country on imperial business. Here again, April and May witnessed an increasing number of attacks on them, attacks that followed the same pattern of starting small and then building up. The attacks, though violent, tended to be disorganized and not pushed through all that effectively.

Alexander Reid, a British engineer, was traveling with a group of British up the Wei River when they were successively set upon by mobs on the riverbanks. The mobs "discharged fire-arms, bricks and clods of earth" at the British, but there were only a few minor injuries, and each mob let the boats by without chasing them up the river. A gunboat they encountered acted to protect them from further attacks, firing "blank shot to frighten" the Chinese attackers. The British managed to pressure a local magistrate to arrest four villagers and give them several hundred "strokes with the Bamboo," and the expedition continued safely under armed escort. Notable about the attacks were the mixture of weaponry available, the ineffectiveness of the assault, and the lack of persistence. Reid had a further encounter with the Boxers, one that illustrated the centrality of the drought to the movement: Trapped by a group of Boxers on the way to Tianjin, Reid said sarcastically, "The priests . . . very kindly and considerately shouted that if the 'Foreign Devils' were sacrificed, rain would come." Luckily for Reid, his Chinese escorts managed to talk the Boxers out of the ritual, and they escaped.[29]

Local officials worked to control the Boxers, especially after a late-February decree by the throne "stringently prohibited" the sect, but quickly found themselves unable to do so.[30] In April, a local magistrate could still force a group of Boxers to move out of their yard next to a missionary compound away across the village, where they would be "less likely to molest" the missionaries. He could admonish them "in open court . . . to the effect that . . . they will be very severely dealt with if they interfere with Christians."[31] By the middle of May, however, the magistrates were finding themselves impotent in the face of the sustained growth of the movement, a growth that was no longer confined to Shandong but, instead, was national across northern China.

## THE LOCAL BECOMES NATIONAL

It is worth examining the growth of that movement, as histories of the Boxers have tended to neglect the catching of the fire. The gestation in Shandong has been minutely examined and the full conflagration in the summer of 1900 resolutely detailed. What has not, however, been treated deeply was the moment when the local went national. At the end of 1899, the Boxers were, if troublesome, very much the local revolt of a local society. It was little more than the Qing had dealt with before, dealt with, in fact, on a regular basis. Even as late as the middle of May 1900, Charles Jameson could laugh at the ideas of Boxers marching on Beijing as "Chinese fairy tales."[32] Within two weeks of his laughter, however, the Boxers did exactly that.

And that is the great difference: in the spring of 1900 the Boxer movement exploded across northern China. It became something the Chinese had not seen since the Taipings, forty years before. Even the Taipings had had a leader and leadership and structure. The Boxers had nothing similar; what local leaders there were were soon superseded or made irrelevant by the spread.

The reasons for that were both straightforward and mysterious. The growing resentment over foreign intrusion was not limited to Shandong. Neither were the continuing natural disasters. The drought that had started a year earlier was general across northern China, and hunger was rampant. As one foreign observer put it, "There is an awful famine pending in the interior. All along our route . . . is a desert and the mortality by famine this year must be enormous."[33] In that densely populated area, Chinese, living as always on the bare margin of starvation, had almost a universal sense of desperation and impotence. That latter was perhaps the most critical: the drought meant that the daily routine of agriculture was largely at a standstill; the Chinese (though frantic to gather food) were at leisure.

Into this field, planting and nurturing the seeds of rebellion was easy. The main tenets of the Boxers proved compelling. The physical and mystical rituals gave the peasants something concrete to do, with concrete results. Here was a way to gain power: invulnerability, both martial and physical. The Boxer message, "Support the Qing, exterminate the foreigners," targeted just those whom the peasants blamed for their plight. To boot, it was a simple and memorable slogan, easily portable from town to town. If we understand the first part as being less the idea of *support* than it was of reminding the Qing of their duty, then the slogan stands as even more attractive. The Boxers were not so much backing the imperial throne as they were forcing that throne to its duty.

The foreigners attacked were those the Chinese saw on a daily basis: the missionaries and the railway workers and engineers. Both of those exemplified the kind of modernity that, from the peasant perspective, had so disrupted Chinese society. In a sense, the Boxer movement was deeply conservative, concerned with ensuring the triumph of tradition over progress; the inherent contradiction of the movement was that they aimed to enforce tradition in a radical way, one that disrupted and overturned the central and dominant structures of Chinese society and government. The Boxers were conservative in message but radical in action.

The result was a deeply decentralized organization, linked more by a unity of message and method than communications or leadership and identified by the wearing of a red sash. Individual groups of Boxers acted largely without regard for other Boxer groups, but with the same consistency of aim. They attacked the foreigners available to attack and ignored the local officials when those officials tried to stop them.

But we should not mistake that larger decentralization for weakness or a lack of intelligence. One of the main methods that the Chinese government had used to suppress previous secret societies had been by arresting and locking up their leaders. The Boxers did not rely on leaders to spread or act, and that made it hard for the government to target them. On a military level, the lack of structure gave the Boxers a tactical flexibility that the more traditionally organized Chinese armies lacked.

To get a sense of this, it is worth examining two Boxer attacks in some detail. The first was carried out by a Boxer band in the middle of May against a company of Chinese troops. On May 22, a small unit of mixed infantry and cavalry led by Colonel Yang Futong was patrolling in an area that bordered on northwestern Shandong. They had encountered a group of Boxers five days earlier and dispersed them with rifle fire, killing a large number of them. The ground they had to cover that day was crisscrossed with irrigation ditches, making it especially difficult for the cavalry to ride their horses. One of Yang's men warned him of the potential for ambush, but the colonel ignored the warning and had his cavalrymen dismount and lead their horses. The subordinate proved to be accurate, and as the Chinese force worked its way through the ditches, a concealed band of Boxers launched an ambush that carried them right into the middle of the Chinese soldiers.

The success of this bold tactic remains something of a mystery. Some histories have said that Yang "wanted to try to disperse them and was reluctant to give the order to open fire," but this seems strikingly odd, given the previous encounter.[34] More likely, Yang was taken by surprise by Boxers launching an assault out of the irrigation ditches and getting in among the Chinese soldiers before they could respond. The result was a confused melee, in which Yang and three other soldiers were killed. The remaining soldiers managed to drive the Boxers off, but not before the colonel's body had been mutilated: "[Yang] was wounded in more than one hundred places so that no part of his skin was left intact. His face was unrecognisable, his innards lay open and the thumb and index finger of the right hand were cut off. He was killed with such viciousness that it was terribly painful even to look at him."[35] Though later reports would put the Boxer numbers in the thousands, this seems unlikely. It would be nearly impossible to conceal that number in such a way that Yang's troops got close to them without knowing they were there. Rather more likely was that the Boxers numbered several hundred, a reasonable figure for concealment.

What is notable about this encounter was that the Boxers had clearly reacted to the earlier incident not with irrational rage but with calculated planning. They chose ground that was good for an ambush, in terms of both forcing the cavalrymen to dismount and giving the ambushers cover in the ditches. They waited until the Chinese troops put themselves at a disadvantage before attacking, and then they focused on coming to grips with the soldiers so that their weapons, largely farm implements and other close-combat weapons, would be effective. Yang's wounds, in this evaluation, seem to be less deliberate mutilation than the result of a focused attack with axes, scythes, knives, and other common implements. The relatively low number of fatalities among the Chinese soldiers also reflected that limited weaponry and suggested that while the Boxers could effectively find ways to get close to their enemies, actually managing to inflict substantial casualties was a challenge.

The second attack, on a British unit, showed some of the same characteristics. The British had established the First Chinese Regiment, manned by Chinese soldiers and commanded by British officers. As May 1900 began, it was stationed in Weihai, in Shandong. At first, the area seemed calm; the "almost friendly and quite peaceful disposition" of the locals led the British to reduce patrols outside the wall from thirty men to twelve.[36] It was just after the change, on May 5, that one of its officers, a Major Penrose of the Royal Engineers, went to inspect the camp boundaries. While he was out, the unit was ambushed by a group of locals. The ambush was quite sophisticated, waiting until the British were in a sunken, dry riverbed before launching the assault. The Boxers used the cover afforded them to get to close quarters:

> The party was suddenly attacked by a large crowd of Chinese, armed chiefly with agricultural implements and stones. Major Penrose was the main objective, and he was very severely handled, especially with a bayonet, wrested from him, and which he had taken from one of the escort after emptying his own revolver into the mob. Sergeant Pillay and the other man of the Royal Engineers also put in some good work with their pistols, while Mr. Schaller formed up the escort, and kept the crowd off Major Penrose, who had, by that time, fallen. Things now began to look very serious, for the crowd, though losing rapidly, showed no signs of giving way. Individuals, possibly imbued with Boxer notions of invulnerability, repeatedly tried to come to close quarters again, after once being driven back, several with more than one bullet in their bodies.

Note that the Boxers had gotten close enough to take Major Penrose's bayonet away from him. Driven off by rifle fire from the soldiers, the Boxers tried to get close again, a situation that would effectively neutralize the superior weaponry of the British.

The tactical sophistication did not stop there. The British attempted to retreat up a hill toward the camp but discovered that the Boxers had set up *another* ambush point from the top of the hill:

> As soon as things began to look serious they withdrew up the hill on the right of their track, and still main-

tained a running fight in the direction of the camp, about half-a-mile off. The Chinese had allowed for this, and a large number now appeared above the party, and began to throw great stones at them.

Penrose's party was, at this point, in serious trouble. But the fight was taking place within hearing range of the camp, and other British soldiers intervened. Lieutenant George Brooke was a witness to this from the camp:

After lunch about 2 pm we were surprised by hearing some shots fired. On looking up the valley we saw a large mass of men moving in the direction of the shots which turned out to be Major Penrose's escort who were being attacked. All available men in camp turned out and went to his assistance and only got there just in time.[37]

Penrose's party was saved by the intervention of troops arriving from the main part of the camp, but even then the Boxers were not done, luring the saviors into chasing them and then mounting a counterattack:

The mob started to run, and some of the men, headed by Captain Pereira, rushed after them. A few turned back, and one put his pitchfork round Captain Pereira's neck, and bore him to the ground, where he would have fared but ill had not one of his men, who was close behind him, bayoneted his assailant.

The Boxers committed a major tactical error by mounting the assault relatively close to camp, allowing for reinforcements to get there quickly. If they had done it at the farthest distance that the party had been from help, six miles, "the party might have been wiped out before it was even known in camp that they were in danger."

What is notable about both the attacks was the sophisticated planning that went into them. Both were on ground that must have been carefully chosen for its advantages, at a time also in the Boxers' favor, and executed in such a way that the Boxer attackers succeeded in closing with their targets. That neutralized, to a certain extent, the great advantage that both the official Chinese troops and the foreign forces had in firepower and weapons technology. A rifle, whether single shot or repeating, became not much more than an unwieldy club when the enemy was within touching distance. It is noticeable, in the British case, that having revolvers may have saved the British officers from Yang Futong's fate.

But despite the solid planning, neither attack was overwhelmingly successful. In neither case did the Boxers manage to inflict major harm to the forces they were attacking. Their weaponry was simply too limited, even at close range. Alexander Reid, the British railway engineer, had a chance to see a unit of Boxers and their weapons close up. He was not impressed. They had "gingals [light guns], shot guns, tridents, pruning hooks, swords, etc."[38] That seems to be an improvement over the ones who attacked Penrose, who did not have firearms of any sort. A force equipped and trained with modern firearms would likely have wiped out their targets to the man.

On a larger note, what these early attacks revealed was that, contrary to the Western perception or even the perception of the Qing, the Boxers were not simply bands of crazed religious fanatics but groups capable of managing effective tactical planning and execution. Limited as they were by their weaponry, two different groups of Boxers had managed successful attacks, and not just against missionaries or railway engineers but against armed and trained soldiers. The question carrying forward into the summer was, could the Boxers manage the same kind of success against forces forewarned and equipped not only with hand weapons but with machine guns and artillery?

To broaden this out, then, we should note that the traditional perception of the Boxers, both at the time and after, was almost completely wrong. That perception, which emphasized the irrationality of the spiritual and martial behavior and the peasant origin of the movement, painted a picture of a force without much in the way of military sophistication. What emerged from the two attacks was rather evidence of a force with a fair amount of military refinement, able to plan, perform reconnaissance, and mount ambushes.

The main flaw of the Boxers in military terms was the same in both instances: a fundamental lack of useful weapons, at least compared with their enemies. Agricultural implements plus knives and stones were simply not effective unless the Boxers could get in among their enemies. That is likely the source of their reliance on ambush, which enabled them to get close to their targets before the latter were aware of the attack, and at least reduced the mismatch in weaponry. Even then, however, the two attacks made it clear that against organized opposition, it was enormously difficult for the Boxers to inflict substantial casualties. In both cases, the Boxers managed a near-perfect ambush, but the fatalities inflicted on the enemy were not overwhelming, and in neither case did the Boxers come close to wiping out the enemy force.

As has already become clear, Shandong itself was a rough-and-ready place, full of bandits, bandit groups, and other folks on the wrong side of the law. In addition, even those who spent most of their time on the *right* side of the law nonetheless found themselves fairly frequently, whether because of government corruption or natural disaster, being forced into illegality. In both those cases, the skills of reconnaissance and being able to hide from government forces were useful. Ambushing tax collectors or rich merchants, given the security likely accompanying them, was good preparation for ambushing a group of soldiers, whether Chinese or foreign. Though Shandong was an extreme example of this, Chinese peasant society in general promoted quite an obstreperous spirit and led to a population frequently willing, often violently, to assert its rights. The Western stereotype of the Chinese, that they were "peaceful and deferential," as one British member of Parliament put it in 1900, could not have been more wrong.[39] They were, in fact, much the opposite. The Boxers were not particularly extreme or particularly unusual in Chinese culture, except for their rapid spread. They were, in a way, the purest expression of that cultural rambunctiousness.

## AN INFORMAL WAR

The rain still had not come in May 1900, and George Morrison's Chinese servant informed him that "eight million men would descend from Heaven and exterminate the foreigners." "Then," he said, "the rain will come."[40] The war between the Chinese Christians and the Boxers widened. What had been small-scale, local, and personal, if violent and bloody and organized, started to become national and international. On one side were the Chinese Christians, the missionaries, and the railroad workers. On the other were the Boxers. The letters written by the missionaries grew more and more plaintive as they began to be drawn into this war. A local bishop, Pierre-Marie-Alphonse Favier, wrote a letter summarizing the situation on May 19 to the French minister, Stéphen Pichon:

> In the prefecture of Paoting-fu, more than seventy Christians have been massacred; near Echoao Icheou, only three days ago, three neophytes have been cut in

pieces. Many villages have been pillaged and burned, a great many others have been completely abandoned. More than two thousand Christians are fleeing, without bread, without clothing, without shelter.[41]

"Pillage and incendiarism," the bishop went on, were "imminent."[42] Favier's words fell on receptive ears in Pichon, who had the bishop's letter copied for the other Western ministers. The Corps Diplomatique of Beijing met on the twenty-first to discuss the situation but could not quite come to agreement on a range of measures. Pichon suggested that the ambassadors ask the Western naval forces off the coast of China to send up a large guard of marines and sailors to protect the embassies, but the other ambassadors thought this too much. On May 26, the group met again, again without setting anything in motion.

The ministers moved slowly partly because of a disbelief that this could become a national issue, and partly because of the inherently slow reaction of diplomatic decisions that had to be briefed and pondered around the world. The attack on the soldiers of the Chinese Regiment, for example, was reported by the undersecretary of state for foreign affairs, William Brodrick, in the House of Commons six days later, but as an isolated incident. Brodrick concluded with the comforting words that the "general outlook was reassuring."[43]

In China, there was a personal and imperial element as well. Pichon was seen by a number of the other ambassadors as a hysteric, prone to see the most disturbing portents in the evening shadows. They thus tended to disregard his dire warnings as overexcited ramblings. In the meeting on the twenty-sixth, Pichon's words were confirmed by the Italian ambassador, but the latter too could be dismissed as coming from a power still resentful over the rebuff of 1899.

But the corps could not ignore things much longer. The crisis was spreading rapidly, whatever their delays. The war came closer to Beijing every day. There were seemingly no generals, no leaders driving it closer. It grew toward the capital, perhaps best understood as the organic outrage of a peasantry in despair. Buffeted from so many different directions, the Boxers offered up a target to blame and sheer physical immunity to the dangers of this new modern world.

The first Boxers appeared in Beijing in late May 1900. Soon crowds, wearing the red sashes, were in the city itself. They brought an interesting power dynamic to communal interactions in the city. What had been a relationship among mostly dominant Westerners and Chinese soldiers and civil servants and the much more subservient civilian Chinese acquired another player. The Boxers were not Western, and they were not soldiers or civil servants. They were, at the root, ordinary Chinese, though they did not behave that way. They strutted and swaggered and made themselves large in the streets. They put on physical displays to demonstrate their prowess. They tried to own the public spaces. Ordinary Chinese they appraised for supposed infractions against Boxer beliefs. Soldiers and civil servants they avoided or ignored. Westerners they despised, and members of the embassy population began to feel threatened as these red-sashed Chinese not only did not kowtow to them but stared with open hatred. Suddenly a simple walk to the market or through the streets of Beijing had to be treated with some wariness. This was an unfamiliar feeling for most of the Europeans. They were used to being dominant, socially, culturally, and politically. They understood when the Chinese government tried to manage them with politeness and obstruction. This open hatred was both simpler and more confusing. They were nervous enough to begin taking some physical precautions, like fortifying their compounds. As Mary Porter Gamewell, whose husband was a civil engineer, wrote:

Mr. Gamewell had, early in the progress of affairs, called masons and built solid brick work over the outside of all gates in our walls that could be dispensed with, thus providing against their being fired by the Boxers, who were daily assuming a more threatening attitude in the city. He also had barbed wire stretched across the courts to prevent a rush of the enemy in case they should break into our premises.[44]

Adding to the worries was the increasing number of reports of violence from outside Beijing. Chinese Christians were dying, and so, in a shift, were Western missionaries. Refugees were beginning to appear in the capital, carrying horrific tales of bloodshed along with them. No one knew quite what to do. On May 27, a bloodied and exhausted Belgian railroad engineer staggered into the embassies to report that the train line was being destroyed by the Boxers at Fengtai, the junction between Beijing and the coast. The next day, the station there was burned. Claude MacDonald, the British ambassador, called a meeting of all of the heads of the foreign legations for the next day, and at that meeting it was decided to send down to the ships gathered at Dagu for soldiers to guard the embassies. The message reached the fleets quickly over the telegraph, and sizable contingents of soldiers, Russian, British, Japanese, and American, left for Beijing on May 31. In addition to the guards, MacDonald called the British residents in the rest of Beijing to come to the security of the embassy and started to think about how to defend the legations.

The streets of Beijing began to take on a distinctly hostile air. The attitude of the Boxers seemed to have infected all the Chinese against the Westerners. Threatening omens seemed all around, from the rumor that the railway lines were being torn up to use as the raw materials for weapons, to the signs appearing in Chinese shops, "Swords Made Here." "It was a queer reversal of the Scripture saying that swords shall be beaten into plowshares."[45]

The arrival of the guards on June 1 brought some temporary calm to the embassy personnel, as well as a certain amount of bravado. If the locals got out of hand, Robert Coltman wrote, "a machine gun will now have something to say in one's behalf."[46] The confidence was short-lived, and the Westerners began "briskly" assembling their defenses. Frank Gamewell continued his good work: "Walls were built across the wide compound and deep ditches were dug beyond the barbed wire checks." The church was turned into a final redoubt, with bricks piled on the roof "to be hurled upon any attacking party." The defenders stockpiled food and boiled giant cauldrons of water to purify it.[47]

Tensions continued to rise. On June 9, a racetrack just outside the city walls was burned down by a crowd of Boxers. A number of young European men rode out to view the fire, and in a confrontation between the two groups a Boxer was shot and killed. MacDonald telegraphed to Admiral Edward Seymour that he needed a much larger guard to protect the embassies, and the admiral promised one quickly. On June 11, the Japanese chancellor, Sugiyama Akira, went down to the train station to await the supposed arrival of this force. Instead, he was set on by Chinese troops and cut to pieces. The war had come to Beijing.

It was an impromptu war, with fluid rules on both sides. The forces within the legations began gathering outlying Westerners and Chinese Christians. Gunfire started, from legation forces, from imperial troops, and from the Boxers. On June 11, it was still possible for a force of marines to go to the train station to wait for Seymour's arrival. On June 13, the last telegraph line was cut, repaired, and then cut again, this time for good. On June 14, several hundred Boxers "with flaming torches and firebrands" set upon the legation. The picket of marines out front drove them back, leaving four Boxers dead and two wounded.[48]

By June 17, large crowds of Boxers had settled in around the legations, and the Western forces were beginning to put together a sustainable defensive line. The critical defensive feature was the Tartar Wall, which overlooked the legations. If the Chinese took that, they would be able to fire down into the Westerners, to devastating effect. To prevent this, the Americans and Russians held the west end of the wall, while the Germans held the east, with both sets reinforced by British marines.[49]

On June 19, the legations received an ultimatum from Cixi, ordering them to leave Beijing. The allied assault on the Dagu Forts had precipitated an official war to the Chinese, and they were giving the legations twenty-four hours to gather their belongings. They would be, the ultimatum said, escorted to Tianjin by Chinese forces.

The ministers responded with hope but skepticism. MacDonald thought that it was a trap to lure them out of the defensible grounds of the embassy quarter. Once out, as at Cawnpore during the Indian mutiny, the Westerners would be slaughtered. The ministers debated and eventually agreed to send their assent but to ask for a meeting with the Zongli Yamen the next morning at 9:00 a.m. to discuss details.

The next morning, June 20, the assembled ministers waited for a reply. Nothing had come in by 9:30 a.m., and Baron August Freiherr von Ketteler, the German minister, decided impatiently to head to the offices of the Zongli Yamen and wait there for an answer. He took his secretary, Heinrich Cordes, but left without a military escort. Von Ketteler never made it. At some point along the way, he was killed by a unit of imperial troops, commanded by an officer named En Hai. Cordes was severely wounded in the leg but managed to escape.

How it happened has never been entirely clear. Cordes reported that von Ketteler had been ambushed and killed by a single imperial soldier, without provocation and without warning. Later, long after the war had ended, a Chinese eyewitness would testify that von Ketteler had fired a shot first and then been killed by the troops in response.[50] The conflicting stories were never resolved, and by the time the war had ended, no one was interested in disputing Cordes's version. The oddest part of the story would not become known to the legations until afterward: Baron von Ketteler's death had been reported *before* it had happened. A series of newspaper stories, starting in the *North-China Daily News* on June 14, reported the baron's death. *The New York Times* even ran his obituary on June 17.[51] The oddity has been seen as evidence of a Chinese government conspiracy, or simply as inaccurate reporting that had nothing to do with the actual death of von Ketteler.[52]

At the time, no one had any doubt about what had happened. The Chinese government, deliberately and with malice aforethought, had conspired to murder von Ketteler. All the suspicions of the legations were confirmed. German soldiers, in a fury, took the walls of the legation and sniped at those they thought Boxers, killing at least ten. The remaining ministers quickly decided to reject the empress dowager's ultimatum. They would stay in Beijing and be besieged, waiting for a force they could trust to come and rescue them. That night, Mrs. M. S. Woodward remembered, crowds of Chinese gathered outside the walls of the legations and "shrieked, wailed and howled, '*Sha, sha*,' which meant 'Kill, kill.'"[53]

# 4

# EVERY IMPEDIMENT MADE

The war had come to Tianjin as well, as Chinese troops began to surround the foreign quarter of the city. On June 10, at the head office of the Imperial Chinese Railway, all of the Chinese workers failed to show up for work, perhaps sensibly realizing that ownership of the railway building was likely to be contested violently. This was matched by an utter lack of customers as well. The head accountant, who was British, reacted with impressive phlegmatism. In the absence of the rest of the workforce and without customers, the Brit decided to make it a half day for himself and closed the office promptly at 1:00 p.m. Before he left, he gathered all of the "books, vouchers, and documents of any value" and locked them in the office safe.[1]

Clive Mersey, a British traveler working his way through China in 1899–1900, was front and center for the developing crisis. He had reached the Chinese port of Dagu, close to the capital, early in June, planning to head up to Beijing to visit friends at the British embassy. He took the train to Tianjin on June 4, but almost immediately realized that something unusual was brewing. The Chinese travelers, Mersey noted with some bemusement, seemed immensely nervous, and when the train engine broke down, they "at once became panic stricken." Continuing after repair, Mersey noted thousands of Chinese troops lining the railway and, arriving at Tianjin after a journey of nearly ten hours, found that "open revolt" had broken out in the countryside.[2]

The question, for all the foreign powers, was, what to do? Clearly, the limited number of troops already sent as legation guards would not be sufficient if there was a general uprising in China, or if the Chinese government allied itself with the Boxers.

Admiral Edward Seymour was a naval officer, and thus relatively inexperienced in land warfare. But he had long knowledge of Asia, having been a midshipman forty years before in the previous British intervention during the Taiping Rebellion. He seems to have concluded that the enemy he faced was the Boxers, a popular movement, and not the Chinese government and army itself. Given that, Seymour felt he could risk assuming cooperation or at least benign neglect from the Chinese military, meaning that he only needed sufficient troops to deal with the Boxers and a speedy way to get to the capital. Less important was ensuring access to the sea or that Tianjin was held and fortified.

In essence, Seymour felt that as he was facing not a strictly military threat but more a civilian relief expedition, he could take more military risks. The critical element was speed. He decided to put together a scratch force of Russians, Japanese, British, and whoever else was available and hurry northwestward to Beijing, ignoring the Chinese military and brushing aside whatever Boxers he encountered. This would have the advantage of getting the force to Beijing in a few days and putting it in a position to protect the members of the legation.

Seen in retrospect, Seymour's decision was a remarkably risky gamble, built on a racially tinged sense of superiority and a not-inaccurate sense of Chinese decline and weakness. To be fair to the admiral, there was growing pressure from back home to do *something*. A letter from the prime minister to the Admiralty included the pointed, if flowery, remark that "the Marquess of Salisbury would suggest that the Lords Commissioners of the Admiralty should telegraph to the Commander in Chief in China that, in case of danger to the Foreign Legations at Peking . . . he should take such steps in concert with the Commanding officers of the other squadrons as he may consider advisable and practicable for their protection and that H.M. Government desire to have him a wide discretion as to the measures to be adopted." A condensed translation of the prime minister's words might plausibly be that the marquess was devoutly hoping that someone would do something effective, and do it quickly.[3] The pressure on the admiral was obvious. Nonetheless, Seymour was assuming both that the Boxers were not organized or smart enough to destroy the railway and block him and that the Chinese government would have no objection to a military force of several thousand Western soldiers, sailors, and marines blithely marching into Beijing and taking up quarters right next to the Forbidden City. If Seymour was wrong about either assumption, he faced the prospect of being trapped deep inside China with hostile forces all around.

## SEYMOUR SETS OFF

Thus, on June 10, Seymour set off on an expedition. It was not a walk, as Keyes would manage later, but it had something of the same grand air, one of imperial confidence. He had a force of about two thousand, primarily British, but with contingents from most of the other nations present. They gathered at the Tianjin railway station that morning to crowd into a special train that would take them to Beijing. Seymour put Captain Edward Bayly of the HMS *Aurora* in charge of allocating berths to various units, but cooperation was sometimes difficult. Captain Bowman McCalla, the head American officer, demanded space for the American troops in the first car of the train and "wished it clearly understood that Captain Bayly could not boss him."[4]

The confusion and contention meant that the train did not leave Tianjin station until the afternoon. In the first of five trains were half the British, the Americans, and twenty-five Austrians. In addition, that train carried Chinese laborers and railway repair material. Admiral Seymour and his staff also had their quarters there. In the second train was the rest of the British force, the Japanese, and a few French. The third had the Germans. The fourth carried the Russians, the remainder of the French, and the Italians. The last train was a supply train, which Seymour intended to shuttle back and forth between Tianjin and the force.[5]

That tactical arrangement reflected even more clearly Seymour's confidence. The forces on the trains were not organized to disembark quickly, and the supply train would be intensely vulnerable to any substantial enemy force as it went back and forth. Should an enemy force be organized and intelligent enough to cut the rail lines ahead of and behind Seymour's force, his column would almost immediately be in serious trouble. They could not carry enough food and water with them to make up for the loss of supplies. David Beatty, another British naval officer, called Seymour's plan the "maddest, wildest, rottenest scheme that could emanate from the brain of any man." Beatty, however, was only a captain in 1900, and he could not do much more than obey Seymour's orders.

At first, things went quietly. Captain Joseph K. Taussig, an American marine, remembered the countryside that the train took them through:

The country was flat, dotted with the innumerable grave
mounds of centuries. The ground was dry and sun
baked, the crops insignificant and parched. The plain
was studded with villages and cities as far as the eye
could reach. There were no single houses anywhere. All
the Chinese lived in closely crowded communities . . .
This part of the country certainly made a sorry appearance due largely to the extended drought for which the
foreigners were being held responsible by the Boxers.[6]

It was hot. Clive Mersey, who had come with the column to as-
sist Seymour with translation, remembered "the sun at midday
striking down with tremendous heat on the arid lowlands, while
every two or three days a dust-storm enveloped earth and sky
in a burning sandy whirlwind which robbed us of sight, sound
and almost of sense."[7]

During this initial ride, the train passed by a large encamp-
ment of Chinese troops, under the command of General Nie
Shicheng. The passing was peaceful, with the Chinese letting
the allied train go by without hesitation. The belief within the
column was that the general was an ally:

After the murder of the first two missionaries, Mr. Norman and Mr. Robinson, General Nieh [Nie] had engaged the Boxers near Yangtsun [Huangcun] and had
sent into the Viceroy seventy heads in baskets as "a
guarantee of good faith." He now lay there in camp, and
on June 10th we passed him soon after midday, his soldiers coming up to ours and fraternising to the best of
their ability.[8]

General Nie was less an ally than surprised by the appearance
of the Westerners, having had no warning, telegraphing to
Beijing:

Today at noon, over one thousand foreign soldiers suddenly appeared. They carried rapid-firing cannons and railway repair materials to take direct trains to Beijing. I intended to stop them, but a telegram arrived saying that Your Excellency had granted their departure.[9]

The news of the expedition threw the court into a frenzy. They did not trust the Westerners, with years of good reasons, and Seymour's advance was seen as not merely to rescue the legations but potentially to overthrow the empress dowager herself.[10] One court official stood in front of the empress and declared that since he had practiced martial arts as a child, he, too, was a Boxer. More pragmatically, Cixi replaced the pro-Western Prince Qing as head of the Zongli Yamen with Prince Duan, whom the Western governments thought a "bigoted and fanatical conservative."[11]

While the Chinese soldiers had been friendly, the peasants were not. The train riders often saw the peasants working their fields in the distance, but visits to local villages during stops turned up no one, except for a few elders who were unwilling or unable to leave. The rest, the Westerners were informed, had "feared and fled" from the column's advance.

Twenty-five miles or so out of Tianjin, the train encountered a section of broken track, which the Westerners had to stop and repair before proceeding. Seymour camped overnight here. The men in the force were still cheerful and still confident that they would shortly be in Beijing:

As we sat around the camp fire eating our supper of corned beef and hardtack there were remarks of this nature: "Well, tomorrow evening we will have supper in Pekin." "I'll be a pretty sight to dine at the legation with the Minister and the ladies," spoken by one who glanced down at his very soiled uniform. "I hope there are enough beds at the Legation to go round"; this by one as he turned in fully dressed on the hard ground.[12]

Continuing in the morning, the force discovered and repaired more breaks, "at intervals of 2 or 3 miles," remembered Gitaro Mori, a Japanese officer.[13] None of them were major, usually consisting of the displacement of a section of track or two and the scattering of the ties that had supported them. In a few cases, the ties had been burned as well. There was nothing yet that was out of the expedition's repair capability. Seymour remained optimistic, telegraphing back to Tianjin that the force was "30 miles on the road to Peking, repairing railway as advance is made . . . [The] Railway requires repair at frequent intervals, but up to present country quiet and no sign of opposition. Hope to arrive at Peking Monday evening [June 11] unless march is opposed."[14]

It was not to be. As the expedition moved forward, larger and larger chunks of the destroyed railroad appeared, taking longer and longer to repair. On June 11 and 12, the expedition made only three miles, and on June 13, Seymour telegraphed back an update: "progress very slow, railway much broken up."[15] The Boxers were playing a canny game of destroying Seymour's method of advance and, essentially, pinning him in place. The local Boxer leader was a landowner named Ni Zanqing, and his strategy was first to focus on the expedition's ability to move. Cutting up the railway would slow it down and set it up for attacks.[16]

When Seymour tried to send smaller forces ahead to protect the line, they were attacked by Boxer forces. On June 12, while the main force stayed at Langfang to repair the railroad, Seymour sent ahead a group to Anting, thirteen miles north, to "prevent more damage being done to the line." The force of about fifty officers and men was soon under repeated attack by the Boxers, culminating in "a final and more determined attack by about four hundred and fifty Boxers, who charged in line with great courage and enthusiasm, but were repulsed with heavy loss." The Boxers had mounted a frontal assault against a prepared position and lost about 150 men, but the allied troops were forced to retire because their ammunition was running low, leaving the railroad in Chinese hands.[17] The Boxers might have suffered heavy losses, but given that their goal was to hold on to the railway, they had won a tactical victory.

The Boxers finally attacked the main force on the third day of the journey, mounting an ambush from a village close to where the trains were stopped. Numbering only several hundred, they caught the allies by surprise with most of the troops still in their train cars. They "came on us in a ragged line" without any "sign of fear or hesitation." Just out of effective firing range, the Boxers "dropped on their knees, lifting up their hands to heaven."[18] They were armed with a mix of close-in weapons like swords and spears, a few rifles, and an awkward Chinese firearm called a gingal, which required several men to operate. They wore "red caps, belts, and anklets," and a few waved flags of the same color. The Boxers did not attack all that quickly, instead "slowly and steadily advanc[ing], making many salaams and gestures—a most picturesque group." That doomed them, for it gave time for the Western soldiers to deploy into lines on either side of the trains and open up a steady rifle fire. The Westerners, unlike most Chinese soldiers, were armed with repeating rifles accurate to a substantial distance. As a result, the attackers were quickly "riddled with bullets, all, of course, being killed."[19]

The Boxers retreated, leaving behind what observers estimated to be about sixty dead bodies lying on the field. Captain Taussig asked his Chinese servant if the day's events had shown him the fallacy of the Boxers' claims to invulnerability, but the servant demurred, saying that the dead and the wounded were not "good Boxers" and thus were liable to be shot. Good Boxers were invulnerable.[20] That was not quite what Taussig wanted to hear. Worse, despite the victory, both the American marines, armed with .22 repeating rifles, and the British Royal Marines, armed with the Lee-Metford, found that it required several shots to stop a charging Boxer. The Lee-Metford "failed altogether to stop these pertinacious swordsmen, unless it struck a vital spot," wrote one member of the expedition.[21]

The attack had a salutary effect on the organization of the expedition, though. Prior to this, there had been no organized response to a potential attack planned out and agreed to ahead of time. The assault, failure though it was, finally led Admiral Seymour to call a meeting of all the commanding officers and decide on how to respond to attacks in the future.

The Boxers learned from the attack as well. The next attack, near the village of Langfang, was much more effectively mounted than the first. This time the Boxers worked their way much closer to the force before launching the assault, using the cover of the village itself and the orchards close-by. They also abstained from the rituals of the first attack and simply concentrated on getting in among the Westerners as fast as possible.

The allies, somehow, were again surprised. A group of five Italian sailors, who had gone outside the line of sentries to investigate the orchard, were caught in the open when the Boxers attacked. They tried to run back to the protection of the rest of the force, but "they were not speedy enough, and all were cut down by their pursuers."

Most of Seymour's men were gathered around a well getting water, unready for an attack. The sentries opened fire first and the rest of the soldiers slowly joined them. The attacking Chinese, showing the "utmost courage under a withering fire," according to Seymour, actually got in among the Western defenders.[22] "Desperate" hand-to-hand fighting broke out all along the line. Captain McCalla of the Americans shot several Boxers at close range, and one British officer stabbed a Boxer through the mouth with his sword. The allies finally got a machine gun into action, and the "welcome noise" of its firing seems to have inflicted enough damage on the trailing elements of the Boxers that they did not push their attack home, leaving the first few who had gotten into the defenses to be overwhelmed. The attackers retreated, leaving "102 dead on the field. There were no wounded."[23]

Even the partial success of the Boxer attack put the expedition into a bind. The more the column of trains had to stop to repair tracks, the more chances the Boxers would have to mount more ambushes. Should they attempt it with a force of thousands rather than hundreds, the result would potentially be the destruction of the entire column. The Boxers had managed to this point to destroy the rail lines and inflict a small number of casualties on the expedition. The only thing worse would be if the Chinese imperial troops began to fight the Westerners. Unfortunately for Seymour, exactly that was about to happen. On June 13, Cixi, listening to the advice of Prince Duan, had issued an imperial decree ordering General Nie to stop the foreign invasion.[24]

## TAKING THE FORTS

From a military perspective, Seymour's move to Beijing broke a number of rules. He set off by railroad, without any assurance that it would be intact in front of him or remain intact behind him, and without enough men to garrison the line. While such a gamble had worked for William Sherman during the American Civil War, Seymour was not Sherman, and his ad hoc force was not the Union army. Even more important, Seymour set off from Tianjin without controlling his access to the sea. Tianjin was ten to twenty miles inland, on the Hai River. The river ran down to the Yellow Sea. Protecting its mouth were sandbars difficult to cross by naval ships. In addition, four Chinese forts, garrisoned by imperial troops and armed with heavy cannon "opportunistically sold by Krupp of Germany to the Chinese government," watched the mouth of the river.[25] If Tianjin fell to the Chinese and the Western powers were unable to capture the forts, the military requirements of a campaign against China would skyrocket. Charles Dix, a British midshipman, described the topography:

> The Taku [Dagu] Forts are four in number, two being situated on each side of the mouth of the Pei-Ho [Hai] river. To seaward of them stretch large expanses of treacherous mud, just covered by the sea at high water; stakes have been driven into the slime for several hundred yards from the bottom of the embankments, and landing is quite impracticable at any state of the tide. On the landward side stretches a large plain, intersected with small canals and irrigation works, and immediately to the rear of the forts are the villages of Tong-Ku and Ta-Ku respectively.[26]

In addition to the forts, the Chinese had "four perfectly new . . . torpedo-boat destroyers, lately arrived from Germany, all fully manned and equipped and in perfect order," moored up the river.[27] The destroyers and the forts in combination were a not-insignificant defensive force and, if well fought, could have posed serious problems to the Western nations. The defenses were not "impregnable"; the Dagu Forts had been captured by a British force in 1860 on a similar mission, but they had been improved in the decades since, and naval forces attacking land fortifications were always wary.[28]

After Seymour moved north, the man closest to being in charge was Rear Admiral James Bruce of the Royal Navy. Sitting off Dagu in a "desolate anchorage . . . of greenish-yellow water," Bruce quickly grew nervous after losing contact with Seymour.[29] That nervousness grew when, on June 15, the telegraph line between Tianjin and Dagu was cut. On June 16, he telegraphed to London that "situation of affairs over all China very critical, some millions of Boxers in the north."

Bruce finally decided to act when he received reports that the Chinese were sending troops to build up the garrisons at the forts and preparing to mine the mouth of the river. If the Chinese could reinforce the forts and mine the river mouth, the situation would take on a "very grave aspect." "We were face to face with a crisis of the first order," the admiral thought. "If we lost the forts, we lost the entrance to the river, and all communication with our forces at Tientsin and the front." The alternatives were not good: "Our only other available base of operations was Pei-ta-ho about 120 miles to the north, with a destroyed railway, two large Chinese Military Camps in front of us and . . . a country totally devoid of any supplies."[30] Unlike Seymour, Bruce was not going to gamble. Instead, he would build the Western position in China carefully. First, take the forts and then move on to Tianjin. Bruce, if he had a similar aggressiveness to both Seymour and Keyes, was less cavalier about it.

Bruce could not act alone. Instead, he summoned a meeting of the naval commanders present off Dagu and discussed the situation with them. The consensus, after some discussion, was to try to compel the Chinese to hand over the forts peaceably and, if that failed, capture them by force. The explicit goal was "to relieve [the] Commander in Chief." In the week since Seymour had left, the situation had changed drastically. For the moment, the embassies were on their own, and the allied forces in China were simply fighting to preserve themselves.[31]

Bruce, used to the suspicion and mistrust of imperial rivalries, marveled at the cooperation. "Nothing," he said, "can exceed the excellent relationship between the Admirals here, we might all belong to one country and friendly at that." It was a "structure of expediency" put together by the coalition of nations.[32] But even here, he could not help but contemplate a postcrisis situation and what it meant for the imperial powers: "If this should turn out to be the last of the Manchu Dynasty, it would be well to be the strong man armed during the crisis."[33]

Of the powers present, only the American commander, Rear Admiral Louis Kempff, waffled. His instructions from home were to take no action against the Chinese unless provoked by an act of war, and the rear admiral did not feel that such had happened. In addition, the American fleet was focused on the Philippines, and Kempff's superior, Rear Admiral George C. Remey, was proving reluctant to send any forces at all to China. Remey had heard reports that the Filipino junta in Hong Kong was planning to take advantage of the summer rainy season to smuggle arms to the archipelago, and the admiral was worried that sending forces to China would "sap the strength of operations in the Philippines."[34]

On the other hand, American nationals were clearly in trouble in China, and it was Kempff's duty to protect them. He was unlikely to be able to do so without the cooperation of the other Western powers, cooperation that might be reluctant if he refused to go along with their plans. Nor could Kempff put the decision off on Washington. Communications with home were faster than they had been before the spread of the telegraph, but they were still not quick enough to react to the constant changes in the crisis. Kempff was on his own, with a decision to make.[35] In the end, he seems to have arranged matters conveniently. He refused to participate in the attack but did position the American gunship *Monocacy* in the Hai River, near where any action would have to take place, and left it to the commander of that ship, Frederic Wise, to act if necessary. "Captain Wise of the *Monocacy* had orders to protect American interests, but in case of attack by the Chinese government force he was to consider it as a declaration of war and act accordingly." Given where he positioned the ship, such an attack was only too likely to happen, a fact that can hardly have escaped the admiral.[36]

The allies decided to mount a land assault on the forts. They would send an ultimatum to the Chinese commander of the forts, demanding that the structures be turned over to the Western powers by 2:00 a.m. on June 17. Upon expiration of the ultimatum, a force of 904 officers and men, largely British, German, Japanese, and Russian, would immediately land behind the forts on the inland side and attempt to capture them. The guns of the fleet would suppress Chinese defensive fire.

At the same time, another force would aim to take the four Chinese destroyers moored on the riverbank. This force, entirely British, consisted of four ships: the HMS *Whiting* and the HMS *Fame* and their two whalers. Each destroyer would tow a whaler loaded with sailors and marines. They would head up the river, seemingly aiming to go past the Chinese ships, and then, at the last moment, swing in and pull alongside. The first destroyer would lash itself to the first Chinese ship, with its whaler attacking the second Chinese ship, and the second destroyer would attempt a similar pas de deux.

There were drawbacks and vulnerabilities in both plans. Though the ultimatum would have warned them, the preparations for the assault would give the Chinese detailed ideas of how the attack would come. In addition, the attackers on land, aiming first at the northwest fort, would have to cross nearly a thousand yards of open terrain and a moat before they got to the walls. If the fleet could not keep down Chinese fire, the Western attackers were likely to be driven off with heavy casualties.

On the river, if the Chinese sailors in their destroyers were paying any real attention to what was going on around them and could get their guns into action, the British attackers in the

*Fame* and *Whiting* would be in serious trouble. Just managing the delicate maneuver of placing all four ships alongside the Chinese vessels was insanely difficult. It was nonetheless the kind of inspired and lunatic cutting-out expedition that the British navy had been doing for centuries. It may have helped that the commanders of both British ships were in their twenties. The plan surely required the confidence of such a youthful age to be executed.

There is some argument about how firing actually started. The attackers claimed that the Chinese started firing on the Western ships before the ultimatum expired:

> As the pre-arranged hour for starting the bombardment was 2 a.m., and as there were few who felt sleepily inclined, the spare hours were given up to discussing whether the Chinese would accept the ultimatum and run, or whether the allies would find themselves engaged in a few hours' time. This was decided in a most abrupt manner, for at 12.50, or one hour and ten minutes before the allies were going to start, a shell shrieked over the "Algerine" in unpleasant proximity to her topmasts. This was followed by an almost simultaneous fire from every gun that would bear on the little squadron.[37]

The Chinese, by contrast, claimed that the allies had started the firing and thus precipitated a war. The debate was essentially irrelevant: the allies were certainly planning on firing, and the Chinese were acting in defense of their territory. The Western powers attacked the forts for what they thought were sound military reasons, but given the long history of imperial expropriation, they hardly had an innocent leg left on which to stand. The flip side of this was, of course, that the Chinese government, more than was normal in that tumultuous land, had lost control of its people and its countryside. The chaos threatened to engulf European citizens, to whom the Western powers had responsibilities. Given such a situation, the Western powers ultimately had little choice in their actions. But we should not push this too far; innocent actors in summer 1900 China were few and far between, and may well have been limited to those who were simply too young to be anything else.

The assault force for the forts was towed in on lighters attached to tugs. It was a long ride under the guns of the forts, through the darkness of the night. The moon, a few days past full, did cast some light, but not enough to do more than outline the riverbank. As the soldiers moved in, each man was given a "ration of optional cocoa" to sustain him.[38] The force landed to the west of the forts on the north bank of the river and assembled there. A little before 3:00 a.m., it moved into the attack. The first assault did not go well. Moving over the "perfectly flat, hard mud, without a vestige of cover," the attackers discovered that the preparatory bombardment had not, in fact, done much damage to the fort, which was "practically intact." The Chinese now poured a withering fire on the attacking force, inflicting substantial casualties, and Commander Christopher Cradock, the British officer in charge of the force, decided to retreat to cover and wait for a further bombardment.[39]

As Cradock and his men discovered, the darkness made it hard for the fleet's gunners to hit their targets. That went both ways, and for the most part neither the ships nor the forts were hit particularly hard. The exception in the early going was the Russian ship *Gilyak*, which turned on a spotlight to help it find Chinese targets. The intense beam of light attracted every Chinese gun within range, and the Russians found themselves pelted with shells and shot. The ship was sunk and ten Russians killed, with many more wounded.

Commander Frederic M. Wise of the USS *Monocacy* found himself in the middle of all of this. He had refugees on board and shells from the forts sailing perilously close. Mrs. James Jones, one of the refugees, had recently come down from Tianjin because of the risk of a Chinese assault there. "We seemed to have fallen 'out of the frying pan into the fire,'" she remembered. "We and the ships . . . were right in the line of fire and had anything but a pleasant time, the shells whistling above and around us in all directions."[40] Eventually, a six-inch shell crashed through the ship's boat on the stern and then, without exploding, into and out of the hull of the *Monocacy* itself. Wise might have decided that this constituted an act of war and joined the firefight, but concluded instead that the risk to the refugees was too great. He thus moved the *Monocacy* up the river, out of range, and waited for the battle to conclude. Somewhat unfairly, he was roundly criticized for this later by Kempff, who may have been frustrated that his scheming had failed to work.

The sky began to lighten soon after 4:00 a.m., and in answer to Cradock's call for more fire support, the gunboats *Algerine* and *Iltis* moved in as close as they dared and pummeled the fortifications with "good effect." The *Algerine* in particular got so close that the guns of the forts could not be depressed enough to hit it.[41] By 4:30 a.m., the "guns of the fort were practically silenced."[42] At that point, Cradock renewed the advance. The defenders managed to get two field guns working on the side of the fort as the attack came in, but most of the mounted guns either were out of order or had had their crews killed. Captain Hattori, the officer in command of the Japanese units, spotted a path that gave access to the fort, and he "pushed on rapidly, leaving the rest of the allies behind." Hattori decided that "a bayonet charge was the only resource" and led his men up the parapet of the fort. He was shot dead in the assault, but the rest of the Japanese troops made it over and in and swept the defenders from the wall, clearing it for the rest to follow.[43] There was later the story that Hattori, with his troops, reached the top of the wall seconds ahead of the British, and that the Japanese officer turned to extend his hand to Cradock, but was shot dead by a Chinese defender. This seems more legend than reality.

In some regards, the allied forces (particularly the British) treated the attack as more a sporting than a military event. There was a strong sense that each nation's men should strive to outdo those of other nations. In a sense, this competitiveness mimicked the competitiveness of the Olympics going on in Paris at that very moment. Each nation sought not only to win but to represent itself well. And how better than with some physical marker of being first, of being most successful? A British officer described the attack on the forts as a self-conscious race between the Japanese and the British. "The Japanese had volunteered to storm the first fort with the British, and a race ensued between the two, the Japanese winning and getting in first." Once they were inside, "the Japanese flag was hoisted on one of the northern forts, shortly followed by the British."[44] Interestingly, however, two British officers actually involved in the assault claimed that the *British* flag went up first. Charles Dix claimed:

> There was a race for the two flagstaffs: the Chinese yellow Dragons were torn down, and amidst an outburst of cheering the White Ensign was hoisted, closely followed by the red Sun of Japan. I used my pistol for the first time here. My lieutenant and myself were standing in the square cheering our flag going up, with our men taking cover in a passage, when two Chinese nipped out of a gateway about twenty yards away, and came for us with fixed bayonets, firing their magazines as they marched, from the hip. My lieutenant had emptied his revolver and was drawing his sword to defend himself when I chipped in and "bagged the brace."[45]

Tellingly, Dix described the events explicitly in sporting terms: There was a "race" with an "outburst of cheering." The outcome was "closely" decided. He "bagged the brace" of Chinese. In his report to Bruce, Cradock was very careful to emphasize that the British flag had gone up first: "The British flag was in this, as in all successive forts, the first to be run up."[46] Who was correct is open to debate, of course, though one might be forgiven for being skeptical of the reports of Dix and Cradock, closely tied as they were to the success of the assault. Admiral Bruce, from his vantage point offshore, "saw the Japanese Flag flying over the fort and I believe ours went up at exactly the same time," which seems a soundly diplomatic way of resolving the competition.[47]

After the first fort was captured, the attacking forces turned to the others. They found Chinese resistance much lighter, with only "very slight resistance" coming before the North Fort was occupied. Inside the North Fort, the British and Japanese soldiers turned the defensive guns toward the forts on the south side of the river and began adding to the weight of fire. The Russian forces south of the river quickly occupied those forts, and by breakfast time the Western powers had gained control of the banks of the Hai River mouth. The shelling from the ships did little damage to the outside of the forts, but inside it was a different matter. "The forts do not show much damage from the outside, but on entering them a very vivid idea is gained as to the effect of modern shell fire. The place was wrecked and mutilated men and horses were thickly strewn over the blood-stained ground."[48] The attackers cleaned up hastily, "gathering together . . . headless and armless bodies" into heaps and then burning them.[49]

Simultaneous to this was the British attack on the Chinese destroyers. Keyes had to hurry; the firing of the Chinese forts before the ultimatum expired left him distant from the destroyers he was aiming to capture. His ships had moored themselves in the same spot as several Russian gunboats had the past several days. It turned out to be an awkward choice, because the Chinese gunners in the forts had laid their sights on the Russian gunboats during the day and left them, ready to fire, overnight. As a result, Keyes remembered, the first few salvos from the forts were "uncomfortably accurate." Luckily, the falling tide had dropped the ships down in the anchorage, and so a number of the shots sailed overhead to bury themselves in the mud bank on the other side. The Russian ships also anchored there had not had such a "charmed existence," with both the *Koreetz* and the *Gilyak* taking fairly serious hits. The *Gilyak*, with its bright spotlight, brought it on itself, but the *Koreetz* had remained dark. A Chinese junk loaded with mines had also been hit and blown up next to the *Whiting*. All in all, it was no place for the British to remain.[50]

Keyes ordered the boarding party into the whaler that would trail behind the *Fame* as it moved off and "ran forward to weigh the anchor." Just as he did, another shell hit the *Koreetz* just ahead of them, and the crew on the deck of the *Fame* was "smothered with smoke and soot." Commander Colin Mac-Kenzie, in the *Whiting*, thought that the *Fame* had been blown up and was relieved when he came around the next bend in the river and found Keyes waiting for him. The two ships, trailing their boats, moved up quickly on their Chinese targets, worried that the defenders would inflict damage as the British closed.

But the Chinese crews of the ships did not react quickly to the outburst of shots, and Keyes and MacKenzie were able to put their ships alongside the targets without taking any hits. It was a deft feat of navigation sailing against the current to put the ship and its towed whaleboats directly against the side of their targets, but they managed. The boarding parties jumped aboard and fought their way through what Keyes later reported to be "the exchange of a few shots and a hand-to-hand scuffle." The Chinese crew was either summarily pushed overboard or "shoved down below with the hatches closed over them."[51] Commander MacKenzie reported similarly: the attackers were greeted with "smart small-arms fire . . . but no casualties were suffered [and] the whole four destroyers were . . . carried with a rush."[52] Keyes ordered his men not to shoot the Chinese crewmen clambering up on the bank, claiming that he was "rather squeamish" about shooting men in the back. He regretted it in a moment: "[Letting them go] was a mistake which no foreigner would have made . . . as they came back and started sniping us from the dockyard walls by way of thanks."[53] This "heavy sniping" from the dock may have been Chinese troops ashore rather than the escaped crew, as the latter was unlikely to have been able to secure weapons that quickly after being so heartily dispossessed of its ship.[54] The British got all the ships—captured or not—under way and set off for a secure anchorage, which they managed within a few hours.

Admiral Bruce greeted the success with "enormous relief."[55] The allies had worked together relatively well on both land and sea, and the casualties had been minimal on their side. The fighting did illustrate one issue that would continue. The Westerners began to assume that all civilians were Boxers and to treat them that way. Thus, one observer noted after the fall of the forts that "as soon as it was daylight we saw in the distance a black mass of Chinese hurrying from the forts and the villages round about. It is feared they will make for Tientsin and join the Boxers."[56] The assumption that any fleeing Chinese were Boxers (or would join them), as opposed simply to being civilian refugees, shaped how the allies treated Chinese civilians, much to the negative.

The Chinese, for their part, believed that the attack on the forts was an act of war.[57] The conservative politicians within the court convinced Cixi that now was the time to fight. The Boxers would serve as useful irregulars, and those elements of the Chinese imperial army that were trained and equipped to

Western standards could fight the invading force. Now was the opportunity to show how much power "self-strengthening" had created. On June 21, 1900, the throne issued a declaration of war, arguing that "the foreigners have been aggressive towards us, infringed upon our territorial integrity, trampled our people under their feet, and taken our property by force."[58]


## BESIEGED

At that moment, in the middle of June, the military situation hung in the balance. The allies held the entry point to the Chinese mainland at Dagu but were penned in Tianjin by substantial Chinese forces and had to protect the civilian residents there and elsewhere in northern China. They had not had time to build up a large reserve of forces. Seymour's expedition had ground to a halt halfway to Beijing, and the Westerners in the legations were surrounded by units in the capital city. If the Chinese could keep the Westerners confined to Tianjin and Dagu, or even drive them out of the former, the situation would require the commitment of enormous numbers of Western soldiers and ships to overcome. Such a concentration was possible, but the throne could always hope that the political infighting among the Western powers, not least between Japan and Russia, would prevent it. On the flip side, the Chinese faced not one Western power but eight, and most particularly they faced not only the largest of the empires in the British but the Japanese and Russians, local to the conflict and with enormous military resources in the immediate area. The balance was close, but Cixi seems to have decided that she had no choice. It all came down to the Chinese army. Could the newly trained units manage better than before? Could the army, as it had not in 1860 or 1894–1895, hold against the soldiers of the imperial powers?

The Chinese troops arrayed at Dagu had not done well

against the Western forces. By contrast, those who started to move against Seymour's column did much better. The first thing that Seymour's people noticed on June 17 was the disappearance of the imperial troops from their positions protecting the railway between Tianjin and Beijing. Where they had gone, no one was sure.

Boxer tactics had changed. Their spears and swords had been replaced by rifles, and they had learned that pushing home their assault would result in heavy casualties.[59] Instead, now that the forces were moving largely by foot, the Boxer units mounted ambushes in which they fired one or two volleys and then broke off the attack. The point seems to have been not to inflict serious casualties on the expedition but to make it break from its march and deploy into skirmish lines or, even better, take up defensive positions of its own. The "flat fields interlaced with mud walls and thousands of grave mounds" offered numerous opportunities for just such tactics.[60] Sometimes, the Boxers figured, they didn't even need to use weapons, preferring firecrackers instead. Upon coming on a village and hearing a fusillade of gunshots, the troops took to the ground, only for a Japanese captain to realize what was going on. "He simply shouted 'Firecrackers!' . . . The mixed line of American, British, French, and Japanese rushed forward on the double, all yelling at the tops of our voices," but they were too late to capture the Chinese responsible. "Firecrackers," Captain Taussig remembered glumly, "were added to the list of defensive weapons."[61] The allies responded to these new tactics by simply burning all the Chinese villages they encountered, to prevent their use by the Boxers.

The Boxers successfully slowed Seymour's advance down considerably. The repeated necessity to break into skirmish line or go to ground and then clear out the village ahead left Seymour's expedition unable to make any substantial progress on June 17 and early on the eighteenth. Combined with the continued wrecking of the railroads, the column began to resemble nothing more than someone running in deep sand, slower and slower and with more and more effort.

On June 18, Seymour traveled on the supply train back to Yangcun to help organize efforts to repair the lines behind them. He left Captain Guido von Usedom, a German officer, in charge of the main body of the force near Yangcun. It was here that the Chinese army finally showed itself by mounting a sizable assault on the forces under von Usedom. Early on the morning of the eighteenth a mixed force of Boxers and Chinese imperial troops attacked the Westerners. The Chinese seem to have outnumbered the Western forces, although perhaps not substantially.

The Chinese forces, despite repeated attempts, could not close with the Westerners, and by the end of the day they had suffered heavily, with an estimated five hundred dead. The Westerners had suffered only about five dead and a number wounded and held the field. Despite the victory, von Usedom decided "that it would be futile to attempt to make Pekin under these circumstances, and even to hold Lang Fang," so he ordered a retreat back down the line to join up with Seymour. Seymour was shocked to hear from von Usedom of the encounter:

> [The troops] had had a severe engagement with . . . [a] great force estimated to be fully 5000 men (including cavalry), large numbers of whom were armed with magazine rifles of the latest pattern. The banners captured show them to have belonged to the Army of General Feng Fu Hisang . . . It was thus definitely known for the first time that Imperial Chinese Troops were being employed against us.[62]

Von Usedom's decision was curious, to say the least. He was certainly in command until Seymour came back, but retreating essentially made it enormously difficult for the admiral to push his forces back up the line. Given the newly active Chinese army and the likelihood that the Boxers would be ripping up the twenty-five miles of rail line left abandoned by the retreat, the Westerners would be unlikely to return without interference. Retreating in the aftermath of a victory seems somewhat weak-kneed.

Still, a strong case can be made for von Usedom's actions. With the Chinese army in play, having the various parts of the expedition separated from each other up and down the rail line was extremely dangerous and risked having each of those elements cut off and defeated in isolation. At one station between von Usedom and Seymour, the admiral had left one officer and thirty men, hardly enough to hold against a sustained attack.[63] Traveling back down the line, von Usedom gathered up those forces left behind him, and by the time he reached Seymour, nearly the entire force was together again, almost for the first time since setting off. Finally, von Usedom may have recognized that the chances of continuing to Beijing were essentially gone, and this was his way of pushing the admiral to recognize the same thing.

Seymour's hand was certainly forced, both by the actions of the German captain and by the Chinese army itself. Taking the rail line all the way into Beijing was simply no longer possible. Without the train to carry wounded and supplies, the column could not advance. And even if it could, Clive Mersey thought, "to arrive [in Beijing] without food and ammunition, and with a number of wounded, would be of little help."[64] Seymour contemplated his situation. They were "cut off from our base," and "it seemed unlikely that we could get nearer Peking than Anting or a little beyond it" on the train. He thought about heading back to Yangcun, where the railroad joined the Hai, leaving the train, and heading up the river to Beijing. This was the route the British had taken in 1860, and it had the promise that, unlike railroads, the Boxers could not tear up a river. But it required a substantial amount of shipping to carry supplies and wounded. Seymour sent messengers back to Tianjin to have them gather such ships, but they never returned.

In the end, by June 19, Seymour decided to head back to Tianjin and regather his forces there. They would take the train back to Huangcun and then follow the river into Tianjin, helped by four junks that the Germans had liberated, or so they claimed, from Boxers. None of the allied forces were "skilled in handling such craft," which slowed the retreat.[65] Nonetheless, the expedition made reasonable progress on foot, going eight miles in the first day. The Chinese continued with their harassing fire, shooting from each village and retreating before they were engaged by the Westerners. Advancing thus required constant fighting, whether with rifle fire or bayonet.

Seymour, perhaps still lost in his dreams of superiority, did not realize that this was a deliberate tactic and thought that "the charge with bayonet was always very effective, the cheers of the men as they advanced appearing to intimidate the Chinese, who without waiting to receive the charge would fall back immediately."[66] Mersey was more clear-sighted about the difficulties this caused:

> Nearly every one of these villages was held by Boxers in more or less force, but always sufficient to make us halt the junks, deploy, and form firing line. These positions, with their high mud-walled houses, clusters of timber and treeless zone outside, were easy to hold, and the first lesson we learnt was that the attack must always be prepared to lose four or five times as much as the defence.[67]

The attackers were still entirely Boxers, but on the twenty-first a unit of Chinese cavalry appeared in the distance and began to shadow the force without engaging. The sense here was of a slow trap closing in on the Westerners, with the irregular forces providing harassment, while the regular forces set up some sort of advantageous battlefield for an engagement. Seymour, however, did not make the connection, failing to wonder where, exactly, the Chinese army was and why it hadn't engaged. This lack of insight led to an unwelcome surprise at Beicang on June 22, where he found a substantial force of Chinese troops arrayed in a fortified position along the river. It was, Seymour thought, "a very strong position, from which we were unable to dislodge them." Continuing along the river was a necessity because of the junks.

Seymour's situation was now desperate. The forces, burdened with wounded, low on ammunition and food, hardly had the resources for a substantial battle. It is a sign of Seymour's dawning desperation that rather than decide himself, he called an emergency conference of his officers. They decided to try to sneak past the Chinese during the night. This did not hold out a substantial chance of success, as the noise of nearly two thousand soldiers, sailors, and marines marching could hardly be concealed. Nonetheless, the column started out at 1:00 a.m. in the attempt. Within minutes, "fires were seen at one or two places . . . evidently signaling our advance." After about a mile, the advance guard came under heavy fire from a village on the bank. The marines "then fixed bayonets and carried the position without further opposition." But at the same time, the junk carrying the force's fieldpieces and machine guns was sunk by fire from Chinese artillery. The Westerners managed to save the machine guns, but the fieldpieces were lost. Despite the alert, the Chinese defenders did not react well to the allied column. Rather than sallying out of their fortifications to cut off the force, the Chinese preferred to remain behind their walls and snipe at the Westerners as they went past, sniping that was largely ineffective because of the dark. Much to everyone's surprise, by the time the night had ended, the allied force had successfully made it south of Beicang, with Tianjin close ahead.[68]

That did not mean, however, that the expedition was free from worry. Seymour could not know for sure, but he had to have guessed that there were a substantial number of Chinese forces in the Tianjin area proper and that he would have to fight his way through them to get into the foreign enclaves. Even then, Tianjin might only be a temporary reprieve, as the admiral did not know whether the foreign forces in the city were linked with the fleet offshore. He might break into Tianjin only to discover that he had to break out again, this time to Dagu. Or it might be no reprieve at all, as Clive Mersey thought: "We had heard salvoes of heavy guns all day, and for aught we knew Tientsin had already been captured, and we might still have to cut our way through to Taku [Dagu] and the sea." In any case, breaking into Tianjin might no longer be possible. The column was desperately short of supplies, particularly ammunition and food, and was substantially weighed down by the growing number of wounded. Seymour had snuck by the Chinese the previous night; that likely wouldn't be possible against the Chinese at Tianjin, and neither he nor his officers could guarantee the outcome of a full-scale battle between the fresh Chinese troops, supplemented by Boxers, and his weary force. The imperial confidence that had brought him to this situation had leached away, leaving Seymour, now a "little despondent," wondering what to do.[69] He was not the only one suffering from the strain. Captain H.T.R. Lloyd of the Royal Marines wrote later that his senior NCO had essentially broken under the strain: "My Sergeant major was in such a state of collapse that at each halt, he fell on his face shouting out 'My God, my God!'" Eventually, the man refused to move, and Lloyd had to have two of the marines half carry, half drag him.[70]

"The Chinese kopje: not so easy as it looked
from a distance." (Library of Congress)

ABOVE: North China: Shandong to the south, Beijing to the northwest
(Library of Congress)

BELOW: The plan of attack at Dagu (British National Archives)

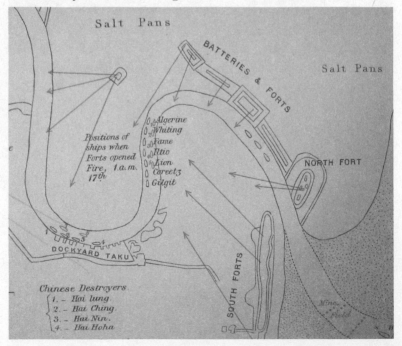

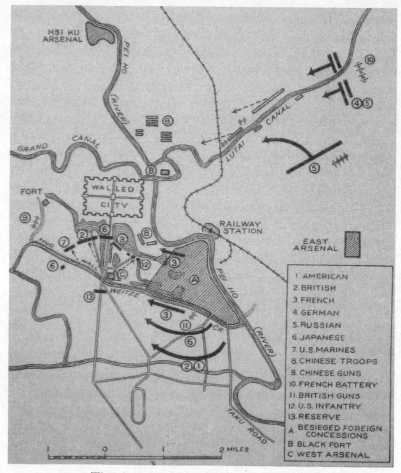

The plan of attack at Tianjin (*Military Review*)

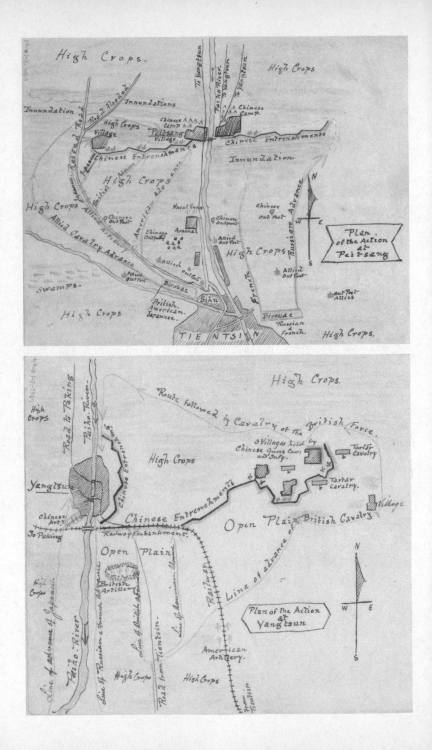

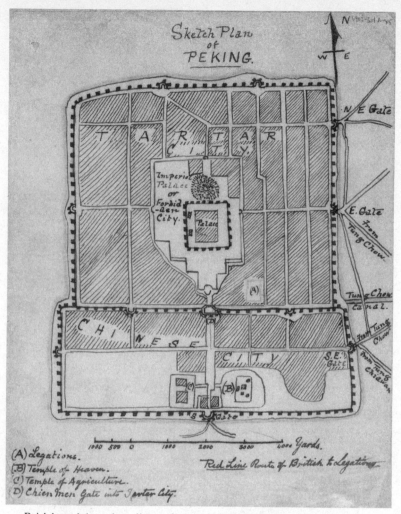

Sketch Plan of PEKING.

British and American lines of entry into Beijing (National Army Museum)

Chinese Christian refugees (Library of Congress)

The Tartar Wall, to be held at all costs (Library of Congress)

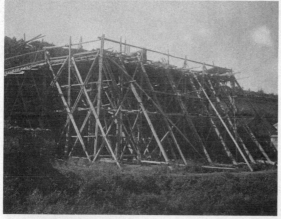

ABOVE: Repairing a sabotaged railroad (National Army Museum)

LEFT: Fortifying the legation wall (National Army Museum)

BELOW: The center of the legations. The board was used for messages and news. (National Army Museum)

A group of Boxers in Tianjin (Library of Congress)

A wrecked fort at Dagu (National Army Museum)

The Tianjin railway
station, much abused
(Library of Congress)

LEFT: Chinese soldiers at
Tianjin (Library of Congress)

BELOW: A Japanese mural
of the turning point at the
Battle of Tianjin (Library of
Congress)

American soldiers treating wounded Japanese after the Battle of Tianjin (Library of Congress)

Watching an execution at Tianjin (Library of Congress)

French soldiers in camp (Library of Congress)

A Chinese family eating in the ruins of its house in
Tianjin (Library of Congress)

A body floating down the Hai River (National Army Museum)

Chinese junks used as a supply chain (Library of Congress)

A village destroyed by coalition forces on their march to Beijing
(Library of Congress)

"Are our teachings, then, in vain?" (Library of Congress)

American soldiers camping in the Forbidden City (Library of Congress)

The body of Captain O'Reilly and his men (National Army Museum)

Public executions (National Army Museum)

Punishment (Library of Congress)

"A disturbing possibility in the East." (Library of Congress)

American soldiers saying goodbye
(National Army Museum)

Chinese Christian refugees leaving
Beijing (Library of Congress)

The empress returns. (National Army Museum)

# 5

# "THE FAULT OF NATURE"

Seymour was saved by a stroke of luck. Between Beicang and Tianjin lay the Xigu Arsenal, an enormous fortified structure that the Chinese used to store mass quantities of ammunition, food, and other supplies. It was this fortification that the expedition came upon the morning after it had snuck through the Chinese army at Beicang. It was an imposing edifice with enormously high and thick walls but, strangely, only held by a small force of imperial troops, a singular and fatal neglect by the Chinese. Seymour quickly set his forces to capturing it, a task that, despite the small force arrayed inside, took them most of the day. The main part of the force fixed the attention of the defenders by firing from the front of the arsenal, while a smaller force of Royal Marines, under Major James Johnstone, circled around behind them. Johnstone's force reached position in late afternoon and attacked, a "startling surprise" to the defenders. They seem to have mistaken his force for a much larger Western one coming up from Tianjin, for "without more ado, the Chinese abandoned their wonderfully strong position and fled," leaving the arsenal to the allied force.[1]

Here was safety. The wounded, now numbering about 230, could be protected without burdening the defenders, and the enormous walls of the arsenal provided a ready-made defensive position for the healthy combatants. The remaining issue was food. By the time it took the fortress, the expedition was down to three days' worth of rations. They could not stay for long, the men thought. Worse, the Chinese began attacking the arsenal almost as soon as it was captured. An assault hit the walls on the morning of June 23 and was beaten off, but the defenders were now getting low on ammunition as well as food. It was, Seymour noted carefully, a "somewhat precarious position."[2]

It was to get much less precarious almost immediately after that morning attack. It was only after it was beaten off that Seymour thought to make a "thorough search" of the armory. Doing so produced a pleasant surprise. Within the walls were "about fifteen tons of rice" and "immense supplies of guns, arms, ammunition, and war material of [the] latest pattern." Seymour estimated that it held about "£3,000,000 worth of warlike stores." The allies were overjoyed: the "discovery gave us what we most needed, viz food and ammunition." Much of it was familiar, guns and ammunition from Germany making up a substantial part of the stores. Captain Taussig waxed eloquent:

> There were stacks and stacks of modern rifles— Winchesters, Mausers and Manlichers; and hundreds of thousands of rounds of ammunition. There were field guns and siege guns by the score. There were magazines containing immense stocks of both black and smokeless powder. That this place was so easily taken seemed a miracle. It was our salvation.[3]

The expedition had breathing room. The problem was that the arsenal was, if anything, *too* large. Seymour's force had had no sleep for almost two days, and so the admiral decided not to man the outer walls, but pull in around the armory and the hospital. Only "small picquets . . . put out at short distances" kept watch. Like so many of Seymour's decisions, this resulted in near disaster:

> At 3 o'clock in the morning we were again attacked by masses of Boxers and troops combined. They had got in over the outer walls during the night and had concealed themselves in the long reeds, whence they poured volleys into us. In the action that resulted while clearing them out we again suffered considerable losses.[4]

The trick now was to get into communication with the forces in Tianjin and let them know that Seymour and his men were close by. Seymour tried first on June 22 to send a small force of Royal Marines in a wide loop away from the river toward Tianjin. It was a dangerous mission, and Captain H.T.R. Lloyd, one of the marine officers, wrote later that he and his fellow officers "decided to keep one round in our revolvers in case we were taken by the enemy, in order to commit suicide."[5] The force was discovered fairly quickly, and the Chinese defenders aroused against them. "Active resistance" and the loss of four marines led the force to return to the arsenal.[6]

On the next day, Seymour took a different tack. He found a native Chinese, the servant of Clive Mersey, who was willing to take a message to Tianjin. The Chinese man scrambled down one of the walls that day with a message "which he was to eat if caught."[7] His escape was covered by a raging dust storm, and he managed to get past the Chinese soldiers around the arsenal. Sensibly, the man had almost immediately eaten the message, not trusting that he could do so when he was approached by Boxers or troops. Later, he was, in fact, captured by Boxers, tied to a tree, and interrogated, but he steadfastly claimed that he was a local. They released him, and on June 24 he managed to sneak into the foreign enclave at Tianjin. French sentries there fired on him, but "by semaphoring with his arms, he at last conveyed to them that he had a message." Given the rough suspicion with which all Chinese were held by the Westerners at that moment, that itself was quite an accomplishment.[8]

## RELIEVING TIANJIN

The capture of the Dagu Forts meant that the way to Tianjin was essentially open to the Western powers. But simply capturing the forts did not end the matter. The attack on the forts had led the Chinese forces around Tianjin to begin shelling its foreign enclave and cutting off communications with the coast. One of the last messages to get through to Admiral Bruce came from W. R. Carles, the British consul. It was straightforward and desperate: "The foreign settlements are being shelled and the [defenders] are being driven in. Reinforcements are *most* urgently required." British phlegmatism did command Carles enough that he signed the message "Your obedient servant."[9] Herbert Hoover, then a young mining engineer, would write of the situation in the foreign enclave. There was so much artillery and rifle fire coming into the enclave, he said, that at times the streets "were simply canals of moving lead."[10]

By June 21, Admiral Bruce had lost contact with both Seymour and the foreign enclave: "No communication from Commander in Chief for seven days or with Tientsin for five days." He did not have "sufficient strength" to relieve Tianjin. Privately, he wrote that "matters [were] generally as bad as can be."[11]

He heard from Tianjin first. A resident of the city and member of the Tianjin Volunteer Corps, Mr. J. Watts, volunteered to try to make a dash to the coastline, carrying messages.[12] Accompanied by three Cossacks on fast horses, Watts left the night of the nineteenth and made a high-speed run down the river line, avoiding Boxers and Chinese troops alike or, in one case, simply riding through and past a group of soldiers before they could react. Watts delivered his messages, which led Bruce to write a second telegram to the Admiralty on June 21. It was not good news. Allied forces at Tianjin were in peril: "Casualties have been heavy. Supplies of ammunition insufficient. Machine guns or field guns required . . . Russians at railway station hard-pressed. Chinese maintain incessant fire with large guns on European concession, nearly all which burnt."[13]

The allied forces could get to Tianjin by railroad, by river, or overland. The railroad was out of action, and there were not enough ships to carry the men to the city. Overland became the only viable option.

The first force to set out for Tianjin was a mixed Russian and American force, with a large number of Russian soldiers supplemented by a smaller group of American marines. The attack on the *Monocacy* had been enough for Admiral Kempff to associate the U.S. forces with the other Western powers, but he was limited in the number of fighting men he had available. A portion of the American marine force was in Beijing itself, holding the legations. On June 18, the first of a flow of reinforcements began to show up when the USS *Newark* arrived from the Philippines, carrying a force of marines under Major Littleton Waller. It was those marines, supplemented by more from the USS *Nashville*, who set out to Tianjin on June 19, about 140 strong. This was not an organized assault; there had been no meeting of the commanding officers of the various powers to decide on a further plan of action. Kempff ordered Waller to go with the first foreign contingent, in this case, the Russians. Waller's men thus headed off, leaving behind the British and Japanese forces at Dagu. On their march, they "overtook" the Russians, and the two forces joined up. They took the train as far as it still went, to about twelve miles from Tianjin, and then camped overnight on June 20.[14]

The next morning saw a disagreement. The Russian commander wanted to advance, while Major Waller felt that the force was "much too small to begin active operations." The Russian won the argument, Waller claimed later that he was "overruled in council," and the group began to advance toward Tianjin.[15] It reached the imperial arsenal on the outskirts of the city at about 6:30 a.m., where it came under fire, "lightly at first, but presently heavily, and with considerable accuracy." For "two hours of sanguinary fighting," the Russians and Americans tried unsuccessfully to take the armory. Both the marines and the Russians had casualties. Private James J. Sullivan, a marine, remembered that "[we] had some men seriously wounded and we not having or the Russians either a single doctor or stretcher and us Marines having absolutely nothing but depending on the two Russian nurses who worked liked horses caring for the wounded."[16] The gun crew of the marines, which was leading the advance, was particularly hard-hit, with all but one being wounded or killed.

Who decided to retreat and exactly when remains up for discussion. In some accounts, the Russians withdrew without telling the Americans, leaving the "small force of Marines to cover their retreat entirely unassisted, which in their customary gallant manner they were able to do."[17] In another, the issue is gently ignored: "The Marines, during the retreat, took up the dangerous position of rear guard, and successfully fought off all pursuers."[18] In any case, both Russian and American forces made it back to their starting point, though the marines had the unpleasant experience of a four-hour retreat, carrying their wounded, while engaged with the enemy. Waller's first brief message back to Kempff was terse and gloomy:

I have to report that we made an unsuccessful attempt to relieve Tientsin this morning. We were surrounded and nearly overpowered. My loss is 4 killed and 7

wounded, 5 of the latter being slight . . . I was really
forced into this much against my better judgment.[19]

Several days later, when he came to write a more detailed report, Waller lauded his men: "I feel that I cannot do them justice. They have made history, marked with blood, if you please,
still glorious and brilliant." For the debacle of the first attack,
he blamed himself: "I tried to get into Tientsin to help the besieged. I failed. I lost a gun. If there is any fault it is mine."
What caused the shift? Perhaps the fact that the allies had since
successfully taken Tianjin, a victory that dimmed prior difficulties. Waller, upon reflection, may have recognized that he could
not have been "overruled" since he was technically not under
anyone but Admiral Kempff's command.

Despite the confusion, both forces made it back to safety
relatively intact and waited for reinforcements. They were not
long in coming, with a large group of Russians, British, Italians,
and Germans showing up at about 5:00 p.m. on the same day.
Waller gratefully "decided to act in cooperation with the British, under Commander Cradock," and thus escaped from the
Russians.[20] The combined force now numbered more than two
thousand men, and it marched to the railhead and camped,
aiming to start toward Tianjin at about 4:00 a.m. the next day.
Unlike the previous day, the Chinese defenders failed to mount
a strong defense. Sullivan noted that they shot "high" and over
the attackers, and "we killed several and they ran like sheep as
they could not understand us keeping on coming while they
were firing. We drove them before us like sheep." A British
midshipman quite enjoyed the attack:

> The best fight I had was coming into Tientsin as that
> was at close quarters and we could see the brutes. I
> managed to shoot two to my great satisfaction and was
> most anxious to slay one with my cutlass. I ran after

him but couldn't catch him before he reached the main body. He kept firing at me from his hip with a repeating rifle but luckily always missed, so eventually I had to shoot him.[21]

The Western attackers successfully pushed the Chinese back into Tianjin and made into the walls of the foreign enclave shortly after noon on June 23, much to the relief of the besieged in the city itself. "Shouting and cheering and crying and weeping for joy" greeted them.[22] Sullivan did not mention it in his diary, but the marines also were given bottles of beer by the grateful residents, ample reward in the June heat.[23] Herbert Hoover later said that he could not "remember a more satisfying musical performance than the bugles of the American Marines entering the settlement playing 'There'll Be a Hot Time in the Old Town Tonight.'"[24]

## FINDING SEYMOUR

The foreign enclave in Tianjin had been, if not liberated, at least opened to access. It was still besieged by Chinese forces on several sides, but the Western powers could begin building up their forces and supplies along the riverside route. The railroad needed to be repaired and boats and barges to carry supplies up the river gathered and provisioned, and crews hired. In an odd twist of fate, Frederic Wise of *Monocacy* ended up as head of the railroad effort. As an American, he was the only nearby officer who the British and the Russians would agree could handle the rails. Both sides worried about the other gaining an advantage if one of their officers was in charge. But Wise, though acceptable, knew little about railways, and repair expertise was somewhat scarce on the ground. Eventually, Wise found an American marine who had been a railroad section hand in civilian life and was "the only man out of 2,100 who could set out a fish-plate and spike down a rail."[25]

Finding boats and crews proved more of a difficulty. The British officer in charge of such logistics complained of the problems: "[The] 'Russians are shooting inoffensive natives, no hope of obtaining transport.'"[26] The Russians would get a bad reputation during the campaign, with a number of observers reporting that they attacked and killed innocent Chinese civilians. During the chaos after the capture of the Dagu Forts, as a group of three hundred Chinese laborers tried to escape from the dock opposite one of the forts, the Russians fired on the crowd, and the "whole three hundred were either shot or drowned."[27]

The Russians were not the only offenders. The Japanese also gained a reputation for ruthlessness. Oddly in that age of scientific racism, Japanese ruthlessness was seen as laudable, while the Russian behavior was barbaric. In any case, all of the Western powers traditionally relied upon native workers to do the unglamorous jobs that supported a modern military force. In this instance, the violence made it difficult for the Western powers to hire local laborers. Killing them or scaring them off simply made the job harder.

Despite this difficulty, the next steps remained to drive off the Chinese around Tianjin and to rescue Admiral Seymour. The latter, unexpectedly, came first. The arrival of Mersey's servant brought news of the admiral, news reinforced by the actions of the Chinese forces around Tianjin. A number of the Chinese guns were pulled from their bombardment and sent north, where they could be heard shelling what would turn out to be Seymour's force.[28]

Beset by attackers, low on food, and "encumbered with sick and wounded," Seymour's force needed to be rescued.[29] Rescued it was. Captain Bayly of the British marines met with the Russian commander, and the two set up a joint force of a thousand Russians, six hundred British, and some three hundred others under the Russian colonel Shirinsky. The force, guided by Clive Mersey's servant, set off on an overnight march on June 24 and arrived in front of the arsenal containing Seymour's force at 7:00 the morning of the twenty-fifth, encountering surprisingly little Chinese resistance.[30] Mersey, on the wall of the arsenal, described their arrival: "Early one morning the welcome cap and lance of a Cossack were descried to the south, then a European bugle was heard, and finally on the opposite shore appeared the welcome relieving force, some eighteen hundred strong." "We were," Mersey finished up with some understatement, "truly glad to see them."[31] The forces were able to get to the tired Europeans quickly and without much in the way of fighting. They escorted Seymour's forces back into Tianjin proper, bringing the wounded and blowing up the arsenal behind them. Here, the official British account of the rebellion was gently critical of the decision to destroy the arsenal, saying "the occupation of this place might have been of great advantage to the Allies." Having dared that much, however, the report backed away quickly, doubtless aware of the political implications of such a criticism. "On the other hand, its retention was not considered feasible by the authorities on the spot, who were in the best position to judge."[32]

At best, Seymour's ill-fated expedition was a gamble that did not come off. At worst, it was a terrible misreading of the situation. Seymour had acted in an imperial fashion, without any recognition that the situation was different. It had almost cost him his entire force.

Certainly, the situation still looked grim. Admiral Bruce, by late June, was clearly worn out, writing vengeful missives to the Admiralty. In one, he wrote he thought that "there should be no half measures this time, and the Imperial City of Bejing should be razed." More, "with the destruction of [the] Taku [Dagu] forts, Summer Palace, and finally the Imperial City of

Bejing, every other Chinaman in China ought to commit suicide, which would usefully and materially reduce the population."[33] By then, the admiral had likely been short of sleep for
more than ten days and must have been near the end of his
mental endurance. But the mind-set he revealed would be mirrored in future allied behavior. The sheer confusion and chaos
of the situation, the lack of understanding of the enemy, and
the seemingly contradictory events caused a simmering anger
on the part of the Western forces that would often be taken out
on anyone identified, rightly or wrongly, as an enemy.

We should pause here for a moment to appreciate the careful
nature of the allied progress at this point and not get distracted
by the sometimes chaotic ways in which that progress took
place. At the tactical level things were very much ad hoc, but at
the strategic level the allies were cementing their control over a
gateway into northern China (Dagu) and then the nearest and
easiest connection to Beijing (Tianjin). Relieving the foreign
community in Tianjin was a part of that, but controlling the
route to the capital was critical as well. In the absence of Seymour, the other commanders had started the solidification of
the allied presence in northern China. The quasi-conflict that
had led up to this point was over. Now it was full-scale war.

## ORGANIZING THE CAMPAIGN

No one was particularly ready for the crisis. China was, if a major imperial interest, a distant one. The Europeans had their
own local "sick man"—the Ottoman Empire—about which to
worry. As the French minister for foreign affairs, Théophile
Delcassé, put it: "The sick man who sits yonder at Pekin upon
the tottering throne of the Manchu princes, preoccupies the
European chancellories just as much as he who agonizes at
Constantinople upon the worm-eaten throne of the autocratic

and bloody sultans."[34] Meanwhile, the Americans were struggling against an insurgency in the Philippines, and the British were locked in a war in South Africa against the Boer forces. Memories of the "Black Week" of December 1899, when British relief expeditions following the railways to the besieged garrisons at Ladysmith, Mafeking, and Kimberley were defeated by Boer forces, had worrying echoes with the experience of Seymour's expedition. Though the war was going better in the summer of 1900, with General Frederick Roberts successfully relieving the besieged towns and capturing Pretoria, the Boer capital, it was still a much larger commitment in terms of casualties and manpower than the British had expected. Unbeknownst to them, there was a long guerrilla campaign still to be fought. Given the situation in South Africa, a major campaign in China was not a particularly appealing one for the British, but one that seemed unavoidable at the moment.

The British were handicapped in their June organizing effort because both Seymour and MacDonald were incommunicado. "The two officials who have authority to act . . . cannot issue orders," wrote one British undersecretary to the prime minister, Lord Salisbury.[35] W. R. Carles, in Tianjin, assumed MacDonald's responsibilities by default, but he was not familiar to the British cabinet, and thus an unknown factor. The cabinet was forced to rely on newspaper reports, and the notation "according to the *Daily Mail*" became frequent in Foreign Office files.[36]

In mid-June the British nonetheless set about building a force from whatever resources were available. They sent a thousand men from Hong Kong and pleaded with the Japanese and Russians to send four thousand each. Salisbury wrote, with some understatement, that "time may prove to be of importance if the Admiral is in difficulties."[37] The problem with this plan of action was that Japan and Russia were rivals in China, keeping a wary eye on each other and neither wishing to allow an advantage to slip from it. Both moved cautiously, when they moved at all. The Japanese believed the "previous agreement between Powers absolutely necessary on the question of command and spheres of action."[38] In addition, committing the British to fight in such a coalition meant, as Salisbury put it, that "they would have our policy in their hands."[39] This was a particularly worrying element for a nation still dreaming of "splendid isolation." The result was British waffling throughout the process. The London *Times*, for example, talked one moment of Japan as a "young and vigorous recruit to the Concert of Civilization" and within a week was lamenting the "considerable risks in allowing Japan to land a large army in China."[40]

There did not seem to be any choice, however, given the severity of the crisis. The wild card was the Germans, a new imperial power itching to throw their weight around. Salisbury solved the latter problem by confining his negotiating to Russia and Japan, ignoring the Germans. "I can deal with two; three is impossible."[41]

The business of putting together British forces was perhaps not as political, but certainly no less complicated. The British had a thousand men in Hong Kong they could send immediately. After that, the forces would have to muster from around the globe. Men to fight in China came from all over the British Empire, including Canada, South Africa, and, most critically, India. The latter was the only major source of manpower in the British Empire whose forces could reach China quickly, and it was to India that the British government turned. The day after the capture of the Dagu Forts, the secretary of state for India wired Lord George Curzon, the viceroy of India, to "make all arrangements at once to send three battalions Sikhs or Punjabis; one company sappers; one cavalry regiment native; one battery field, if possible, if not, horse artillery, as an expeditionary force."[42] Curzon responded quickly, promising "promptitude" in sending the forces to China.[43]

Ironically, the dispatch of Indian forces actually helped the situation in India. Since the mutiny of 1857, the British government had been careful to keep a balance between white and native troops in India. That balance had been upset by the sending of a number of white units to fight in South Africa. The fear was that without the moderating influence of British units, the Indian soldiers might rise in revolt. Add to that a famine in western India and general unrest throughout the country, and the government of India, oddly enough, felt "relief" to see Indian troops leave the country for China.[44] Such a sentiment may have been unfair to the Indian soldiers, who seem to have been quite eager to fight for the empire and were bitterly disappointed at the lack of Indian units being sent to the Boer War. Amar Singh, the Rajput nobleman and officer, thought it "joyful news" that he and his unit were going to fight the Boxers.[45]

Moving thousands of soldiers and their dependents was an enormously involved process. Supplies had to be gathered, including, for example, twenty-five hundred pounds of "compressed vegetables." The British paid for family members to travel with their soldiers, at least for the officers, so their travel had to be organized. The horses for the cavalry, transport, and artillery units had to be shipped and supplied. Those thousands of animals ate eight hundred tons of fodder per month, dwarfing the food requirements for the soldiers themselves. The conflict broke out so suddenly that the preparations were rushed, at best. The intelligence office designated to prepare information packets for the expedition, stationed in Simla, India, would protest afterward:

> The outbreak of the war was so sudden that it was not found possible to get out a very full military report on

Northern China, and the information available in Simla on these subject was really very limited, but on the whole the notes furnished to the troops when the expedition started were very fairly correct.[46]

The temptation to translate this as a statement that the intelligence briefings were wrong, but for good reasons, is almost inescapable. Such protests also ring a little hollow, given that, within living memory, a British expedition had captured the Dagu Forts and then marched on Beijing, but the lack of such institutional memory is perhaps not surprising.

Adding to the complication was the fact that, though the forces came from India, the funding came from London. The Exchequer, which controlled the government budget, was a notoriously penny-pinching institution, and Curzon had to clear through it "all important questions of expenditure." Actually, it was worse. He had to report to the secretary of state for India, who would refer it to the Chancellor of the Exchequer.[47] The layers of decision makers made the prospect of an extended campaign a difficult one. Should the British get involved in a serious and ongoing war, running it simultaneously out of London and Delhi was a recipe for inefficiency and confusion.

But the British were practiced at this kind of deliberate parsimony and inefficiency. It was, in essence, how they ran most of their wars, and they were skilled at extracting maximum benefits from whatever resources, whether financial or emotional, they could find. To give an example of this, the British sent three hospital ships to China to treat the casualties of the expected campaign. Those hospital ships came from multiple geographic and financial directions, as the undersecretary for foreign affairs, William Brodrick, explained in the House:

Three hospital ships are being provided. One by the Government of India; one, the "Maine," by the gener-

osity of the Atlantic Transport Company and the benevolent exertions of American ladies; and one by the
munificence of his Highness the Maharaja Sindia of
Gwalior.[48]

Thus, in essence, the British government was paying for only
one out of the three hospital ships in the theater. The maharaja's support was "made on behalf of himself, his mother, and
his wife, to testify their loyalty to Her Majesty the Queen Empress," and reflected a kind of imperial reserve that could be
drawn on in times of crisis.[49]

The Chinese Regiment at Weihai was a conundrum. It was
close at hand, but there was some controversy over whether it
should go. Admiral Bruce did not "desire" the Chinese Regiment, worrying about its reliability, but the regiment's commander sent a strongly worded plea on its behalf: "Please insist
on regiment being employed at Beijing. If there is fighting and
we are not used, future of regiment very doubtful. Men can be
trusted and are asking to go."[50] In the end, the British came to
the delicately logical conclusion that it would be dangerous to
leave the Chinese Regiment in place, where local loyalties
might cause friction.

The United States was in a remarkably similar situation.
Fresh off fighting an overwhelmingly successful war with Spain,
the United States had gotten involved in another war in the
Philippines. Those islands had been acquired as part of the
peace treaty with Spain, at the cost of $20 million. The acquisi-
tion had not been much to the liking of the Filipinos, who,
unsurprisingly, preferred independence. The United States
refused, and a conventional war broke out in the spring of 1899.
American forces had won the conventional war handily, but it
had been followed by an insurgency that they struggled to put
down. By the middle of 1900, American units and ships were
scattered throughout the Philippines, fighting a small war drawn

over a large canvas. It did not seem to be going well, but the only immediately available troops for China had to come from the Philippines. The Americans, unlike the British, would thus have to weaken their effort in one war to fight another. Reluctantly, Washington ordered that the Fourteenth and Fifteenth Regiments from the Philippines be sent to China.

General Arthur MacArthur, the commander in the Philippines, was the father of Douglas MacArthur and, like his son, did not suffer foolish decisions quietly. He screamed bloody murder at the reassignment of the two regiments, arguing that it would cripple his war effort. "Force in Philippines has been disseminated to limitation of safety . . . evacuation of territory now occupied . . . would be extremely unfortunate . . . Loss of a regiment at this time would be a serious matter." He did confess at the end of the telegram that he could, if absolutely necessary, spare *one* regiment. Perhaps to preempt questions as to why he had not previously noted that his force was stretched so thin, MacArthur said, "[I] have not cared to emphasize this feature of the situation."[51] The secretary of war, Elihu Root, might well have asked exactly *why* MacArthur had not cared to pass on such critical information, but, knowing whom he was dealing with, ignored the complaints and ordered MacArthur to send a regiment "as soon as possible." Root further admonished MacArthur to make sure of the "tact and judgment of the commanding officer," giving the general permission to replace the commander if need be.[52]

To a certain extent MacArthur's complaint was valid, but it was the start of the rainy season in the Philippines, when campaigning was difficult anyway. As long as the units returned to the Philippines by September or October, MacArthur's position would not be too damaged.

The rainy season did, however, make it extremely challenging for the American unit, the Ninth U.S. Infantry, even to get to the ships that would carry it to China. It was dispersed into smaller units, spread throughout the Central Luzon island of the Philippine archipelago, fighting a counterinsurgency war against the Filipino *insurrectos* led by Emilio Aguinaldo. Colonel Emerson Liscum, the commander of the Ninth stationed in Tarlac, received an abrupt telegram from the American headquarters in Manila on June 17. The Ninth, the telegram said, "will be concentrated in Manila, with the least possible delay, for transfer to Taku [Dagu], China." It was not as simple as all that, of course. Not only did the Ninth have to be pulled out, but another unit had to be inserted in its place, to garrison and fight its former positions. "Relieve the regiment with the troops most available for accomplishing it speedily," another HQ telegram directed. Units of the Ninth were not to wait for the relief to arrive, but pack up and head out immediately, leaving behind any supplies they had accumulated. They would head for the nearest railway line, to be picked up there and sent to Manila. This put the local Filipinos cooperating with the Americans in a difficult situation, as they would be left to the mercy of any *insurrectos* in the area while American units were gone. Brigadier General James Franklin Bell, the commander of the Central Luzon area, was aware of the problems of leaving the Ninth's area unfortified, that it would be "inhuman to leave these people at the mercy of the . . . insurgents," but the best he could order was for the units to leave any captured or extra guns they had with the local *presidente*.

Liscum telegraphed back the next day that a number of his units would not be able to make the trains: "I have flooded streams to contend with . . . I am at a loss to know how the company from Gerona will get here, as the washout at El Bendio is 200 yards [greater] in extent than last year, until the river becomes fordable." Worse, as Liscum pointed out on June 19, a "well-defined case" of smallpox had appeared at the company at La Paz. In the middle of all of this, Liscum received a telegram from the assistant adjutant general in Manila that General Loyd Wheaton was "anxious that the Ninth Infantry should present a good appearance when it goes where troops of other nations are. You will therefore please have new uniforms for the regiment." Liscum's response to this was not recorded and, in any case, is not likely to be printable.

Remarkably rapidly, given the conditions, the regiment gathered itself. The company with the smallpox case was left behind, and the others, by hook or by crook, found ways to get to a railway. It was not easy:

> The adjacent country and the town itself were flooded, and the natives were using boats to move about the town. The company commander succeeded in hiring thirty-five carabao carts, with native drivers, to handle the baggage, and began its march at 5:45 a.m. For more than three hours the company wallowed through waist-deep water, following no road, but keeping as close as possible to the course of a trail . . . Frequently the men blundered into deep holes.

After twelve hours of marching, the exhausted column reached Tarlac, to get on the train. If it did not have Boxers shooting at it, as did Seymour's column, the differences were not otherwise all that great.

At Manila, the regiment boarded the transports *Logan* and *Port Albert*, which carried it to Nagasaki, Japan, to pick up coal.[53] Thankfully, the trip was smooth and the men had a chance to recover, though even then the stresses of getting to Manila caused sixty-one men to go on sick report aboard ship. At Nagasaki, the ships were joined by the USS *Brooklyn*, and the combined force arrived at Dagu early in July. Getting ashore proved almost as difficult as did getting to Manila. Some of the companies were sent in over the sandbar in a Chinese junk that required constant bailing if it was not to sink, and the others on an open lighter pulled by a tug. The tug missed the tide, and these latter companies were thus stuck in the open water and the burning sun for an entire day before the next high tide arrived and they could head in. All the companies were exhausted by the time they reached Tianjin on about July 10, only to discover that rest was difficult owing to the mosquitoes and the incessant Chinese bombardment. In a sense, it was something of a relief to go into action on July 13, though that relief would prove short-lived.[54] The Ninth was, in any case, a "hard, tough bunch of soldiers," and they managed.[55]

In command of the American forces was to be General Adna Chaffee, then serving in Cuba. Chaffee, born in Ohio in 1842, had joined as a private in the Union army in 1861, risen to the rank of brevet captain by the end of the war, and then remained in the service during the long decades of the Indian Wars in the West. He had done well there, and well in the Spanish-American War, and had been chief of staff to General Leonard Wood, the American commander in Cuba. Now he was ordered halfway around the world to help put out the fire in China. Theodore Roosevelt, then vice president, wrote to Chaffee that he was in "charge of our destinies in China . . . I only wish I were to have a regiment under you. It would double-discount the vice-presidency." Chaffee's reaction to the prospect of having a force of nature like Roosevelt under his command has not been recorded.[56]

Chaffee's role was carefully delineated for him by the American government. He was to go to Nagasaki, Japan, first. There would be further orders. If the situation in China had eased, he would likely be ordered directly home. If it had continued to worsen, he would be ordered to China. What he was to do there, Root wrote to him, was to take the forces under command and use them "for the protection of the life and property of American citizens and American interests in China wherever the Chi-

nese Government fails to render efficient protection." Chaffee
could "confer freely" with the generals of the other powers, and
if the situation demanded it, he could "act with the forces under your command concurrently with the forces of other powers." But that did not mean that Chaffee could ally himself with
the other powers, and, the general was sternly enjoined, he was
to "avoid entering into any joint action or undertaking with
other powers tending to commit or limit this Government as to
its future course of conduct."[57] The rivalry of empires would
not be pushed aside for such a small matter as an international
crisis.

Even as Britain and America gathered their forces, so too
did the other powers. The two closest geographic powers, Japan
and Russia, were able quickly to get together the most troops.
By June 26, Rear Admiral Bruce could report that there were
over twelve thousand troops in the Dagu area.[58]

## TROOPS IN THE DAGU AREA, JUNE 26

| NATIONALITY | NUMBER OF TROOPS |
|:---:|:---:|
| Japanese | 3,752 |
| Russian | 3,735 |
| British | 2,300 |
| German | 1,340 |
| French | 421 |
| American | 335 |
| Italian | 138 |
| Austrian | 26 |
| *Total* | 12,047 |

Arriving at Dagu was often a shock, as Captain Gordon Casserly of the Indian Army remembered:

> All around a heaving, troubled waste of muddy sea, bearing on its bosom the ponderous shapes of war-ships—British, French, Russian, German, Austrian, Italian, Japanese. Close by, a fleet of merchantmen flying the red ensign, the horizontal stripes of the "Vaterland," or the red ball on white ground of the marvellous little islands that claim to be the England of the Far East.

From the anchorage, the incoming troops were loaded onto smaller ships and ferried to shore, to Tanggu, where they caught the train to Tianjin. The train was, to say the least, multinational. Casserly, again:

> Leaning out of the windows was a motley crowd of many nationalities. Out of one appeared the heads of a boyish Cossack and a bearded Sikh. The next displayed the chubby face of a German soldier beside the dark features of an Italian sailor. When the train stopped, a smart Australian bluejacket stepped out of the brake-van. He was the guard. In the corridor cars were Yagers, Austrian sailors, brawny American soldiers, baggy-trousered Zouave and red-breeched Chasseur d'Afrique. Sturdy little Japanese infantrymen sat beside tall Bengal Lancers. A small Frenchman chatted volubly with a German trooper from the Lost Provinces. Smart Tommy Atkins gazed in wondering disdain at the smaller Continental soldiers, or listened with an amused smile to the vitriolic comments of a Yankee friend on the manners and appearance of "those darned Dagoes." And among them, perfectly at his ease, sat the imperturbable Chinaman.

At each railway station was an officer delegated with the responsibility of sending the troops getting off the train to their billets, or of finding billets and supplies for them. At the Tianjin station, Casserly found an old companion, a Major Whittal of the Hyderabad Contingent. Whittal's fluency in Russian, French, and German had gained him the "scarcely enviable post" of railway station officer at Tianjin, a job that "required the possession of a genius for organisation and infinite tact and patience." Casserly went to say hello but had trouble getting through the "French, Russian, or German officers and soldiers crowded round" the major, complaining of a wide range of problems.[59] Whittal was the perfect example of the imperial cadre. Multilingual and able to handle the demands of many different nationalities, he was, in many ways, the foundation of empire.

## AT THE LEGATIONS

Meanwhile, at the legations, the siege continued. The defenders had managed to create a reasonable set of fortifications to protect their territory, thanks in large part to Frank Gamewell's engineering efforts. The fortifications centered on a compact core of legations, including the British, French, and Russian. Outlying embassies, like the Belgian, had been abandoned and their inhabitants brought within the main lines.

There were sustained attacks in late June as imperial troops began to join with the Boxers. But direct attacks were not frequent; rather, fire was a favorite weapon. On June 20, Private R. G. Cooper of the Royal Marines reported that there was "constant sniping . . . The Austrian Legation is in flames . . . very heavy continuous firing." The next day, he reported the "burning of the Italian and Dutch Legations" and "another daring attempt at the north end of the Legation to fire the buildings. Only slight damage was done, but the Hanlin and

some houses adjoining the Legation were completely gut-
ted."[60] The Hanlin that he mentioned was the Hanlin Yuan,
the "imperial center for scholarly studies," which, among other
things, contained a library that rivaled the comprehensiveness
of the ancient library at Alexandria. Like that library, the Hanlin burned with most of its contents lost.[61]

On June 24, a mixed force of Boxers and imperial troops
infiltrated through buildings close to the western wall of the
legation defenses and set fire to them. They used the cover of
smoke to fire sustained volleys at the defenders. The fire was
contained with some difficulty, and Captain Lewis Halliday led
twenty of his Royal Marines in a sortie against the attackers.
They made a hole in the defensive wall and charged out. Halliday was shot almost immediately in the chest, "the bullet
fracturing his shoulder and carrying away part of the lung."[62]
Halliday fell against a wall, saying to the first marine through
the hole, "I am wounded," and then he nonetheless managed
to shoot three Chinese, covering the exit of the rest of the marines. "Carry on," and don't "mind me," the captain told his sergeant, walking back to the hospital under his own power.[63]
The marines obeyed, mopping up the rest of the attackers.

The most critical portion of these defenses was the chunk
of the Tartar Wall held by the legations. This stretch of the
wall, sixty feet high and nearly twenty-five feet wide, overlooked and dominated the grounds of the various embassies,
and its loss would have made the defense nearly impossible.
The two marine captains were John T. Myers and Newt H.
Hall. There seems to have been something going on with Hall,
as Myers took command of the marine position atop the wall for
five days running without sleep, while Hall remained in the
legations. Myers was finally ordered by Claude MacDonald to
get some sleep, and Hall took over, with an order from Edwin
Conger that the minister would bring charges against the marine "if you leave until you are absolutely driven out." But while

Myers was gone, Hall allowed the Chinese to build a new wall closer to the marine position, which included a fifteen-foot tower overlooking the marine line. When Myers returned, he immediately mounted a counterattack and captured the Chinese position. Myers was severely wounded, however, which left command (again) to Hall.[64]

It was a strange siege. The Chinese never pressed their advantage as they might have. From the beginning, they were willing to shell the legations and snipe with rifles, along with the occasional small-scale attack. The use of fire was widespread, but the Chinese never really followed up with a full-scale attack on all of the walls of the legations. They certainly had the force to do so, and they would have overwhelmed the defenders if they had. Later, military officers looking back highlighted this oddity:

> The perimeter established around the legations was closely hemmed by Chinese buildings, and had the attackers made use of the artillery the Chinese were known to have, or had they even made an all out infantry attack, the legations must have fallen. Instead, they surrounded the area, shot at every movement, set fire to buildings, and made piecemeal attacks, continually trying to edge forward.[65]

Captain Myers would write later that "there were no 'military operations' that would justify the name during the siege. It was all a matter of 'sitting tight' behind a barricade." He could offer no real reason for the Chinese reluctance to attack, suggesting only that the Chinese were afraid of foreign "spirit soldiers" who would defend the legations.[66] But if the Chinese, for whatever reason, were not attacking, they were still pinning the legations tightly, and relief seemed even further off.

Outside the legations, things were drastically more danger-

ous. The whole north of China was covered by Boxers and by
Western missionaries fleeing them. Some managed to make it
to the coastline and were taken off by ship. A group fled to
safety through the Gobi Desert to the north riding on twenty
camels and nineteen horses. But some did not. In Taiyuan, the
capital of Shanxi Province, forty-five Westerners, men, women,
and children, were slaughtered in the middle of July. Depending on the source, it was either the provincial governor, Yuxian,
who oversaw the killings or a mob of Boxers. Whoever did it,
the Westerners were still as dead.[67]

## TAKING STOCK

Once rescued, Admiral Seymour sat down and wrote a lengthy
report to the Admiralty on June 27 outlining his experiences
and the reason for the expedition's failure. He was blunt. He
admitted that the expedition had "failed" and blamed it on
the Chinese government. "Success was only possible on the
assumption that the Imperial Troops, with whose Government
we were not at war, would at least be neutral; their turning their
arms against us, and certainly conniving in the destruction of
the railway . . . made failure inevitable." It is interesting to note
Seymour's use of the passive voice and the assumption that an
army should remain neutral when a large foreign military force
passed through its territory. Nonetheless, the admiral was more
straightforward in the next part. "For the undertaking of the
expedition, for its conduct, and its issue, I am responsible." His
rhetorical falling on the sword was undercut a bit by the fram-
ing of the report, which, as noted, laid the fault entirely at the
feet of the perfidious Chinese government and military. Nonetheless, his taking of the blame was gallant and, it should
probably be said, accurate. Noticeably, British army generals involved in the Boxer crisis either remained tactfully silent about

Seymour's decisions or were critical. Seymour would later write perhaps the most ruefully accurate evaluation of the expedition and his role:

> Whether success or failure attends you, England nearly always approves an officer who has evidently done his best. I never could understand why anyone minds taking responsibility. You have only to do what seems proper, and if it turns out badly it is the fault of Nature for not having made you cleverer.[68]

The expedition ended up losing 285 men—65 killed and 220 wounded—a not inconsiderable number, although nowhere near the casualties that the British had experienced in some of their nineteenth-century colonial wars, nor, it should be said, anywhere near what the British were currently suffering in the Boer War. But, more critical than the casualties, the expedition had been roundly rebuffed, driven back to its starting point by a mixed Chinese force. That was noteworthy. However we may look back and see that Seymour was taking a substantial gamble and that the force was undersized and under-provisioned, it was still the military representative of the world's dominant powers, and the "sick man" of Asia had managed to defeat it. The Chinese may have missed a chance to destroy the force completely, but they had forced it to return to its starting point, bruised, hungry, and glad to be safe. As one observer put it, "The contrast between the jaunty smartness of the column when it started for Peking, and the ghastly bedraggled footsore men who came back, was too marked to be pleasant."[69] That was a victory the likes of which China had not seen for almost a century. China was, if not winning the war at that moment, at least not losing it.

# 6

# THE BATTLE OF TIANJIN

The memory of the Battle of Tianjin has largely been lost. Even within the Boxer War itself, Tianjin has taken something of a lesser place to the siege of the legations, Seymour's failed march to Beijing, and the ultimate relief of the Western embassies. The British government awarded a medal for service in the China operation, with clasps for capturing the Dagu Forts, the defense of the legations, and the relief of Beijing but not for the defense of Tianjin.[1] This was a mistake. The battle, which took place in mid-July, was, along with the later battle at Beicang, likely the turning point of the entire affair. At Tianjin, the Chinese fought the hardest, and at Tianjin the outcome was most in doubt. Western forces could have lost here, a loss that might not have changed the ultimate outcome but would have required a much lengthier and more determined campaign to overcome. Victory at Tianjin essentially crippled Chinese resistance just as it was getting started.

In addition, Tianjin seems likely to have been the last great flourish of the Boxers themselves. They were out in force in the Tianjin area from mid-May onward, as Edward Seymour discovered to his cost, and by mid-July they had been reinforced by a substantial number of imperial troops. The forces arrayed against the European powers were large, numbering (by Seymour's estimation) roughly twenty thousand troops of the Military Guards Army under General Yu Li and an indeterminate number of Boxers.[2] The imperial troops were well trained and equipped. The Boxers were highly motivated. Together, they were a formidable opponent, but the grave difficulty that they faced was communication and coordination. The Boxers, especially, had little in the way of organized units or commanders, and they were viewed suspiciously by the regular troops.

Tianjin had its advantages in geographic terms. Unlike the Dagu Forts, the first line of defense, Tianjin was beyond the range of the powerful guns of the Western fleet. Unlike the last line of defense, the walls of Beijing, Tianjin was not harboring the throne itself. The Chinese could theoretically lose Tianjin and not lose the war. The city had a large number of European civilians in residence, and it was at the end of an extended supply line of road and river leading down to the coast. The Chinese held strong positions there, most notably the thick walls of the city itself. With the European forces tied to their supply lines, the Chinese had the freedom to maneuver as they wished.

Even more, the forces arrayed against the Chinese gave the dynasty an advantage. The Western armies in that July month were a hodgepodge from different countries, different services, and different areas of empire. They had no overall commander, they did not share a common language, they were suspicious of each other, and any cooperation they managed was tenuous at best. To give an example of the difficulties small and large that the Western contingents encountered, none of the Japanese spoke English, and none of the British or Americans spoke Japanese. The result was incomprehension until both sides discovered an understanding of French. Throughout the campaign, thus, the British, Americans, and Japanese communicated with one another in French, with the French officers serving occasionally as both interpreters and mediators of meaning.[3]

On a political level, the cooperation was undermined by years of imperial suspicion. The Russians and the Japanese were local rivals, edging warily around each other in the Pacific. The Russians and the British were rivals in southern Asia, where the "Great Game" had been a diplomatic watchword for decades in India and Afghanistan. The French and the British were old rivals in Europe, now only slowly beginning to come together to face the nascent but building German threat. The Americans were new arrivals, peppery and full of vinegar, but having some difficulty holding on to the Philippines, the imperial spoils of their war against Spain. All the powers were waging war in China not merely to save their legations but to establish and firm up their spheres of influence and control. The question in the middle of July was clear: How long would such tenuous cooperation last under pressure?

The answer, at least in those several days, was that it would last long enough. A committee of generals and admirals met several times during early July and agreed upon a course of action. With the European section of Tianjin secured, albeit subject to severe shelling at times by the Chinese, it was time to capture the Chinese section of the city and drive off the Chinese forces. Thus would Tianjin become a foundation for the drive up to Beijing, a campaign many thought would require tens of thousands of men and last at least until the end of the year. Having captured Dagu and the river up to Tianjin, the allied forces, by conquering the city, would gain a solid logistical base into the interior of China, most critically up to Beijing itself.

## STRATEGIES

From the Chinese perspective, the question was, what strategy to take in this war? The goal for the imperial court was, at the very least, to prevent another Western conquest and sacking of Beijing on the order of 1860. Such a sacking risked the collapse of the dynasty itself. At most, it was to force the Western armies to give up their position in Tianjin and Dagu and retreat to their ships. If the latter was not particularly achievable and the former was the bare minimum, a more reasonable compromise goal was to hold up the allied coalition for as long as possible and hope that rivalries within the imperial alliance would fragment it and lead to negotiations between the Chinese and various Western powers. If, for example, the Chinese could negotiate a separate peace with Russia, the room for maneuver of the other powers in the area would be gravely curtailed. That would quite likely lead, the Chinese might hope, to a general peace and a chance for the dynasty to continue with self-strengthening. In reality, though, the empress dowager was bailing a lifeboat in a storm, simply hoping to survive one wave to the next. It had worked for decades, after all.

Such goals required two main strategies. First, the throne had to get the Boxers under control. While this peasant rebellion dominated both the capital and northern China and attacked foreigners of all stripes, the Chinese government was unlikely to be able to manage any kind of real negotiations with the Western powers, military successes or not. Second, and somewhat contradictorily, the Chinese had to repeat the military success that they had managed against Seymour's column. The contradiction lay in the critical role that the Boxers had played in that success and the possibility that trying to bring them under control would make them useless militarily against the Western forces.

There were two obvious strategies. The first was to fight at Tianjin before the allies could build a substantial force in the area. The advantages of this Tianjin strategy were several. The allies were still disorganized, without even an overall commander in charge of the forces. The Chinese had a substantial number of units in the area, and they held well-built and well-defended fortifications. The disadvantages were also several. Tianjin, though not on the sea, was nonetheless close enough to provide a relatively short supply line for the allies. The allies also had a base to fight from in the foreign enclaves to the south of walled Tianjin. But perhaps the most worrying element for the Chinese was that fighting at Tianjin would require the imperial army to do something it had not managed well for most of the last century: stand toe-to-toe with a Western army and, at the very least, fight it to a draw. Defending Tianjin meant gambling that the reforms of the previous five years, since the catastrophic war with Japan, had been enough to revitalize the forces in the Tianjin area. To this strategy, the Boxers could contribute irregular forces that might well help weaken the Western armies, but they would not be able to manage the same kind of ambush and sabotage that had proven so effective against Seymour.

The second strategy might be called the Boxer strategy. It involved essentially replicating the situation of the Seymour expedition by allowing the Westerners to hold Tianjin and then march on Beijing. That march would be harassed, as Seymour's column was harassed, by the Boxer units in the area, while the Chinese army would shadow the column, without looking to engage the main body. That would force the Westerners to keep together, prevent them from spreading out to find and destroy the Boxers, and put severe strain on their logistics arrangement. With an effective execution such a strategy might force the allied expedition to give up on its march. At worst, if the invading column reached Beijing, it would still have to get over or through the enormous and defended walls that circled the capital while being attacked from without.

The advantages of the Boxer strategy were twofold. First, it would not risk the Chinese army in an open battle with the Westerners. Second, the Boxer strategy had essentially already proven itself against Seymour. The challenge with the Boxer strategy was that it required a great deal of faith in the Boxers. They had to execute their harassment effectively against a potentially much larger force. That required an awful lot of trust in a movement that the court did not truly understand.

The court was split. The moderate factions, whose power was centered on the Zongli Yamen, argued for continuing negotiations. Yuan Chang, of the Zongli Yamen, argued eloquently that the legations should be allowed to leave Beijing. Conservative Manchus, most notably Prince Duan, argued for resistance. Cixi waffled, ordering Ronglu to prevent Boxer attacks on the legations but allowing Chinese forces to build up in the Tianjin area. By default and without much forethought, the dynasty adopted the Tianjin strategy.

The Chinese increase in and around Tianjin strengthened the areas they held with fortifications and artillery emplacements. Estimates of the number of Chinese troops in the area vary a fair bit, but the British believed there were roughly twenty thousand to thirty thousand troops there by the end of June.[4]

On the allied side, the major question concerned who would command the unified coalition forces. While the council of senior officers had served surprisingly well in taking Dagu and relieving the foreign enclave of Tianjin, it could not be a lasting solution. As Lord Salisbury, the British prime minister, put it in a discussion with the French ambassador on July 3: "Advice coming from such a Council might represent the opinion of a less competent majority, and not that of the most weighty members of it."[5] This is perhaps a bit rich coming from him, given how badly Seymour had just managed the relief expedition, but the British were never shy of confidence. What Salisbury's comment reveals is the degree to which command of a campaign in China was a matter of imperial rivalry. Heading the campaign would be not only a person but a nation.

Of the powers in the area, a number could be eliminated from consideration immediately. Italy and Austria-Hungary did not have sufficient forces in the area, nor were they large enough imperial powers to be worthy. The United States was still too minor a power, for all its emergence in the previous few years. Russia and Japan were both local powers and were both committing substantial troops to the effort, but they were rivals, and neither would see the other at the head of such a relief column. France's sphere of influence was southern China, and that was where the lion's share of its troops remained, eliminating it from consideration. Of the two remaining, Britain was the obvious choice. It was the senior and most dominant imperial power, and northern China was within its sphere of influence. Some members of Parliament simply assumed that a British officer would command.[6] But British prestige had slipped because of the chaotic embarrassments of the Boer War, and Seymour's defeat had not helped. More, as the dominant imperial power, Britain inspired resentment and jealousy as well as respect, and it was this that played against it. As one British officer in the expedition would write later, "The English were the most unpopular nation in Europe; the Boer War was on; there had been little incidents like Agadir and Fashoda! I don't know whether the Germans or French hated us most."[7]

In addition, the Germans lobbied hard for the position, seeing in it a chance to increase their country's imperial prestige and to repay the Chinese for the murder of von Ketteler. The kaiser appealed directly to the czar for his support, and Nicholas II of Russia proved willing to aid a fellow emperor, especially if it meant poking "the modern Carthage" (Britain) in the eye with a stick.[8] Their chosen candidate was Baron Alfred von Waldersee, a former chief of the Imperial General Staff and close friend of Kaiser Wilhelm II's. Salisbury, faced with this united front, decided that he had no choice but to go along, wiring the Germans graciously that "Her Majesty's government will view with great satisfaction an arrangement by which so distinguished a soldier is placed at the head of the international forces."[9] The British prime minister was an old campaigner, however, and the setback here inspired him to begin thinking about an Anglo-Japanese alliance to counterweight the Russo-German cooperation.

Von Waldersee's appointment did not come without protest. The French, who still burned with the desire for revenge against Germany for their defeat in the 1870–1871 war, were not pleased that a German would lead French troops in China. A member of the French parliament complained that the Germans were "most brutally aggressive" and that putting one in the lead would send the wrong message to the Chinese.[10] But the French did not have the weight to overrule the Germans, Russians, and British, and so von Waldersee was it.

The count was from the beginning a commander in absentia, having to make the long journey from Germany to China to take up the role. Even moving quickly, he was unlikely to reach China before September, and such a late arrival threatened to stretch the campaign well into the frigid north China winter. Relieving the legations quickly would have to give way in the face of imperial rivalries.

## OPENING THE ROUTE

Meanwhile, however, Tianjin had to be taken. In the first week of July, the allies began to build their numbers in the foreign enclave there, helped by the arrival of a number of units from abroad. Despite these new arrivals, building up forces in the Tianjin area meant, necessarily, scrimping on them elsewhere. This was potentially risky, but there was little choice. Thus, the forces holding the Dagu Forts were stripped to the absolute minimum. One of them, for example, was held by a hundred

British and thirteen Italian sailors. Considering that the forts were within easy reach of the Chinese army at Beicang, this was a substantial risk, as one British midshipman remembered: "It does seem rather ridiculous that a hundred should expect to hold a fort of which the ramparts are more than a mile round against ten or twenty thousand." The defenders mostly spent their time playing cricket, "socker," and reading and sleeping.[11]

The Chinese were the first to act. Their strategy included constant shelling of the defenders (the British soldiers referred to the largest Chinese gun as the "Empress Dowager") and sniping from concealed positions close by or even within the foreign settlements.[12] Both of these were effective. It was relatively easy, it seemed, for Chinese to infiltrate near to or even in the foreign enclave at Tianjin, and the result was a constant barrage of small-arms fire. James Ricalton, a photographer, was almost one casualty. He was talking to a soldier in the street when the soldier suddenly exclaimed: "'Come out of this! Didn't you hear that bullet come between us?' We were not more than three feet apart. We concluded our confab behind a wall."[13] Frederick Brown, a minister living in Tianjin, remembered the experience: "The greatest danger was from the hidden riflemen, who seemed to be firing from every building in the settlement, especially from the warehouses. To show oneself in the streets was to be shot at."[14] Luckily for the Westerners, the snipers were not particularly good shots, and so casualties remained relatively low.

Captives were treated harshly. A Chinese infiltrator who "fired a revolver point-blank" at a civilian and missed was "seized and executed."[15] Such immediate slayings seemed to be the order of the day. When a nest of seven snipers was discovered, they were "instantly shot" by the British.[16]

The Western powers tried to restrict Chinese movements in the area by requiring signed passes to move, but that did not reduce the amount of fire and resulted in a fair number of dead civilian Chinese. As one British woman remembered: "One poor huckster returning home and perhaps not understanding things, upon being challenged by the German sentry ran, and was at once shot dead! This seemed to most of us very like murder."[17] The artillery fire was also effective, and the foreign enclaves found themselves under a constant barrage of shell and shot. The accuracy was enough so that the Westerners began to be suspicious, the idea of the Chinese themselves managing it being apparently unthinkable. It had to be Westerners at the guns, or so the rumors said: "One [report] was that before hostilities actually broke out, the Chinese forcibly detained eight of their Russian gunnery instructors, and compelled them, at the point of the bayonet, to lay their guns for them." Captain A.A.S. Barnes, with the Chinese regiment, who related this story, was skeptical of it, but only because he preferred the story that involved "the foreign-trained gunners from the Taku [Dagu] forts" making their way to Tianjin and serving "the guns there with that accuracy of which we had daily demonstration." Either way, the accuracy was down to foreign influence.[18]

In any case, both the sniping and the artillery fire meant that by the first week in July, the city was locked down:

> Hardly a house but had been struck by shells, the valuable contents of the warehouses going to form barricades to keep out the bullets which lay thick about every street, and studded every tree and wall. It was indeed a different spectacle. Women and children were to be seen no longer, and the two clubs were both turned into hospitals, which by this time were nearly crowded with wounded officers and men.[19]

The effects of the constant shelling and the sniping began to wear on the civilians in the concessions. Most Western civilians had to retreat to the "large cellars" of the buildings for refuge and left them only rarely. The sniping made even the shortest journey a risk, and the constant shelling interrupted rest and brought fear. By the beginning of July, one observer remembered, all in Tianjin "were worn out by broken sleep and apprehension."[20]

## SKIRMISHES

These harassing efforts were supplemented by attacks aimed at capturing the railway station at the northeastern end of the foreign enclave. This was a worthy goal as, at a single stroke, it would isolate the forces in Tianjin from their supply line down to the ocean and make it more difficult to use the train lines to get up to Beijing. On July 3, the Chinese started by mounting a heavy artillery barrage on the foreign city and the Russian camp. The next day, the bombardment continued, and Chinese forces began to move in the area near the Western Arsenal. This turned out to be a "demonstration" to draw allied attention, and the Chinese units involved retreated under cannon fire from the British guns. But it had done its job of drawing scrutiny and thus allowed the real Chinese attack to go in with tactical surprise. This was helped by "rain and thick mist" as well as a heavy preparatory bombardment, and the attackers got into the railway station itself. "The fighting was stubborn," the British account of the battle recalls, and the British were forced to rush reinforcements into the station to help the "roughly-handled" defenders. Captain Barnes was part of the relief. He and his men "doubled through the French Concession, up one road and down another, with the bullets . . . whistling their vicious note over our heads." It started to rain, and they could only see a few feet in front of them. They reached the station eventually:

Here the din was appalling. Rifles incessantly crack-
ling all round, bullets pattering on the corrugated iron
or singing away over the Settlement, and a perfect
deluge of rain falling impartially on the lot, made a
combination of noise that was bewildering, to say the
least of it.[21]

After several hours of confused fighting through the ruins, the
Chinese forces were driven off, leaving fifty dead behind
them.

Undeterred, the Chinese tried again several days later. This
time, they attempted to move a force around to the southwest
of Tianjin and the foreign settlements, hoping to come south of
the city and cut off the communications that way. Before they
could manage it, however, a scouting party of Japanese cavalry
discovered their position on July 8 and warned the rest of the
allies. This led to the creation of a joint British, Japanese, American, and Russian force of about two thousand men who, on
July 9, sortied out to attack the Chinese units. The British,
Americans, and Japanese were together under Major General
Fukushima, but the Russians had refused to be commanded by
a Japanese officer, so the British general Arthur Dorward commanded them. The joint force found the Chinese units occupying a small village and after a short but sharp fight succeeded in
driving the imperial troops off.

Emboldened by the success, the Western force finished by
linking up and marching on the Western Arsenal, about one
and a half miles away. The Chinese defenders did not mount an
accurate fire on the attackers, and the British, Americans, Japanese, and Russians fought their way into the arsenal with minimal casualties. The Chinese defenders successfully retreated
to the native city, destroying the north wall of the arsenal as
they did. Unfortunately for the allies, that made the arsenal
useless as a strongpoint. Without the north wall, it was "so ex-

posed to fire from the south wall of the native city . . . that its occupation by the Allies was decided to be undesirable."[22]

The Chinese tried again on July 11, mounting another assault on the railway station. This time the fighting was even fiercer, with the Chinese soldiers again getting in among the defenders, who had to resort to hand-to-hand combat to push them back. French, British, and Japanese reinforcements arrived and were thrown in immediately to stabilize the defensive lines. The Japanese spotted another Chinese attack forming and threw themselves into an impromptu assault, which broke the imperial forces before they could launch their own attack. The day ended with the Western forces still holding the railroad station, but tentatively at best. They had suffered about 150 casualties during the day's fighting. Chinese casualties, Admiral Seymour wrote, "must have been very heavy, but cannot be accurately given."[23]

The Chinese forces in these attacks consisted of both imperial troops and the Boxers. When the Boxers attacked, they did so with a degree of pomp and ceremony that struck the Westerners. "They moved toward us led by huge figures in head masques and women in white turbans and red sashes carrying red and black banners," wrote the American sailor Wendall Brown. "Groups of spearmen carrying red tasseled spears, gingal crews, swordsmen, riflemen and archers were flanked by bands of blaring trumpets."[24] Needless to say, the slow pace of the attack meant that these Boxers suffered heavy casualties.

It is interesting to note the difference in tactics between the Boxer bands around Tianjin and the ones who had attacked Seymour's column. The latter had tried the same ritualistic attacks early on, but had learned the hard way to attack faster and to come from cover at closer range. One of the great strengths of the Boxer movement was its decentralized nature, but in this case it meant that the lessons of Seymour's advance had not made it to the Boxers at Tianjin.

This particular attack was interesting in another way. The Russians had planned to mount an assault on a Chinese artillery unit near the rail station. To do so, they were planning to pull a number of soldiers from among the defenders of the station. If the plan had been executed, the Chinese attack would have hit the railway just as it was particularly undermanned. The Russian attack, however, was called off for logistical reasons, and so the defenders remained and proved crucial. The coincidence of timing, however, led to speculation that the Chinese were getting intelligence from within the foreign enclave and had deliberately planned to assault at the most propitious time. The forces were dependent on local Chinese for manual labor of all sorts, a population that seemed to many to be "overrun with spies."[25] Given the decades-long presence of Russia in China proper, that one of these Chinese might have known enough Russian to overhear the plans and report seems possible, if not overwhelmingly likely. But in any case, like the sniping, the suspicion that they were being spied on built the sense among Westerners that all the Chinese were enemies, not just the soldiers and Boxers.

By the middle of July, then, while the positions of the forces remained essentially the same, there had been near-constant fighting. The British, for example, had lost fourteen killed and fifty-three wounded in the two weeks since Seymour's return.[26] The Chinese forces had come close to breaking into Western defenses several times but had not quite managed it. The Western forces, by contrast, had broken into defended Chinese positions. The Chinese were nonetheless demonstrating a level of sophistication and operational awareness in their planning (most notably in the "demonstration" before the first assault on the railway) that was being undone by their tactical inadequacies. For whatever reason (better equipment, training, or motivation), the Western soldiers were proving superior.

## ASSAULT

By the middle of July, the coalition forces were strong enough to plan an assault on the walled city of Tianjin. The council of senior officers set the date for July 13 and put in command General Dorward. The plan for the attack was hammered out by the council, and each force had its role to play. It would take place from both the south and the east of the native city, with the Russians and Germans attacking from the east and the British, Japanese, Americans, French, and Austrians attacking from the south.

The defenses that the attackers faced were somewhat daunting. The main Chinese forces were located in the inner walled city, a fairly formidable defensive position. Even to reach that position required all the Western forces to clear a mud wall that ran around outer Tianjin and then work their way through the residential areas before coming up to the main walls. That distance was anywhere up to a mile, and it meant that the attack would be funneled into the streets and subject to fire as the forces advanced.

The attack started early the morning of the thirteenth, and things started to go wrong almost immediately. Just getting to the mud wall proved difficult for the attackers coming from the south, with the allied force coming under fire as it approached. There was only one gate to get through the mud wall, and it was swept by both small-arms fire and artillery rounds. Once inside, the troops discovered that the ground ahead of them was, to put it mildly, conducive to the defense. It was swampy with numerous holes and ditches filled with water, hard to move through, and offering only minimal cover. Farther in, the suburbs of the walled city consisted of numerous small houses that offered well-concealed positions for defenders to fire on the advancing troops. On the right, before the foreign enclave, were the ruined remains of more Chinese houses, which offered further refuge to Chinese soldiers. The only way through this was a raised causeway running north to south between the inner city and the mud wall. Anyone moving along the causeway, the troops soon discovered, came under intense fire from the walls of the inner city, troops hidden in the houses of the suburbs, and two guns of the Chinese artillery positioned out to the west. This "little Thermopylae," as one observer called it, was not a promising vision at that early morning hour.[27]

Worse, there was confusion about what exactly to do. This centered on the Ninth U.S. Infantry, only recently arrived in Tianjin. Colonel Liscum had not been invited to the conference of officers who finalized the plan, a problem as he was the senior American officer present at that time. It may well have been the confusion of the last few days before the attack rather than any intent to exclude the Americans, but the result was that Liscum only had a shaky idea of the plan, one that he chose not to share with any of his subordinate officers. That morning, as a result, where the Ninth was supposed to go remained somewhat mysterious. A visit from a staff officer bearing a message from General Dorward did not clear things up enough, and rather than ending up on the extreme left of the allied line (along with the U.S. Marines), the Ninth found itself on the extreme right. Worse, no one seems to have done much of a reconnaissance of the ground beforehand. Liscum's Ninth Infantry had some excuse, as it had just arrived in Tianjin on July 9. But Dorward does not seem to have been terribly well informed either, a point an American officer made later: "It appears, however, that [General Dorward] had made no adequate reconnaissance of the ground or of the enemy's position." As a result, the Ninth had to "wade through ponds" and came under "withering rifle fire" from the right flank.[28] Dorward later gave a halfhearted apology, in which he said:

"I blame myself for the mistake made in taking up of their position by the Ninth Regiment, not remembering that troops wholly fresh to the scene of action, and hurried forward in the excitement of attack, were likely to lose their way." The British general was gracious enough to follow that up by saying that the Ninth "gallantly . . . prevented a large body of the enemy from . . . inflicting serious loss on the French and Japanese."[29]

Thus the Ninth found itself taking fire not only from the north—the inner city and suburbs—but also from the west, the ruined suburbs outside of the foreign enclave. The soldiers went to ground in a graveyard, surrounded by low burial mounds. It was swampy, and the men found the foxholes they were digging filling with water almost immediately. Moving forward was impossible, as someone advancing was likely to be shot right away from both the front and the side. Moving backward was equally difficult. In fact, simply raising one's head above the level of the burial mounds was likely to draw a bullet. The casualties began to mount, and attempts to evacuate them foundered under fire.

Liscum took a battalion of men to attack the Chinese on the flank but, after charging across a flat area, discovered that there still remained a small but impassable pond before them. This stopped the assault dead, with the force of men hung up on the side of the pond without real cover. Liscum was killed almost immediately, and his men went to ground in the mud and water. They were still terribly vulnerable to Chinese fire, but getting up to retreat would have been worse. By midmorning, then, the Ninth was pinned down in two separate areas, its commander was dead, and the unit was suffering continuing casualties.

The experience of the Ninth, though extreme, echoed that of the rest of the southern assault. None of the other forces could manage to get to the Chinese defenders and instead ended up pinned down. On the far left, a U.S. Marine unit found itself in a similar predicament. Dug in, the marines kept time as the day whiled away by looking at the watch on their dead captain's outflung arm. They watched nervously as a large force of Chinese cavalry lurked close by, seemingly maneuvering to get into position for an attack. Had they done so, had the Chinese been an "energetic foe," one American army officer who analyzed the action later that year thought, the Western force might well have been "annihilated."[30]

Neither the British nor the Japanese had much more success, though they did not get into quite the difficulties that the Ninth did. The Japanese made repeated attacks on the main gate of the walled city but were repulsed each time. The fire from the defenders was simply too heavy for the Japanese engineers to get a charge placed and fuse set and lit. The British, meanwhile, were pinned down farther away from the wall, unable to move.

Despite the lack of overall success, it was a day for individual heroism, of all sorts. During the attack on the walled city, for example, the British naval brigade was brought under a "very heavy cross-fire." Able Seaman McCarthy fell to a bullet out in the open. Basil Guy, a midshipman of the HMS *Brawler*, tried to lift and carry him to safety, but "not having sufficient strength to do this," Guy instead remained with the seaman. Kneeling there, with the rest of the brigade now under cover, Guy found that the "entire fire from the city wall was concentrated" on the two of them. One witness later recalled that the "ground around Guy was absolutely plowed up" by bullets. He bound the wound as well as he could and then went to get help. Returning with a stretcher team, he helped load and carry McCarthy off the field. Tragically, as they were carrying him off the field, another bullet struck McCarthy, killing him. The midshipman survived and was awarded the Victoria Cross for his gallantry. He had turned eighteen years old the month before.[31]

Meanwhile, to the east, the Russians were experiencing similar difficulties. They, along with a small German contingent, had moved out of their camp early in the morning and marched to the northeast to get in position to hit the walled city from the east. As with the attack from the south, a hearty duel soon developed between the Chinese guns and the Western artillery. The Chinese arsenal on the eastern side, hit by one of the Western shells early on, exploded with a roar and rattle that shook troops for miles around and unhorsed a fair number of Russian Cossacks. The noise was loud enough to be heard down in Dagu, and Captain Bayly thought the column of smoke went six hundred feet in the air.[32]

The Russians and Germans managed to clear the Chinese from the mud wall but could not get over to attack the main Chinese lines or the fort. The problem was the same as for the southern attack. Once over the mud wall, there was little in the way of effective cover on the move toward the native city. The troops were exposed to both rifle and artillery fire as they moved into the assault, and it was simply too far to go. The walls of the city offered enough protection to the Chinese defenders that the Western artillery could not suppress their fire, and the small clusters of peasant houses between the two sets of walls offered concealment for Chinese troops to move closer and snipe. This was the one battle that was fought on terrain highly favorable to the defenders, and in that context the Chinese soldiers put on an exemplary display of tenacity, sticking "very pluckily" to their defenses.[33]

By late in the day, then, the allied assault had essentially been repulsed by the Chinese. Captain Barnes, with the Chinese Regiment, did not take part in the battle and so watched from walls of the foreign settlements. He could see clearly that things were not going well:

> The [Chinese] fire never seemed to slacken, or give the
> Allies a chance to get up to the wall . . . It was . . . a dis-
> mal day, for all the time there came in a mournful pro-
> cession of wounded, British, American, and Japanese,
> in stretchers, in carts, in rickshas, and hobbling pain-
> fully along, which told its own tale of the desperate
> fighting among those ruins.[34]

A "dismal day," as Barnes put it, seems a reasonable evaluation
of the effort. Despite all the heroism on the side of the Westerners, at the end of the day the Chinese still held much the
same positions as they had at the start of the day. As Barnes did,
James Ricalton watched the attack from the concessions, and
like that of Barnes his conclusion was grim: "Night is coming
on, and the ponderous gates are still closed and intact . . . To
charge these walls would mean destruction and slaughter; to
retreat meant the same. It is defeat."[35]

"The foreigners were actually defeated," said one analysis
later, in what seems a tone of wondering surprise.[36] Later, the
search for answers to this setback would give credit not to the
Chinese but to the designer of the fortifications, who, perhaps
fitting into the allied preconceptions, was a Westerner. The
"excellence" of the fortifications, Captain Henry Leonard of
the U.S. Marine Corps wrote later, was due to being "planned
by 'Chinese' Gordon, Gordon of Khartoum."[37] Leonard might
have noted that Gordon had been dead a decade and a half by
that point, the victim of his fatal underestimation of another
non-Western force, but that irony would have undercut his
point. Such an excuse came later, however: that night, the
American war correspondent Sydney Adamson reported that
the mood among the Western officers was "despondent. On the
face of it we had failed."[38]

That failure was transformed overnight. The Japanese, who
were closest to the walled city, used the slackening of fire as

darkness fell to their advantage. They planted "tins of gun-cotton" against the south gate and set a fuse. The fuse, sputtering in the dimness, was put out three times by Chinese fire, until finally a Japanese engineer "took a box of matches, ran forward, and touched the powder. Immediately there was an explosion, which blew man and gate to atoms."[39]

The Japanese unit involved then charged in the outer gate, managed to scale the inner wall under fire, and then captured and held the inner gate until morning, when they could be substantially reinforced. It was an impressive performance.

When dawn came, Western forces pushed farther into the city, driving the Chinese army before them. The assault was hampered by the thousands of civilians fleeing along with the Chinese forces. There was little discretion about whom the Western soldiers were shooting, and Charles Dix, a British midshipman, remembered Western soldiers on the walls of Tianjin firing "volleys into masses of fugitives pouring out of the west gate, among whom were many women."[40] But by the end of the day on July 14, the allies held all of Tianjin. They had triumphed: a close-run victory, but a victory nonetheless. Allied casualties were about two thousand killed and wounded. Chinese casualties were estimated at around ten thousand, though this was a Western figure.

In retrospect, the battle was not particularly well run. Dorward opened himself up for serious criticism in a number of ways, from not effectively reconnoitering the ground ahead of time, to mounting an assault over fire-swept terrain during the daylight hours, to not keeping particularly tight control over his units during the actual assault. Even the success of the Japanese blowing the gates came at their own initiative, rather than Dorward's orders. An American army critique years later (which was also quite hard on Liscum) would lay at Dorward's feet "glaring examples of poor tactics," "almost total lack of unity of command," and the absence of even "the most rudimentary military learning."[41]


## AFTERMATH

Tianjin itself was a "picture of desolation" after the siege and battle, "changed from a rich and important city of over a million inhabitants to a burned and battered heap of ruins."[42] Adamson, who entered the next morning, reported that the walled city was "strewn with corpses. Men had been killed in every act of life."[43] The buildings of Tianjin were largely destroyed, and there were countless numbers of dead bodies lying about, both civilian and military. Charles Dix remembered going into the walled city with some dismay:

> The further one went into the city, the more horrible were the scenes with which one was confronted. Shrapnel, common shell, and lyddite had spared no one; every type was to be found there lying where they fell, killed, one might almost say, by an accident, male and female, old men and little naked children.[44]

Adamson spoke of the "fetid smell of human flesh." Not all of the bodies were dead. Adamson, again:

> Just within the gate a strange creature sat. He was naked to the waist. His left arm above the elbow had a piece cut out to the bone. The wound was glutted with coagulated blood. His pelvis was smashed and his right thigh was crushed to a jelly. It was loose, and the lower leg seemed to hang to his body by some pulpy flesh and the bloody rags that were his clothes. He sat watching the rush of human beings through the burning streets

with an imbecilic smile, sometimes raising his arm with
a gesture of appeal.[45]

The Chinese were in no position to help their own
wounded, and the Western forces did not have the capacity to
help, even if they were interested in doing so. Likely, then, that
most died where they had been wounded. The capture of the
city also provoked a wave of refugees fleeing the occupation.
James Ricalton remembered the scene in the main street of
the walled city:

> This street and the surrounding houses were a holo-
> caust of human life. A day later that long thoroughfare
> was a slow-moving line of homeless, weeping human
> beings—their homes in ashes, without food, friendless,
> and, in many cases, their kindred left charred in the
> ruins of their homes.[46]

Nor did the destruction stop then. Possibly driven by the
sheer violence of the battle, a wave of looting followed the capture of the city. An American marine reported that "soldiers of
all nations joined the orgy . . . Men of the allies staggered
through the streets, arms and backs piled high with silks and
furs, and brocades, with gold and silver and jewels."[47] Some
managed to rationalize their actions. Henry Savage Landor, a
British correspondent, thought "it certainly seemed a pity to let
so much beautiful and valuable property be wasted. Was it
not, then, the lesser evil to allow these men, who had fought
hard, to reap what benefit they could from the misfortune of
others . . . ?"[48]

Looting would later become an international scandal, and
so it is worth investigating in more detail. Captain Barnes, of
the Chinese Regiment, dealt with it in his memoirs, though
reluctantly. "It would now seem to be the time to attempt

some vague description of the looting of Tientsin [Tianjin] city, of which we have all heard," he starts out, before reassuring his reader that the looting was "mainly and most systematically by ex-Chinese soldiers, Boxers, and other ragamuffins, who took advantage of the encouragement held out to the inhabitants to return, to enter the city in disguise as coolies, etc., and regularly clean the place out." Perhaps realizing how unlikely it sounded that such "ragamuffins" could manage to strip the place bare under the noses of those they had just been fighting, Barnes does then concede that "of course, it must not be imagined that the troops looked on passively at this, for this is rather more than flesh and blood can be expected to stand," so it was not unreasonable that the Western soldiers ended up with "one or two or even more, unconsidered trifles, that were, at the moment, ownerless." The waffling continued, with Barnes waxing eloquent about the Chinese houses. They "were a sight one can never forget. In some, the profusion of rich furs, silks, wearing apparel, clocks, watches, musical boxes, looking-glasses, china-ware, cloisonné, and other articles of priceless worth, was something to live for and to see but once. I verily believe that one could have taken a few cart-loads of the above-mentioned away from many houses." Just in case anyone worried that this was perhaps entirely too rhapsodic, Barnes hurried to assure his readers that "we had no carts." Finally, after all of this, Barnes settles on his last word on the situation, one that echoed Landor's:

> When men have been exposed to all sorts of danger, through no fault of their own, from a city that has, more or less voluntarily, sheltered hordes of the most cruel fanatics the world has ever seen, you must not be too hard on them if their human nature gets a little the upper hand of their finer feelings.[49]

Barnes reconciled himself to the looting eventually, but not without a great deal of textual effort.

Not all Westerners rationalized the looting. James Ricalton was condemnatory, and given the details he related, it is hard not to see his point. Ricalton witnessed looting not only of empty Chinese homes but of the refugees fleeing:

> Men and women were fleeing, carrying their precious heirlooms—their jewels, their furs, their silks, their embroidery, their money. These much-prized valuables were snatched from them, and they dared not protest; they could not protest; they could not even tell that they were not Boxers.

Ricalton did not see much in the way of justification:

> Looting from an enemy bent on taking your life as well as your property is justifiable by a natural *quid pro quo* equivalency, or by the law of reprisal, as well as by the Old Testament code; but indiscriminate plunder of friend and foe is robbery, and robbery is robbery even in war . . . Shamefully looted China has had a lesson in the ethics of Christian armies she will not soon forget.[50]

What both Barnes and Ricalton failed to note was that looting violated the Hague Convention of 1899, which all the combatants had signed. Perhaps the convention was so newly minted that its proscriptions had not quite been taken on board by the military and overcome the long tradition that allowed looting after the capture of a city: "After all, there is precedent without end, for in nearly every instance where a city has fallen by direct assault, and where there has been only flight, not surrender, on the part of the defenders, the town has been sacked."[51]

In any case, whatever the moral status of the looting, it is clear that in the several days after the capture of the walled city, the Western forces, enlisted and officer alike, spent much time acquiring booty for themselves. A thriving black market arose in such looted goods and found eager customers in those who had arrived late or those who had disposable income and the means to get the acquisitions home. The practical reality was that enlisted men sold to officers, an interesting mercantile relationship that complicated the more normal military one. Haggling, it seems likely, might be difficult when done with a superior officer.

There was another, much less pleasant form of cleaning up required in the city. The first requirement of occupation, from a military perspective, was to deal with the bodies. There were simply too many to handle this gracefully, and so most of them were either buried in mass graves, burned in pyres, or dumped in the river. Captain Barnes of the Chinese Regiment was one of those detailed to gather the dead: "On the afternoon of the 17th I was informed that as soon as I was able to report the south-west quarter of the city clear of corpses . . . I had to burn them, in all, some thirty. Selecting a fine open yard, we set to work to build a pyre."[52] The job had still not been finished weeks later. George Newell, an American soldier who arrived at the beginning of August, wrote of Tianjin that "it is all one big ruin now."

It must have been a ferice [*sic*] battle for the dead are still lying in the streets every where you go, & on which the dogs and hogs are getting fat. When we first got off the train here the first thing I seen along side of the rail road track was a drove of hogs and dogs fighting over & at the same time tearing to pieces a dead Chinaman.[53]

For several weeks after the battle, sailors on ships moving up or down the Hai River reported dead bodies having to be cleared from the side wheels.

The allies had conquered Tianjin and destroyed it in the process. Now they needed to rebuild it. To do so, they established the Tianjin Provisional Government (TPG). The allies posted an open letter to the inhabitants that said that the TPG would "protect everyone wishing to deal in a friendly manner with foreigners" but would "punish without mercy everyone who causes trouble." It continued apocalyptically, "Let the bad people tremble! But the good people should feel reassured."[54]

Each Western power sent a single officer to the head council of the TPG, and they set about their architectural, municipal, and criminal justice responsibilities with some vigor. The TPG started redesigning the city on a European model, with broad avenues and buildings in a checkerboard pattern. They initiated work on a sewer system and electric tram line and began offering free health care to the population, including small-pox vaccinations. They aimed to establish a freshwater supply system throughout the city. They began to put together a police force to patrol the city, effectively enough that both the Japanese and the German consuls eventually requested that the TPG police patrol their foreign enclaves as well. It turned out to be a remarkably effective occupation, and when the foreign powers returned Tianjin to Qing control in 1902, they had built the foundation of a modern city.[55]

But until the TPG managed to get things in something that resembled order, living in Tianjin was hazardous for those not affiliated with one of the militaries. Even Western civilians had their own problems. James Ricalton found himself close to starvation, and only scrounging staved it off:

One day during this period of scarcity, while on the street, I saw a potato drop from a passing commissary wagon. This I seized, and following the wagon for a half-mile picked up in all seven potatoes and one onion. With these I returned to my room in a mood of triumphant forage.[56]

The situation for Chinese civilians was unimaginably difficult, whether they had stayed in the city or fled to the countryside. One newspaper wrote of the Chinese city as a ghost town: "The Chinese city is almost deserted, where before lived a population of nearly a million souls. Some have come back, but very few."[57] Those that had come back did so at the risk of their lives. The Chinese permitted in Tianjin by the allies had to carry passes, and soldiers were known to "wantonly kill" those without, or even those who had not pinned the pass to their breast so that it was immediately visible.[58] The war may have moved north from Tianjin, but the violence had not.

# 7

# THE SECOND EXPEDITION

The conquest of Tianjin was only the start, the first act in what seemed to be shaping up into a long campaign. The most critical goal—the relief of the legations in Beijing—was still far distant. In a sense, the capture of Tianjin was, to use a Churchillian phrase, the end of the beginning. Now the allied forces would have to organize an expedition to march on Beijing, and one that would stand more chance of success than Seymour's. Just what that expedition would find when it got to Beijing was unclear. The uprising had created a media frenzy, and even the American presidential campaign had fallen to "a subordinate place in the estimation of the American public, whose interest is fixed on the extraordinary possibilities of the situation in the Flowery Kingdom."[1] In England, *Attack on a China Mission* was being filmed in the garden of a rented house in Hove.[2] Into this frenzy, and even as Tianjin was being captured, the news broke that the legations had fallen to Chinese assault, and all the inhabitants slaughtered. The story appeared in the *Daily Mail* of London and seemed authentic, with details about how the Europeans had died.[3] The story, however, was undone by a telegram from Edwin Conger, encrypted in the State Department cipher, that reached the allies on July 20. The encryption strongly suggested its authenticity, and, decoded, it was an urgent plea for help. The Americans were "besieged . . . under continued shot and shell . . . Quick relief only can prevent general massacre."[4] The Westerners in the legations were still alive, and relief was still possible.

The reality on the ground was quite a bit more prosaic. Within days of the capture of Tianjin by foreign forces, the Chinese besiegers declared an informal truce in their sporadic attacks on the walls of the legations. This was barely in time, for the legations had been suffering substantial casualties in the defense of the walls.[5] For the next two weeks, as Captain Edmund Wray of the Royal Marines wrote later, there was a "cessation of hostilities . . . except for sniping on both sides."[6] Annoyingly, the Chinese snipers kept shooting down the American flag flying over the U.S. embassy during this period, an insult that the marine private William Horton took personally. Every time the flag came down, Horton would climb up the pole and reattach it.[7]

On July 19, to confuse things even more, the Zongli Yamen sent a message to the legations asking them to leave for Tianjin and promising safe conduct there. The ministers refused, trusting neither the government, the Boxers, nor the troops to honor the promise. Most befuddling of all, on the following day, July 20, the Yamen sent the legations "four cart-loads of watermelons and vegetables . . . as a sign of good feeling."[8] Robert Hart, the British head of the Imperial Maritime Customs Service, was sent a "special allotment" that included not only watermelons but a hundred pounds of flour, and two blocks of ice.[9] No one knew what to make of that. Food was running low. The Chinese Christians had been segregated into a separate part of the defended area and left essentially to fend for themselves for food, given only the supplies that the Westerners would not eat. But when the government offered to take the Chinese Christians off their hands because "the pressure in our midst of so many converts must be inconvenient, and that as popular feeling was now quiet and tranquil," Claude MacDonald noted that "it did not seem worthwhile to consult the converts as to whether they wished to facilitate their own massacre."[10]

## GASELEE PLANS A WALK

On July 27, Kaiser Wilhelm II of Germany gave a speech to departing German troops at Bremerhaven. He exhorted them to demonstrate the might of imperial Germany. "The task that the old Roman Empire of the German nation was unable to accomplish, the new German Empire is in a position to fulfill." He continued with their mission: "You are to revenge the grievous injustice that has been done." Then, diverging from his written statement, the kaiser added:

> Should you encounter the enemy, he will be defeated! No quarter will be given! Prisoners will not be taken! Whoever falls into your hands is forfeited. Just as thousands of years ago the Huns under their King Attila made a name for themselves, one that even today makes them seem mighty in history and legend, may the name Germany be affirmed by you in such a way in China that no Chinese will ever again dare to look cross-eyed at a German.[11]

The words were so grossly exaggerated that the German Foreign Office edited out the kaiser's addition when it issued a printed version. His improvisation, however, summed up one side of the imperial world of 1900. Making China bleed would bring the Germans international reputation and make them "mighty in history and legend." Thus did the conquest of faraway places give status at home.[12]

The kaiser's words were irrelevant as they left his mouth. The imperial world was not going to wait. The inherent silliness of delaying until the German troops and Count von Waldersee arrived was clear. Sir Alfred Gaselee, the newly arrived British commander, began to lobby the other commanders to send a second expedition immediately.

This feeling was increased by another message that the allies received on July 21. It was from Claude MacDonald and had been carried from Beijing by a sixteen-year-old Chinese man named Lin Wu Yuan. Lin had made it out of the embassy quarter in Beijing, "let down over the wall by a rope," and then, "without being molested," had made it out of Beijing and down the main road to Tianjin. He was not stopped by either imperial troops or Boxers, but in one village he was forced to stay and work for eight days by the villagers. Lin "saw a few parties of Boxers in villages, but none on the road." He reported that the Hai River was "in high flood" and that "crops everywhere look[ed] well. Villagers are attending to their farms, but there is a Boxer organization in every village."[13] Most notable was the lack of Boxers on the road and the multiple hints that the drought was beginning to lift: the river in flood, the crops in good shape, and the villagers "attending to their farms." The missive echoed Conger's grim picture of the situation at the legations:

> Enemy are enterprising but cowardly . . . Our casualties up to date 44 killed and about double that wounded. We have provisions for about 2 weeks [but] are eating our ponies. If the Chinese do not press attack, we can hold out for some days, say 10, but if they show determination it is a question of 4 or 5, so no time should be lost.[14]

In the message, MacDonald reported that "British Legation . . . repeatedly attacked by Chinese troops on all sides, both rifle and artillery fire . . . Food sufficient for a fortnight at most. Ammunition running short . . . Important that relieving force when near should advance rapidly to prevent attack on Legation by the retreating Chinese forces." He also noted that sixty-two defenders had been killed since the siege started.[15]

It had taken Lin two weeks to get to Tianjin, meaning that time seemed almost up for the legations. Gaselee knew of Mac-Donald's military background and had no reason to think that the minister was exaggerating the seriousness of the situation. In addition, Gaselee was worried about the campaign lasting too long. Should it take the allied forces months to make their way to Beijing, they might find themselves in the middle of a Chinese winter. That would not be particularly worrisome except that if the Hai River froze, it would interrupt the key supply line the British planned to use.[16] The Americans were worried about the same thing, noting that the Hai River became unnavigable around December 1, "so it was necessary to provide not only the landing of the troops with their horses, transportation, ordnance, and current supplies, but for the delivery in China, not later than the middle of November, six months supply" for that force.[17]

In addition, Gaselee could see the advantages of moving quickly, while the Chinese were still disorganized and scattered after the defeat at Tianjin. Colonel A. G. Churchill, a British liaison with the Japanese, summed up the military case for moving quickly by pointing out that the Chinese had been "very much demoralized" by the defeat at Tianjin, that delaying would give them time to rebuild and reinforce their troops, and that bad weather which would slow movement was likely "at any time."[18]

Finally, it must be said, Gaselee may well have been considering the advantages of stealing a march not only on the Chinese but on von Waldersee and the Germans. The kaiser might have won the political battle to get a German commander in chief, but Gaselee was there on the ground. Imperial rivalries did not stop simply because the imperial powers were working together. The British Foreign Office was happily using the collection of warships off Dagu to get pictures of foreign ships that it needed for intelligence purposes.[19] It seems hard to imagine that Gaselee did not have imperial advantages in mind as well.

There were dangers, of course. In the aftermath of Seymour's expedition and the fight around Tianjin, estimates of how many allied soldiers were required to take Beijing had jumped substantially, to over fifty thousand men.[20] In addition, the allies had suffered major casualties in the previous week's battle and needed some time to rebuild. Many of the troops arriving in Tianjin were not ready to move immediately; the horses of the Sixth U.S. Cavalry, for example, were so weakened by their ocean journey that they needed time to recover. Finally, the allied supply line would be a tenuous one, running back down the Hai River to Tianjin and then along the Dagu to the coast. It would require a substantial number of troops to protect, troops that would be a drain on the advancing allied force. The force itself would only be able to carry about a week's supply of rations with it, which meant that any supply cutoff could quickly have dire consequences. Admiral Seymour's expedition stood as an urgent warning about the risks of such a gamble. As Frederick Brown put it:

> The sole excuse for undertaking the march with twenty thousand men fewer than military experts deemed necessary for the capture of Peking in the middle of the "rainy season" is to be found in the urgency of the situation. It was daring in the extreme, and had it ended in failure would have been characterised as a foolhardy undertaking.[21]

From London, Major General Sir John Ardagh dismissed the idea of a "small or moderate sized" second expedition as doomed to failure. The "serious loss of prestige" that accompanied the repulse of Seymour's expedition would be redoubled by the collapse of a second attempt. Ardagh summed up the practical reasons not to go immediately as well, pointing to the "heterogeneous composition of the international forces, the subdivision of command, and the jealousies which undoubtedly exist among the nations concerned." All of these would "greatly impair their collective efficiency and render unity of action almost impossible."[22]

Despite this, however, Gaselee pushed to start to Beijing as soon as could be managed. "Early forward movement essential in spite of our weakness," he telegraphed the War Office on July 30.[23] His brother-in-law, a fellow British officer, Robert Francis Gartside-Tipping, spoke of Gaselee's agitation: "I have seen Alfred daily . . . he seems well . . . I know he is chafing much, as we all were, at the enforced delay here, when those poor people are still shut up in Pekin. God send that we may rescue them all right with small loss to ourselves and them."[24]

Gaselee's case was assisted by the continuous stream of troops arriving, including further British units and American, French, and Japanese forces. In the last ten days of July, fourteen British troop transports passed through Hong Kong on their way to Dagu.[25] The arrival of the general in command of the American forces in China, Adna Chaffee, on July 29 also brought an ally. Chaffee, like Gaselee, saw no reason to wait. Between the two of them, they convinced all but the French commander of the urgency of moving, and at a five-hour meeting on August 3 the assembled generals agreed to move the next day, with even the initially reluctant French holdout finally assenting.[26] Again, imperial buccaneering had won the way.

The command arrangements were ad hoc. Though Gaselee and Chaffee had gotten the expedition moving, they had no formal authority to command the force. Von Waldersee was the only agreed commander of the international coalition, and he was still at sea at the beginning of August, unlikely to arrive for several weeks. The result was, as Chaffee put it, that the "troops of each nation were under the control of their own commanders, who gave the necessary orders." At the highest level, the actions and movements of the force would be decided by the "conference method" in which all the senior officers got together every day and decided on the next day's plans.[27] Needless to say, it is hard to imagine a riskier or less recommended command arrangement than the one with which the allies ended up.

The council planned for a force of just under nineteen thousand men: eight thousand Japanese, forty-eight hundred Russians, three thousand British, twenty-one hundred Americans, and eight hundred French.[28] The assembly of that force required some fairly impromptu arrangements. To feed and supply nearly nineteen thousand men demanded a substantial amount of supplies daily, and more if the force was fighting regularly and using its ammunition. The allies had no time to build enough boats to carry the supplies, and there were not enough willing sellers, so they took the simple and brutal expedient of stealing Chinese junks from their owners, a task that Charles Dix, the British midshipman, found distasteful:

> The work of collecting junks off the river was a task not looked forward to by either officers or men, consisting, as it did, of turning whole families out into the banks, from what had been their sole living place; but the orders were to get junks, and empty ones are not found floating about in war-time even in China.

The one empty junk they did find still had the corpses of eight Chinese who had been slaughtered aboard much earlier.

Dix recalled that that particular junk was "allowed to go on floating."[29]

The supply situation was improved by a concerted effort on the part of Russian military engineers to repair the railway between Dagu and Tianjin. This eased one bottleneck. But others remained. Dagu itself was not a terribly useful port. The sandbar off the harbor mouth limited the draft of ships that could come into the river and dramatically slowed the off-loading of supplies.

In addition, the supplies themselves had been hastily packaged and sent to China, with the attendant consequences. Some were hard to shift by hand. Ammunition boxes that weighed four hundred pounds, for example, were easy to lift using a transport's crane but almost impossible to carry by hand onto a wagon or into a junk.[30] Some supplies were macabre. Charles Henry Martin, an American captain, wrote that a great store of coffins was sent with the American forces.[31] Some supplies were simply not useful. Gartside-Tipping, commanding the First Bengal Lancers, remembered that the British soldiers and cavalrymen were issued greatcoats as part of their supplies. The August nights in northern China were certainly cooler than the days, but it is hard to imagine that many of the issued coats did not get tossed aside as soon as the march started.[32] Had the campaign lasted into the fall months, the loss of the equipment could have been a serious problem, but it is hard to criticize the soldiers and marines when the daily temperatures were over a hundred degrees.

But if the arrangements and supplies were often a hodge-podge, they did serve the purpose of getting a force together and moving. George Newell, the American private, wrote home on August 3: "Well from what I hear I think we start to advance tomorrow. Pekin is 80 miles from here an we expect 3 good battles between here & there. Pekin itself from what I hear from men that have lived there say that it wont be hard as this place was to take."[33]

The troops arose at 3:00 the next morning, and the force began marching at dawn. The force that left was a mixed bag, to say the least. Smedley Butler, an American officer, looked on as "French Zouaves in red and blue, blond Germans in pointy helmets, Italian Bersaglieri with tossing plumes, Bengal cavalry on Arabian stallions, turbaned Sikhs, Japanese, Russians, English" set off for Beijing. Included also were at least a dozen newspaper correspondents embedded with the force.[34] It was hot; as soon as the sun came up, the temperature rose until, as one marine remembered it, it was like marching through a "blast furnace."[35]

Tagging along on this walk was, of all people, Roger Keyes. The naval officer loathed the idea of missing the climactic moment of the war and had lobbied Seymour to go along as a liaison with the army. Seymour, irritated and less forgiving than Bruce, refused. But Gaselee was an old friend of Keyes's family, and the young lieutenant found a willing ear in the general. Gaselee intervened with Seymour, and Keyes, to his delight, found himself seconded to the British army for the duration of the expedition.

It took a long time to get the entire force sorted and arranged in column. The Americans, who were toward the back, did not begin moving until 3:00 p.m.[36] But eventually, the force wended its way north, following the Hai River, with a highly mixed supply train behind it. There were Chinese laborers, or coolies, as the Westerners referred to them, wagons of all assortments, and the indigenous supply forces of the various national units. The march gave the various units a chance to size each other up, out of camp. "The Japanese are pleasant little men," Lieutenant Colonel H. B. Vaughan of the British wrote, "always cheerful and happy looking, and very like the Gurkhas in appearance."[37]

On the river itself was a motley collection of boats, lighters, and junks in every shape and variety. One quartermaster described the scene:

> The sight presented by the enormous amount of road transportation is said to have beggared description; it included pack animals of all kinds, horses, ponies, mules, donkeys, carts of all shapes and sizes . . . Everything on wheels had been impressed into the transport service, even the cows bearing packs for the Japanese, and loaded camels plodding along with the Russian trains.[38]

The land that they moved through was almost entirely flat and cultivated, an "absolute plain," as one British officer remembered it. The crops, despite the drought, had reached above head height, and so the soldiers found themselves fighting through field after field of grain, unable to see ahead of them. Only the officers on their horses were lifted above the plants, but their view did not extend much further. There were few hills, and the sense grew quickly of moving through a featureless land that went on forever. It is telling how far the officers had to go to get a sense of the land ahead of them: "Two long bamboo ladders were lashed together at one end, and the lashed ends raised, forming a double stairway to nowhere in particular, which was kept in position by guys, and from the apex of which an extensive view could be obtained."[39]

This was not an improvisation, but in fact standard British equipment, "portable field observatories" with special ladders designed to fit together and give a view from thirty feet aboveground, which "enabled a look-out man to see above the tall crops easily."[40]

## BATTLES

By an odd coincidence, July 27, the day of the kaiser's speech, was also the day that Chinese policy firmed up. The failure of the moderates to manage any successful negotiation with the legations had turned Cixi away from them. She looked instead to Li Bingheng, an old warhorse, who advocated strong resistance to the Western attack. Cixi was trapped in a corner: she could not safely get rid of the legations, as they refused to go; she could not control the Boxers; and she could not, apparently, stop the Western powers at Tianjin. Li promised her that he could defend Beijing, and she listened. Yuan Chang, the moderate member of the Zongli Yamen, was executed on July 28 to signal the shift, and the Chinese found themselves, perhaps for the first time, with a set strategy. It was to fight.[41]

It was thus that, as the second expedition neared the first sizable village north of Tianjin, Beicang, it found a substantial concentration of troops:

> Imperial troops and Boxers, were holding a very strong position at a place called Peitsang [Beicang] about 12 miles to the north of Tientsin . . . The Chinese were strongly entrenched, had many guns, and . . . their position extended on both banks of the river Paiho [Hai], being 6 to 7 miles in length.[42]

The Chinese commander was General Dong Fuxiang, who the allies believed was strongly pro-Boxer. The Westerners thus moved forward cautiously, expecting a major battle almost immediately. In more normal times, the allies would have used their cavalry to outflank the Chinese defenders, while the infantry held them in position. "Flanked out and started on the run," Charles Henry Martin called it. But "herein lies our weakness," the American captain continued. "Cavalry is short . . . [we] cannot cut them up as we might."[43]

Instead, the Russians and French advanced along the left bank of the Hai, while the Americans, British, and Japanese moved along the right bank. The plan was to have the Japanese attack the eastern flank of the Chinese defenses, break into the defensive line, and then roll it up. The Chinese would be prevented from reinforcing the flank by near-simultaneous attacks along the line by the Russians, French, Americans, and British, in that line order. The river would stop the Chinese from moving forces quickly across it, and when the defensive line crumbled and the Chinese began retreating north, the allied cavalry would come in behind them and carve them up.

The Chinese forces near Beicang were, as the scouts reported, a mixture of imperial troops and Boxers. They had had several weeks to fortify themselves and had dug long lines of trenches with raised walls of dirt, "cleverly screened" by straw.[44] The imperial troops were armed with "modern magazine rifles and Krupp quick-firing guns, and fired smokeless powder."[45] The Boxers, it appeared later, were still armed with their various hand weapons, though some had been given old rifles. It should be noted that the Chinese troops were thus better equipped than some of the allies, not least the Japanese, who had single-shot rifles firing (extremely smoky) black powder. The Japanese government had "decided that they might safely take the opportunity of using up their surplus stock of black powder as it was not considered necessary to waste any of their new smokeless powder on an enemy so little formidable."[46] The Japanese soldiers were about to pay a price for that decision.

The Chinese had taken two steps unknown to the allies. They had built a bridge of boats across the Hai, allowing relatively rapid reinforcements in one direction or the other. In addition, they had cut the riverbank on the western side of the Hai and allowed the water to flood the ground to the south of their defensive fortifications.

The coalition forces attacked the morning of August 5. The French and Russians attacked on their side of the river, and the British, American, and Japanese on their side. The French and Russians got a nasty shock upon discovering the flooded plain. Although a unit of Japanese sappers unblocked the river itself with explosives and closed the breach in the side bank by "cleverly . . . swinging a junk into it broadside on, so that it jammed at the sides of the breach," the French and Russians could not get through the floodwaters.[47] In a situation reminiscent of the Battle of Tianjin, the French and Russians found themselves pinned down under heavy Chinese artillery fire. On the other bank, the situation was more positive. Although the allied cavalry found itself struggling to move through the fields, which were "most unsuited to Cavalry, the whole of it being under crops which were growing to a height of from 6 to 11 feet and were very thick," the same crops gave good cover to the infantry.[48] Lieutenant Colonel H. B. Vaughan, of the British, sitting high on his horse, quickly decided that the infantry's lot was a better one:

> The crops were very high, but we could see our shrapnel bursting over the villages in front, one of which was in flames, and towards which we advanced, through intense heat and crops about ten feet high. We could not hear the enemy's bullets owing to the rustling made by our progress through the crops, but in the patches of open ground we heard them patting on the ground, and the soil jumping, and so many struck in one place, that though I had a sprained ankle I thought it advisable to dismount.[49]

The good cover allowed the Japanese to close on the Chinese defenses. The Chinese defenders, however, fought valiantly, and in the end the Japanese had to mount repeated frontal assaults against the Chinese defenses before they broke the line.

The Chinese officers reacted quickly, recognizing that their position was now indefensible. Instead of retreating northward as the allies expected, the Chinese troops fell back along their line to the river and crossed the bridge of boats. They pulled the boats behind them, left a solid rear guard on the western bank of the river, and retreated northwest. The cavalry caught about fifty Chinese stragglers on the east side of the bank and rode them down, and a six-pounder gun was also captured, but most of the Chinese troops escaped. The allies would later find "a quantity of abandoned Chinese umbrellas lying strewn along the road, where they had evidently been left by the Chinese troops in their hasty flight."[50]

Despite the implications of "hasty flight," the Chinese retreat was quite effectively handled. The commanding officers recognized the untenable position that the Japanese success had put their entire defensive line in and reacted quickly to extricate their force. They had clearly planned ahead of time for just such an eventuality, and so they had a ready-made and protected exit for their troops, a path that was not what the allies were expecting. The troops themselves executed the retreat smoothly and with discipline in a difficult situation, and by the end of the day the Chinese had gotten away safely, ready to fight again. Casualties seem to have been about equal. The Japanese in their repeated attacks lost three hundred dead and nine hundred wounded, and the British about sixty dead and two hundred wounded. The other forces did not suffer substantial losses. Chinese casualties were estimated by the allies to be about "1,000–1,500 killed and wounded," a total similar to the allied forces.

Beicang was a clear allied victory; they had won the field

and forced the Chinese to retreat. It was a battle fought "almost entirely," as Major Jesse Lee of the Ninth U.S. Infantry put it, by the Japanese.[51] General Gaselee "accord[ed]" to the Japanese the "whole credit of the victory."[52] But the Chinese had more than held their own, inflicted similar levels of casualties on the attackers, and then retreated deftly to, as it turned out, the next prepared defensive position, up the road at Huangcun. If they could manage to continue this kind of slow defensive wearing of the allied attackers, then the Chinese might be able to extend the campaign into the winter months, when the challenges facing the allies would intensify. If, in addition to the conventional defenses, the Chinese could use the Boxers as irregulars, attacking allied scouting parties and, most critically, allied supply trains, they could potentially, as they had done to Admiral Seymour's column, make the allied drive on Beijing completely untenable. Like the Tianjin strategy, the Boxer strategy showed early promise.

The demonstration of Chinese competence continued the next day. The allies awoke to find that the Chinese rear guard had snuck away overnight and "vacated" the field. This left the Western powers with nothing to do but chase the Chinese up the road, which they duly did. The next town was Huangcun, about twelve miles north.

Here, too, there were extensive Chinese fortifications on the eastern side of the Hai, based partly on the line of the railroad. "Just to the south of [Huangcun] where the Railway curved to the west towards the river and crossed the road at right angles, the enemy had taken up a position and were holding the Railway embankment itself."[53] The raised line of the embankment served well as a ready-made entrenchment for the defenders, who looked down on a deep frontage of grain fields. About half a mile out from the river, the railway curved away south. Here, the Chinese had extended their line away from the tracks, toward three small villages, which were occupied and fortified. Behind this first line of defenses was another line just outside Huangcun itself, curving from south to north. The Beijing road came into the town, crossed the river over two bridges, and then headed almost due north to the capital city. The Chinese had laid out the same defensive scheme as at Beicang: a heavily defended entrenchment based on trenches and strongpoints, with a solid second line of defenses, and then a shielded retreat route northward. On the west side of the river, the Chinese had cut the riverbanks again and inundated the land in front of Huangcun. They relied on this to prevent a flanking maneuver by the allied troops coming up from the west and south. The only Chinese forces actually on the west bank of the river were an artillery unit covering the front of the defensive lines to the east. It was a risky tactic: if the inundated land did not hold back an attack, the Chinese were risking being cut off and their retreat line blocked.

The allies rotated in a new set of troops to lead the attack. The Japanese were still recovering from the previous day, and so the British and Americans were tasked to be the leading elements. The main attack would come against the Chinese line of defenses on the east side of the river. The Americans would attack on the right, the British in the center, and the Russians and French would come up behind them to fill the gap between the left of the British line and the river. On the far right, the Bengal Lancers would cover the American flank and prevent a Chinese counterattack. Meanwhile, on the western side of the river, a section of Japanese forces would come up on Huangcun from the south and hopefully close the door on a Chinese retreat.

As they had the previous day, the Chinese fought hard. The railway embankment was about thirty feet above the plain at that point, and one British observer remembered that the defenders "poured in a deadly fire from above."[54] On the left side of the attack, the British artillery had been able to push up close onto a low rise only a few hundred yards south of the defensive line. This gave them the ability to target the defenders directly, and that, combined with aggressive frontal assaults by the First Sikhs and the Twenty-fourth Punjabis, enabled the British to get into the Chinese lines with fewer casualties than the Japanese had had the previous day.

The Americans had a more difficult experience. The Chinese artillery in the fortified villages at the end of the line could range into the American flanks, and did so with some effect. In addition, the sheer struggle of crossing the fields after hours of marching in the heat proved difficult. Frederic Wise, an American marine sergeant, remembered the assault:

> The plain in front of us was a furnace. Dust rose in thick clouds. There was no air to breathe . . . We advanced a thousand yards. Down on us, every step of the way beat that blazing sun, heavier every second . . . Another thousand yards. My men began to stagger again. They were taut and game, but all in. Here one turned ghastly white. There one dropped dead from heat. More and more men were staggering.

Wise and his fellow sergeants kept his men moving forward by calling the "men everything they could put their tongues to. Anything to madden them."

What spared the Americans to a large degree was the desperate inaccuracy of the Chinese fire, something Wise thought familiar. "Chinese bullets were whizzing over our heads. They were shooting high, as usual." Even the artillery, which was better than the small arms, tended to shoot over their targets. That inaccuracy continued even as the Americans closed with the embankment: "Through the dust and smoke those earthworks came into sight. We stopped, fired, advanced again. Rifle fire blazed out at us. Not a man was hit." Adding to that inaccuracy was the unwillingness of the Chinese soldiers—whether by order or instinct—to fight hand to hand with the attackers. Even as Wise and his men closed, they could see the Chinese "milling about," and when the marines climbed the embankment, it was "empty. The Chinese, each man for himself, were vanishing rapidly amid the tombs in the dust of that endless plain."[55]

Farther to the left, next to the British, the Fourteenth U.S. Regiment under Colonel Aaron Daggett, spared the fighting at Tianjin, had a similar experience. Much as Wise's men had, the members of the Fourteenth found themselves pushing forward through concentrated but inaccurate defensive fire. Artillery fire began to hit them "when within about one and a half miles of the village," coming from "our front and right."[56] Rifle fire started when they were a little less than a mile away from the village. The men of the Fourteenth found a small rise about three hundred yards from the village, and Daggett set them up there to return fire. After the Chinese fire was "nearly silenced," Daggett ordered an assault. The Fourteenth, along with some Sikh soldiers it had acquired in the advance, closed on the village. As in the assault on the Dagu Forts, there was an element of sporting competition in this, as Daggett was careful to note in his official report that the Americans were "a little more rapid in their movements, [and] reached the village first."[57] One of the company commanders called it a "hot race" between the Americans and the Sikhs.[58]

As the men of the Fourteenth closed on the village and the railway embankment, they were hit by artillery fire from three sides, which inflicted "considerable losses." Some of that fire, it turned out afterward, came from Russian and British artillery. They were able to continue forward nonetheless and clear the railway line of the Chinese defenders, who "made some resistance" but were unable to hold against the Americans. Daggett's forces then discovered another Chinese defensive position to their right, "a clump of houses and [a] very extensive wall, surmounted by a pagoda." Daggett decided at this point that his men were "so exhausted that it was impossible to go farther."[59]

There was something odd going on with the Fourteenth Regiment's assault, though. Colonel Daggett mentioned, toward the end of his report, that "for reasons which it might not be best to embody in this report, but which I will state to the General verbally, I deemed it my duty to lead the assault on the village in person."[60] Daggett did not reveal the issue in his report, and what he said to the general was not recorded. In his 1903 memoir, he did not explain the remark, but he did include a cryptic paragraph during his account of Huangcun on the fact that "there is no more important acquisition for an army officer than the knowledge of how to march troops . . . Some officers can march a column of troops to the designated point with the loss of only the feeblest; others will exhaust and disintegrate their commands during the first hours of the march."[61] If Daggett meant someone specific with that discussion, he did not confess it, but one of his captains, Charles Henry Martin, was writing to his wife in a way that indicated he was not a favorite of his commanding officer: "If we had anybody in command who took any interest in the matter I should get a brevet for the fight yesterday, but I fear that Chaffee and Daggett care only for their own promotion."[62] Martin was being unkind to his colonel, and it seems unlikely that he was whom Daggett was thinking of, for the commander had Martin brevetted major at the end of the campaign.[63]

While Daggett's men recovered from their labor, elements of the Ninth U.S. Regiment, marines, and Captain Henry Reilly's field artillery battery moved east of the rail line toward the fortified Chinese villages at the end of the defensive fortifications. They were covered by a unit of British cavalry, which scouted out the villages for them and reported that there were eight companies of Chinese infantry and three artillery pieces in the villages. American counter-battery fire from

Reilly's artillery silenced the Chinese guns and set the villages on fire, after which the Americans continued to advance. As they did, Chaffee received several urgent messages from the British, asking for supporting fire on the center of the Chinese line because the Fourteenth was "suffering severely." Chaffee was reluctant to turn Reilly's guns, believing that the British had plenty of artillery to support the assault and that pulling fire support from his own attack would risk its success, but he did so eventually. Just as Reilly was preparing to fire on the center of the line, Chaffee recognized that the men on top were actually members of the Fourteenth and ordered Reilly to stop.

Despite the confusion, the Ninth and the marines were able to occupy the fortified villages and drive off the Chinese defenders. As at Beicang, it was not clear how much the Western soldiers forcibly evicted the defenders, versus how much the defenders vacated their positions before they could be assaulted in hand-to-hand combat. The Chinese fell back on their second line of fortifications around Huangcun and then escaped across the river to the west side and the road northward to Beijing. None of the allies pursued all that aggressively; the heat was overpowering, and the soldiers had been in action since four o'clock that morning. "The day was intensely hot," Chaffee wrote in his report, "and our men suffered horribly for the want of water and from the heat; quite a number were prostrated and only arrived in camp after nightfall; two of the men so afflicted died on the field."[64]

But if the Chinese escaped without substantial casualties, neither did they inflict them on the attackers. The Americans suffered seven killed and sixty-five wounded, with the British about forty casualties.[65] This was the central dilemma for the Chinese. They could not or would not hold the line against the Western powers effectively enough to exact heavy casualties.

At the root of this inability was the general inaccuracy of

Chinese fire. As Wise noted, Chinese rifle fire tended to pass overhead. Nor was Wise the only one to note this. Colonel Gartside-Tipping of the British mentioned it in the British assault: "The rifle fire of the enemy was comparatively harmless directly our troops got within 2,000 yards of the position as all the bullets passed over head."[66] Such firing over the head was a common problem for troops inexperienced with their weapons. The recoil of the rifle tended to push the barrel high and send the bullet into the air. Even if that were not a problem, it seemed that many did not know how to operate their weapons effectively. One British officer, curious about the inability of the Chinese to hit them even at close range, checked out the Chinese weapons:

> I looked at a lot of their dead who had been firing on us at close quarters and doing little harm. Nearly all their rifles were sighted at well over 1,000 yards, and [I] learnt later that they had imagined, poor beggars, that the more they raised the sights, the more power the bullets would have?[67]

The people most vulnerable were not those closest to such inexperienced soldiers but those farther back, where the bullets going overhead would come back to earth. In addition to the inaccuracy of the Chinese fire, the Chinese soldiers were not willing or able to stand for long against the Western assaults. Once those assaults got in reasonably close, the Chinese units tended to retreat. Wise remarked on the "milling about" of the Chinese soldiers when his marines got close, and this seems to have been common.

The trick, which most of the allied officers seem to have recognized, was to push their men forward as quickly and aggressively as possible. The Chinese could not inflict serious casualties on an attacking force and would not stand to fight that force once it closed on their defenses. What both Beicang and Huangcun established in terms of the campaign was that the Chinese army simply could not hold the Western forces or prevent them from taking whatever position they wanted, nor could the Chinese inflict serious casualties on those Western forces. General Gaselee later summed up this tactical lesson in a standing order:

> The Chinese, however well-armed they may be, are very indifferently trained and are little accustomed to their weapons, consequently we have no cause to fear the enemy's musketry fire and can, as a rule adopt formations that would be quite inexcusable when operating against Boers or Afghans . . . a prompt offensive is usually the most efficacious method of dealing with the enemy.[68]

Despite showing a fair amount of intelligence and organization, the Chinese were discovering that, militarily, they were essentially impotent. "Self-strengthening" had not really worked.

## THE END OF RESISTANCE

Huangcun was the last serious resistance. After August 6, the Chinese never managed to mount a substantial or sustained resistance to the Westerners, not even at Beijing itself. There were two mysteries about this failure. The first was the notable lack of enthusiasm on the part of the Chinese army to engage after Huangcun. Admittedly, they had been subject to a series of defeats, at Tianjin, at Beicang, and at Huangcun. But of all of these, only Tianjin was a major setback in terms of dead and wounded. Though both Beicang and Huangcun ended with allied victories, in both the Chinese did not suffer heavy casualties, and in both they were able to retreat from the field effectively and with reasonably tight coordination. The retreat at Beicang, in fact, had been something of a model, with a carefully shielded line of retreat, disciplined action by the ordinary soldiers, and a valiant rear guard holding the line. None of the battles seemed to indicate that the Chinese armies were breaking under the strain. Certainly, armies throughout history and around the globe have sustained many far worse defeats in succession without showing any sign of fragmentation. So the mystery remains: after Huangcun, resistance by the organized Chinese military disappeared.

As we shall see, there would be evidence of further defensive arrangements but actual resistance by the Chinese army stopped. Some of it came from the disheartening effect of losing three substantial battles in the space of a month: Tianjin, Beicang, and Huangcun. The soldiers were "depressed," as one Chinese report put it.[69] In addition, there seems to have been a growing sense that the court had backed the wrong side and that bringing further troops in would only cause their loss as well. Li Bingheng, who had convinced Cixi to fight in late July, wrote on August 11, "I have seen several tens of thousands of troops jamming all roads. They fled as soon as they heard of the arrival of the enemy . . . I have experienced many wars, but never saw things like these." The next day, he took poison.[70]

Skeptical already of the war waged by the throne, provincial governors like Yuan Shikai of Shandong, ironically the birthplace of the Boxers, refused to send reinforcements to aid the capital, starving the throne of troops.[71] Even the court itself, including Cixi, seemed to be preparing for defeat. On August 8, as the second expedition marched north, an imperial edict appointed Li Hongzhang (the governor of Shanghai) as envoy plenipotentiary to negotiate the "immediate cessation of hostilities."[72] This was hardly the action of a confident government.

In an odd contrast, even as the Chinese gave up attacking

the second expedition, they renewed their assault on the legations. The informal truce held up to August 9, but on that day,
perhaps in response to the news of Huangcun, Chinese forces
attacked the fortified walls protecting the embassies. "In the
afternoon, the enemy made three heavy attacks on the 'Ruins,'
and the Chinese officers in their barricades only 15 yards off,
were heard ordering their men to charge."[73] They failed to
make a dent in the defenses.

But the second mystery was much more perplexing. After
Huangcun, the Boxers started to vanish. For the last week of
the allied march to Beijing, the Westerners were hard-pressed
to find any Boxers whatsoever. Many of the villages that the allied forces came upon were abandoned except for those too
sick, old, or stubborn to travel. Where the Seymour expedition
had been near continually harassed in its long travel up the railway, the allied forces in August found themselves moving without much in the way of threat or danger. The small-scale attacks
that had so frustrated Seymour simply did not occur against the
August group. The sabotage of the railway that had so slowed
the admiral and his forces was not mimicked by any similar
works on the river. In August, the Boxers seem to have largely
disappeared.

The allies did not particularly notice this absence; Seymour
was not there to point out the difference. In addition, the heat
occupied everyone's mind. When they did pay any attention,
the allies chalked it up to their own military superiority and
Chinese pusillanimity. Neither of these particularly apply; the
Boxers had been active against both Seymour and the allied
forces in Tianjin without any regard for Western military superiority or their own supposed cowardice. There is no particular
reason to think that they changed their minds in the following
weeks.

One factor may have been the triumph of a substantial part
of the Boxers' campaign. Though they had failed to drive the

foreigners out of Tianjin or Beijing, and though the military campaign was not faring well, the war against the Chinese Christians had been notably successful. Chinese Christians had, in large part, been either killed or forced to flee their villages. The alternate power structure that so bothered local Chinese had largely been dissolved. The destruction of that rival power group was one of the major goals of the Boxers, and by August 1900 it had been largely achieved.

Let me suggest another reason as well, however. The Boxer movement, as a national apparition, had been created in large part by the desperation and enforced leisure of the extended drought in northeastern China. That dryness had put the peasantry on the edge of starvation, desperate for the reasons behind such heavenly punishment, and with the time to pursue the causes. As one Boxer poster put it:

> No rain comes from Heaven.
> The earth is parched and dry.
> And all because the churches
> Have bottled up the sky.[74]

In July 1900, the rainfall measured at Qingdao in Shandong was about a fifth of an inch, about 5 percent of the normal monthly rainfall.

In great contrast, the rainfall measured at Qingdao in August 1900 was about ten inches, 250 percent of the average. The heavens, it could be said, opened up. The writings of soldiers in the August march on Beijing back this up: starting about August 11, there were numerous references to the rain, during the day but especially at night. After Huangcun, James Bevan wrote that it "rained nearly every night" on the way to Beijing.[75] What both these suggest strongly is that the drought ended—or at least appeared to end—in the second week of August, and what followed was extensive and heavy rainfalls across northeastern China. The coming of the rain would have reminded the Boxers of their responsibilities at home, of fields to be plowed and of crops to be planted. They had no leadership to hold them there, and so the best explanation for their sudden disappearance, it seems, was not military defeat but a decision for domesticity. They had done their duty by Mount Liang. It was time to go home.

## RACING TO BEIJING

Both disappearances were good things, because the coalition forces suffered a substantial breakdown in military order and discipline on the way into Beijing. The allied column began to fragment at both the national and the individual levels on the way up the river. On the national level, each contingent started acting much more independently of the others. As one French officer put it:

> Each contingent acted in that way, generally for itself, without finding it necessary to warn its neighbouring contingent either about the modifications it brought to a plan that had just been consulted, or about an operation it was about to conduct on its initiative, and without worrying about the serious consequences that might result from that for the others.[76]

For example, the Japanese seem to have decided after Huang-cun simply to set off by themselves each day at the head of the column, without waiting to see if the other contingents got moving. As the British liaison with them, Colonel Churchill, wrote:

> On leaving Yangtsun [Huangcun] however, the Japanese appear to have made up their minds that cooperation was impracticable and from that point they accepted the leading position which circumstances had forced upon them and simply pushed ahead as fast as they could without much reference to the other forces which followed on the same road.[77]

The French did the same thing, albeit in a different direction. On the morning of August 8, when the march was beginning again, the French commander told the others that his men were still too tired to start and that "he would follow up the advance later."[78]

As a result of this national fragmenting, the allied column became more and more stretched out. The Japanese led off, starting early to avoid as much of the heat as possible. They aimed to finish before the hottest part of the day. Behind them came the Russians, who moved more slowly than the Japanese but still managed to do most of their marching in the morning. In the worst position were the Americans, who came next. Delayed by the start of the Russians, the American contingent found itself doing the majority of its movement during the hottest part of the day. Behind them came the British, who delayed their start until the middle of the afternoon to avoid getting caught in the same infernal trap as the U.S. forces. Finally, behind them were the French, moving sluggishly, if at all. The result was a long, strung-out column, with those bringing up the rear "practically a day's march behind the Japanese."[79] This created immense vulnerability, and the flanks of the Western column should have offered tempting targets to the enemy. The various units could have been attacked and defeated piecemeal before anyone could come to their assistance. That no one even attempted this speaks to the complete absence of Chinese resistance.

The columns began to fragment at the individual level as well. The heat was so overwhelming that soldiers of all nations suffered from it; many found themselves forced to drop out of marching order and rest by the side of the road. Some fell unconscious. A few died. "The heat this day was intense and very trying. The Americans were said to have had 200 cases of sunstroke," wrote Colonel Gartside-Tipping on August 9.[80] J. W. Mitchell, part of a British telegraph unit, remembered British soldiers "dropping in the roadside like sheep."[81] Smedley Butler wrote of the march:

> There was no shade, not a drop of rain, nor a breath of air. The cavalry and the artillery kicked up clouds of dust, which beat back in our faces. The blistering heat burned our lungs. Nearly 50 percent of our men fell behind during the day, overcome by the sun. In the cool of the night they would catch up with us and start on again next morning. Our throats were parched, our tongues thick. We were cautioned not to drink the water, but no orders could keep us from anything that was liquid.[82]

The Americans fitted a cart with an awning over it and had it follow behind their units and pick up those who dropped out.[83] Even those who did not fall out were not exactly ready for military action, as Lieutenant Colonel H. B. Vaughan recalled:

> At one point we marched through an American detachment; the men were marching slowly along at about two miles an hour, with heads bent and eyes half closed, as though sleeping or dead tired, and though utterly knocked up by the heat, yet determined to stick to it and come into camp on their own feet. I don't think they even noticed us as we passed them.[84]

Soldiers tried everything they could to escape the heat. Sergeant G. F. Cooper of the Royal Marine Light Infantry wrote of pouring buckets of water over his head. "It was what I should imagine an ice cream in Hell would feel like."[85] Simply filling one's helmet with water and putting it on, "letting the water run down all over us under our clothes," gave temporary relief, but they were soon dry again.[86] The effects of the heat were exacerbated by the uniforms of the soldiers. Some Americans, for example, wore felt hats that, though they kept the sun off a bit, also absorbed the heat quite effectively. The marine uniforms rotted away in the heat.[87] "The Japanese," one American remembered, "limped in stiff heavy brogans."[88]

Despite the heat and the breakdown of order, the force still needed to reach Beijing. The day after Huangcun, the commanders of the allied force decided to stop and recover from the encounter and from the exertion. August 7 was thus a day of rest, with much of the forces camped at the intersection of the railway and the river. Bathing in, and drinking from, the river was a general occupation, despite the dead bodies floating in it.

The force started moving again on August 8, marching on the west side of the river, along the road. The day was again intensely hot, and the coalition managed only about six miles, stopping at noon. The men encountered nothing substantial in the way of resistance. The next day, August 9, the march continued through the heat, with substantial numbers of men in all the forces collapsing from it. So, too, on August 10, when the forces managed about twelve miles, struggling through cornfields as the road was in awful condition. More men dropped out due to heat prostration, and the generals took to leaving contingents of the lame behind them at the villages.

What civilians they encountered on the way, those who could not or would not flee the advance, were frequently treated quite roughly. Atrocities were not uncommon, and civilians were often killed out of hand. Henry Bathurst remembered regularly seeing the "corpses of unarmed peasantry" lying on the ground as he marched past. Prisoners, who might be Boxers or not, often suffered similarly. Henry Savage Landor reported on the beating and execution of a Chinese prisoner by a mixed group of American, French, and Japanese soldiers. "With his skull smashed, the man fell, and lay still breathing and moaning, with a crowd of soldiers around him, gloating over his sufferings."[89] Wilbur Chamberlin, who came later, reported that the coalition left behind a "picture of destruction that it would take a volume to describe. The line of march of the allies was a trail of fire and murder."[90] Fred Whiting, an American correspondent, had a similar experience when he came through in August. "The feature of the river, and indeed of all the villages on the line of march . . . was the number of dead bodies everywhere, chiefly Chinese, while the crops . . . were rotting for want of reapers."[91] Another observer spoke of how "some of the foreign troops gave unbridled license to their passion for rapine, robbery, and destruction."[92] The violence against ordinary civilians was an embarrassment to the forces, and as Chamberlin put it, "If the Chinese are a cruel people they will probably be more cruel in the future, for they have the example of civilized nations to follow. Those of our people who have denounced the heathen as inhuman had better keep silent hereafter."[93]

If there was no resistance on the scale of Beicang or Huangcun, there were still indications of resistance, or at least the planning for it. The Japanese, in the lead, occasionally had to push small Chinese imperial forces out of the villages as they passed through, but the defenders were never in such size that the rest of the force had to deploy or even react. The allies did encounter places where it was clear that some sort of defense had been considered, whether it was coming across two abandoned junks loaded with ammunition and gunpowder or finding the tracks of a substantial Chinese force moving along the river. At one point, the Chinese had made a "determined effort to drain the river and flood the country on the right bank," getting, it seemed to the allied officers, within "another two or three hours' work" of completing an "immense ditch" that would have flooded the lands surrounding and lowered the river water substantially. Had they managed such a feat and mounted a defense there, the Chinese might well have been able to make the allied forces attack along the narrow front between river and road on the east side of the waterway. A "great scheme," Captain Barnes of the British called it. But the allies came upon it before it could be completed, and the Chinese fled before them.[94]

As a result of this lack of resistance, the allied forces, despite the heat, made progress toward Beijing. By August 13, they were at Tongzhou, the last village on the river before the force had to strike overland toward the capital. The generals established Tongzhou as a supply depot for all the supply boats coming up the Hai and then met to figure out the plan of attack on Beijing itself. Gaselee had gotten a note from MacDonald in the legations, coded with numbers standing for names. A hasty scribble of numbers at the bottom of the note revealed to the generals that MacDonald was suggesting the best route into the city.[95] The generals used it to allocate which parts of the wall their force would attack. After a long meeting, they agreed to start off together the next morning and lay siege to the city as a combined force. This reflected the sensible military conclusion that the Chinese were likely to defend their capital spiritedly. As if to indicate that, the sound of firing could be heard coming from the capital, suggesting that the legations were being actively attacked. It was, in fact, the last major assault on the legations, a "heavy combined attack on the whole settlement" that started at 7:45 p.m.[96]

One of the sites of the assault was along the Tartar Wall, defended that night by Captain Newt Hall and Private Dan Daly of the U.S. Marines. As the attack grew, Hall left Daly on the top of the wall to go back, the captain claimed, for rein-forcements. Daly, five feet six inches, 132 pounds, and "the most prolifically profane man in the history of the armed ser-vices," held the position alone through the darkness, fighting off repeated waves of Chinese attackers, who took to calling him "Devil" as they attacked.[97] He would be awarded the Medal of Honor for his night's work.

Eventually, as the sound of firing from Beijing ceased, Adna Chaffee, listening from the American positions outside, won-dered if "we were too late, that all was over, that [the besieged] were massacred. The awful thought of defeat, of failure, came over me."[98]

# 8

# "WITH SHUT MOUTHS,
# THEY TOOK THEIR MEASURE"

The plan of the generals was not to be. Imperial rivalries overwhelmed military good sense, aided perhaps by the confidence built by the lack of resistance. The Russian contingent waited until night was well established to pack up their equipment and steal a march on everyone. The Japanese were "roused by the sound of very heavy rifle fire in the direction of Peking" at about 1:00 a.m. and, naturally suspicious of their main rivals in Asia, decided that the Russians were sneaking ahead.[1] They launched themselves after the Russians, though they were kind enough to send a messenger to the British, who then warned the Americans and French, and the officers of the three latter forces hastily woke their men and got them organized for an assault into Beijing.

The Russians would later offer an explanation for this action. A reconnaissance party of Russians, so the story went, had managed to find a clear path all the way to the walls of Beijing and "had found the gates closed, but the walls apparently undefended." They "then sent a messenger back to the Russian general to request reinforcements. Seeing an opportunity, the General ordered an advance of his entire force." When the Russians got hung up by the Chinese defenders, this account continued, the Russian commander then "applied to the Japanese for assistance." The Japanese "at once pushed on to succor the Russians."[2] Thus it was all a misunderstanding. The Russians had been trying not to steal a march but simply to take advantage of the defensive weakness of the Chinese. In trouble, they had called for help from the Japanese. It was a somewhat plausible story, and British Colonel Gartside-Tipping, for one, seems to have accepted it. But there were substantial problems with the story. That a Russian reconnaissance party would have pushed all the way to the walls of Beijing at night and in the rain seems barely possible. Perhaps the Russian commander had his own Roger Keyes with whom to deal. But that the Russian general would decide, as a result of their report, to try to get his entire force moving in that same darkness and rain and mount a full-scale assault of the Chinese capital boggles the imagination. The walls of Beijing were over sixty feet high, and climbing them at night with wet and slippery handholds or ladders would have been a near-impossible task. Even if we accept all of this, that the Russians would send for help to the Japanese does not seem likely. Given all of these contexts, the story seems much more likely to have been a face-saving one that everyone could politely accept and thus not have to deal with the whole issue.

But what exactly the Russians were trying to achieve by getting there first remains unclear. It would have created certain basic gloating rights, akin to the ones that the British tried to claim at the Dagu Forts. Other than playground bragging, there was little reward for gaining the walls of Beijing first. They certainly could not have occupied the city and then denied entry to the other forces; they were not going to get credit for single-handedly liberating the legations; and they would be unlikely to have captured anything or anyone useful in the absence of their fellow allies. The Russian move, more than a century later, smells of the move of an imperial power looking to put one over on the other powers: meaningless except as one small point scored in an endless Great Game. That the Japanese were keeping such a close watch on the Russians suggests that the Russians were not the only ones conscious of the ongoing competition, and a certain lack of surprise on the part of the British seems also to indicate suspicion.

This was war as sport. Perhaps, given the frustrations of the heat, it should not come as a surprise that someone would try to steal a march, to "win" something out of the dry plains of northern China, but it should be noted that the haphazard attack on Beijing was about as militarily dangerous as could be imagined. In the interest of getting there first, or of catching up to the Russians, the allies threw away any kind of force discipline, flank protection, or planning for the assault. What attacked Beijing on that mid-August morning was more a mob than an organized military force.

It is perhaps the most remarkable statement of this whole situation that the Chinese did (or could do) nothing about it. Before the gates of its capital city, the Chinese army proved incapable of mustering more than the most feeble resistance. Almost any kind of assault or ambush of the Western force, spread out as it was, would have stood a substantial chance of success. In addition, the walls of Beijing itself provided a ready-made and massive fortification, easily defendable against even the stoutest force. Western newspapers, like *The New York Times*, warned ominously of the danger, here quoting an "official who has lived in Peking":

> Nothing short of the heaviest artillery could make an impression upon the walls of the Imperial City . . . light artillery would be of no avail, and for this reason the advance of a flying column, even up to the walls of the city, could effect little if a stubborn defense were determined upon.[3]

Passing judgment is a dangerous role for a historian to play, but it is hard to think of an example since the defense of Washington, D.C., in 1814 of a capital so poorly defended. What started as a kind of sporting event, a race to the finish line, ended much the same way.

This is not to say that there was no resistance at all. In fact, in a karmic irony, the Russians got held up by what Chinese defenders there were. The Chinese seemed to have reacted to the Russian attack on the western wall by pouring in the limited reserves they had. The Russians were held for hours by these defenders, unable to climb the walls or break down the gates. The Japanese, the first to arrive, reinforced the Russian attack and also got stuck. By early morning, the largest part of the Chinese forces inside the city was facing the attacks. Russian and Japanese dead and wounded were "lying in heaps" in front of the wall.[4]

The practical effect of this, however, was to denude the southern and southeastern sides of the city of their defenders. That area was right where the British and Americans finally launched their assault the morning of the fourteenth, and, much to their surprise, they found only a "paucity of defenders," as Gartside-Tipping put it.[5] The Chinese general responsible for the movement of the forces, Gaselee reported later, was "so mortified . . . at his mistake that he committed suicide on the spot."[6]

Largely undefended was not, however, the same thing as completely undefended. The American troops, who had been woken from their sleep to assault the city, found themselves fighting their way through the rain and mud, a "miserable lot of human beings," as James Bevan, a marine, recalled.[7]

The Americans wended their way close to the city walls through a suburban congestion of cornfields, canals, roads, and Chinese villagers trying not to get involved. They got lost on the way and had to backtrack three miles before closing in on the walls. Calvin Titus, a bugler in the Fourteenth Infantry Regiment, found himself at the front of the advance with his unit, Company E. Their first encounter was not with the Chinese but with a unit of French soldiers who, under a "very fat officer," had found a large group of Chinese civilians hiding in boats on the Grand Canal and, as Titus remembered it, were "having volley fire into that mass of unarmed men, women, and children." General Chaffee, riding with Company E, angrily stopped the French, and the American advance continued along the canal towpath.

They were covered by tall grass, and there was no rifle fire until they got close to the outer wall of the city. Then a "scattering fire" started that inflicted a few casualties, most particularly during a perilous dash across the bridge that spanned the canal. Smedley Butler, the American marine, was hit in the chest by a spent bullet but saved from serious injury by one of his blouse buttons. The Americans managed to get under cover of the wall itself; it was extremely hard for the Chinese to fire directly at the base of the wall, and there the soldiers congregated. They had made it to Beijing. Now they had to find a way into the city.[8]

## OVER WALLS, UNDER WALLS

The wall itself was made of brick and mortar, and to Colonel Daggett it looked climbable. Standing with Titus, he pondered aloud, "I wonder if we could get up there?" to which Titus, after some hesitation, said, "I'll try, sir, and see if we can get up, if you want me to." Daggett looked over the slender bugler and gave him permission. Titus took off all his gear, "haversack, canteen, pistol and belt and my hat," and began climbing. He could get his "fingers and toes into cracks" in the mortar and used a bush growing out of the wall halfway up for another grip.

Finally, toward the end, he "worked sideways" toward a likely entry spot. When Titus reached the top, he peered through one of the firing slits cut into the wall and discovered that the top of the wall was deserted. Sliding through, he found himself alone inside the bastion. To his right stretched the broad way of the wall itself, twenty to twenty-five feet wide. To his left was a similar wall, but built upon that part was a row of "small matting houses, their backs against the top of the wall where I had just come up." The rest of the troop, were Titus to get a rope down, would have to come up the wall directly under those houses, so the bugler crept around them and carefully looked in to see if there were defenders. He had no weapon with him, and his plan if he found a defender was to pitch him over the wall "so he would drop among our men." Even Titus was skeptical about that idea, unconvinced that he, "a great big 120 lbs!" could manage it, but he crept ahead anyway.

The houses were empty. Titus could see some Chinese defenders farther down the way, around the corner in the fortifications, but their backs were to him. He was not alone for long. The company adjutant, Captain Henry Leonard, climbed up shortly after, bringing a long cord with him. Titus let down the cord, and at the bottom his fellow soldiers tied a rifle and ammunition belt. Titus pulled it up, equipped himself, and began looking around for Chinese targets, while the adjutant lowered the cord and got a rope raised in its place. More soldiers of Company E began to climb, and soon there were seven men on the top of the wall.

The adjutant had also brought with him the company standard, which he draped over part of the wall. He may have been hoping to prevent them from being fired on by other allied troops, but it had the unfortunate effect of drawing the attention of some of the Chinese soldiers in a tower farther down the wall, who began firing at Titus and his fellow soldiers. As was the norm, the fire was inaccurate and inflicted no casualties.

The soldiers on the wall made their way down a ramp and opened a gate to let in the rest of the company. Despite the firing, there were not many defenders in the area, and Titus and the other soldiers certainly seem never to have been counterattacked vigorously or with any real dedication. Nonetheless, it was a remarkable feat of bravery to climb that wall into the unknown, and Titus received the Medal of Honor for his actions. It takes nothing away from that valor to note that the walls which had so concerned the *Times* were surmounted in the end not by heavy artillery but by a bugler of 120 pounds.

The members of Company E were the first Americans to breach the outer wall and get into the Chinese city. There remained the wall around the Tartar City and the Forbidden City, but only the former would have to be overcome to get to the legations. As the Fourteenth Regiment advanced, it met with more resistance, but not enough to hold it up. The race was on to get to the legations, who held a chunk of the southern Tartar Wall looking over the Chinese city. Colonel Daggett of the Fourteenth worked Companies E and G along a road parallel to the Tartar Wall, keeping a sustained rifle fire on the looming wall to prevent the Chinese defenders under cover. Running low on ammunition, Daggett stopped and waited for the rest of the Fourteenth to come up and join them before starting up again. It was several hours into this process when one of his officers, Lieutenant Murphy, spotted a "friendly flag," and then "American marines and civilians called out to us."[9]

"Unfortunately," as Lieutenant Charles Summerall of Reilly's battery remembered, someone else was "better informed" and got there first.[10] It was the British, who had also gotten inside. They had focused their assault on the southeastern gate and found "practically no opposition at that point as we were not expected there." The lead units, the Seventeenth Rajput Regiment and the Twenty-fourth Punjab Infantry Regiment, knocked down the gate and were followed into the Chinese city by elements of the Royal Welsh Fusiliers and the First Sikhs. Gaselee sent the Twenty-fourth, augmented with some cavalry, toward the Temple of Heaven. This would protect the left flank of the British as they attempted to get over the Tartar Wall into the legation area. As they got there, the legation defenders spotted them and signaled from the top of the wall, directing the Rajputs in the lead to a small water gate underneath the massive barrier. The water gate had been crudely fortified from the inside, but the legation defenders pulled away the defenses and opened a gap through which the Rajputs could enter. They did, and then one reported back to Gaselee, who followed quickly. Gaselee's report on this compressed the latter events somewhat to put himself first into the legations: "I with some of my Staff and about 70 men of the 17th Rajputs and 1st Sikhs rushed across the almost dry moat and through the watergate without any loss."[11]

Colonel Daggett of the Fourteenth was not pleased at being beaten and complained bitterly of the situation in his report:

> If my whole regiment had been with me I think I could have accomplished this work two hours earlier and been the first to enter the Tartar City. It will be noticed that I had only two companies with me during the scaling of the walls and silencing the fire along the south wall of the Tartar City.[12]

Just as at the Dagu Forts, the military campaign had become something of an Olympic event, with the silver medal winners (the Americans) still ruing their loss of the gold.

The important thing was that the legations had been relieved, though who was rescuing whom was not entirely clear. Some of the troops, "haggard, with ragged beards . . . dripping with sweat and encrusted with mud," thought they had joined a "garden party":

> They expected to find the besieged in worse condition than themselves, but the contrast in appearance between the rescued and rescuers was surprising. Sir Claude MacDonald was clean shaven and arrayed in immaculate tennis flannels, and Mr. Conger looked equally presentable. Around them was an assembly of ladies looking fresh and bright.[13]

Roger Keyes, still doggedly following along with General Gaselee, reported much the same: "All the ladies looked nice in clean white and light-coloured dresses, strolling about on the lawn. Some of the men who had run in from the barricades looked rather fierce with arms of sorts festooned round them but most were in flannels having a quiet afternoon off." Garden party it might have been, but everyone nonetheless wanted to shake the hands of the soldiers, however much they might have looked like a "disreputable . . . lot of ruffians."[14] Frederick Brown, the Anglican minister serving as Gaselee's interpreter, thought much the same until he was invited to dinner. "I was only too glad" to come, but that feeling did not last the announcement that the first course was "pony soup and brown bread" followed by "mule steak and musty rice." Brown pushed his food around his plate and then escaped back to Gaselee's HQ, where he found the " 'bully beef' and biscuit . . . more to my taste."[15] Some found old friends, even ones they did not realize they were going to find. Colonel Gartside-Tipping encountered Claude MacDonald in the legations, and the British minister reminded him that they had been at Sandhurst together, decades back. The colonel did not at first recognize MacDonald, but then "after a bit of talking, I remembered him—a long, lanky youth there; but had never connected him with our minister at Peking!"[16]

The Russians and Japanese had never gotten out of the positions that they had been stuck in since the previous night, unable to break down the east gate of the Chinese Wall and get into the city proper. The Japanese had "spent 2 or 3 hours endeavoring to place guncotton [at the east gate]," but the defending fire was too intense, and so "eventually desisted until nightfall."[17] Both forces were "startled," unpleasantly so, by the news that the British "had entered Beijing and relieved the legations."[18] Once the sun set, the Japanese—as they had done at Tianjin—set explosive charges at the two closest gates. Blowing them up, they charged into the Imperial City and captured the north and east walls.[19]

That day, the empress dowager, the emperor, and their court fled the Forbidden City and headed west toward the refuge of the mountains. She had bolted similarly from Western forces during the Taiping Rebellion, and it can only have been an unpleasant remembrance for her. They were abandoning the city that was the "physical and material embodiment of imperial power" and leaving it to the allies.[20] Several days earlier, she had appointed Li Hongzhang to be envoy plenipotentiary in charge of negotiating with the allies. Li issued a call on August 15 for the allies not to occupy the capital, so as not to "cause irreparable damages to the present dynasty, and hurt the feelings of 400 millions of Chinese."[21] The horse, of course, was already out of the barn, or, more accurately, the soldiers were already over the walls, with no chance of closing the gate.

Overnight, the allied forces positioned themselves to renew the assault the next day. Frederic Wise and the American marines bivouacked in an "ancient market" just south of the Zheng Yang gate in the Tartar Wall. "It was dark now, raining hard and uncomfortably cold. A hasty supper and the men rolled up in their blankets and lay down on the wet ground in the rain, utterly spent." One of his officers had managed to liberate three quarts of Scotch from the American legation, and he gave one to Wise's commanding officer, Major Littleton Waller. Waller "stuffed it under the folded blanket that served him for [a] pillow and went to sleep." Wise and some of his fellow marines decided that they needed the Scotch more than did Waller, so they deputized Wise to take it from the major. "I crawled up in the dark, got it from under Major Waller's head without waking him," and the marines had an impromptu party. Just to aggravate the major, Wise "crawled back and replaced the bottle, empty." To obscure the evidence further, Wise (and no doubt his comrades) "got a handful of coffee beans, [and] chewed them," thus obliterating "my share of the olfactory evidence."[22] He then went to sleep, surely warmer than he had been a few minutes before.

The next day, the Americans led an assault on the southern gates of the Tartar Wall. The Zheng Yang gate, to the west of the section held by the legations, was surmounted by a multistory pagoda, providing a daunting firing position for the Chinese defenders. This time, the Chinese were ready for the American assault, having reinforced the wall after the allied success of the previous day. American forces deployed to attack the pagoda from a variety of directions. A cannon was hauled up the part of the Tartar Wall controlled by the legations and pushed along the top to bear on the gate. Captain Reilly commanded the gun. He was accompanied by American marines, including Frederic Wise, who would lay down an enfilading fire on the Chinese defenders.

Infantry forces of the Fourteenth Regiment were moved along the streets to the front of the gate, as were elements of Reilly's Battery. Summerall, in command of one of the artillery platoons, found himself behind the gate of a smaller wall in front of the looming gate. It was barricaded from behind, and Summerall used one of his guns to blast through the door: "I placed a gun about fifteen feet from the gate, scratched with my thumbnail a cross on the metal covering of the gate opposite the bar [on the other side] and ordered the gunner to fire at that spot."[23] What Summerall did not mention, but Frederic Wise (watching from the rooftop) did, was that the lieutenant was "under heavy fire" from the Chinese defenders as he did so.[24] It took three shots to cut through the bar and burst open the gate. Through the gate, the Americans could see the route to the Zheng Yang, a few hundred yards away. There were walls flanking on either side. The ground was grass, with a tile road through the middle. The approach was essentially a "great court," bare of cover. From the Zheng Yang gate and its overtopping pagoda came a "heavy rifle fire."[25]

A platoon of Company M of the Fourteenth moved through the opened gate, but, with Wise watching, "they had only gone a short way down the court when, point-blank, a murderous fire opened up at them from the far gate and the walls on both sides of the courtyard. It was a slaughter pen."[26] "They drew a rather severe fire," Colonel Daggett wrote afterward in something of an understatement. The soldiers were forced to flop on the grass and try to get what cover they could. There was little available, given the height from which the defenders were firing. Daggett pushed another platoon into the courtyard and sent Company K to try to flank the defenders.[27]

Trying to continue the frontal assault was not perhaps the smartest move on the colonel's part. Unsupported, infantry could not cross the space without being massacred, and the platoons in the courtyard were running low on ammunition, so Daggett eventually pulled them out and had the two guns of Reilly's Battery work over the defending fortifications. Summerall pushed the noses of his guns through the broken gate and then began hammering the pagoda and "crenellated parapets of the wall in our front" with "percussion shrapnel." From the wall, Reilly with other guns and the marines with their rifles added to the fire. Reilly was standing near Wise, next to Major Waller, when a bullet ricocheted off the top of the wall and entered his open mouth. He fell against Waller and then to the ground. Wise heard "the sound a bullet makes when it strikes flesh" and turned to find Reilly "stretched flat." The captain died immediately. "He never even spoke." The gun crew carried him into an open tower behind them, "tears streaming from their eyes," and then went back to working the gun, still crying.[28]

The defending fire rapidly eased, enough that the men of the Fourteenth could push forward to the Zheng Yang with scaling ladders borrowed from the Japanese. They placed them along the wall and climbed up, occupying each side of the gate. Summerall pushed his guns forward and blew open the Zheng Yang gate as he had done the earlier one. Much to his dismay, and the dismay of the infantry, behind the Tartar Wall was a "similar wall," also occupied. Daggett set about reducing this one, although he (smartly, this time) did not start with an attack from the front. The artillery and the infantry repeated their cooperation and broke through that next wall, "only to see a fourth wall flanked by towers." Summerall might have been forgiven for feeling a trifle discouraged at this point, but the lieutenant kept pushing forward and was only halted from knocking down the gate to the fourth wall—unbeknownst to him, the gate into the Forbidden City itself—by the intervention of one of General Chaffee's staff officers. The allies had decided to halt in front of the walls to the Forbidden City on that day so that all the national forces could enter together.

It should be noted that the Chinese defenders did not sell the wall lightly. During the initial assault on the Tartar Wall, Major William Quinton of the Fourteenth Infantry reported that the Chinese were managing "one of the most severe musketry fires I have ever witnessed."[29] During the day, the Fourteenth U.S. Infantry Regiment expended 31,100 rounds of ammunition, about twice that of the previous day, indicating the intensity of the fighting.[30] Even after the allies had broken down the gate and were working their way through into the Tartar City, the Chinese tried counterattacks to push them back. In one incident that Gaselee reported, a group of fifty Chinese defenders used the cover of some "ruined houses" inside the wall to get close to the Sikhs coming through the gate and then made a "determined effort" to retake the gate, "actually closing with our men" and dying nearly to the last in the attempt.[31] Critically, however, the defenders, while fighting hard, did not manage to inflict substantial casualties on the attackers. Even the Fourteenth Regiment, which had several platoons essentially trapped in the open under fire, lost only four killed and fourteen wounded, not an enormous butcher's bill.[32] The lesson was the same as it had been on the march north: the Chinese soldiers could not inflict heavy enough casualties on the allied forces to slow them down. Only at the Battle of Tianjin had that not been true, and the Chinese had been unable to replicate the relative success of Tianjin at any point afterward. Leslie Groves, a chaplain with the Fourteenth U.S. Infantry, summarized it best in a letter to his wife: "It was a great victory . . . and yet it cost nothing of what you would expect."[33]

Chinese casualties also seem to have been relatively light, even as reported by the allies. The Japanese reported that "the enemy killed up to [August] 17th . . . number not less than 600." Even assuming that number was replicated in the forces defending against the other allied attacks, that still suggested that the Chinese lost substantially fewer than five thousand dead. That was still a large number, but nothing close to the circa twenty-five thousand lost the last time the Qing had tried to stop an invading Western force from taking Beijing, at the Battle of Palikao in 1860. It seems likely that the dynasty had given up on the fighting and thus left the defense of the city to a minimal number of troops. That would explain not only the low casualties but also the way in which the initial attack of the Japanese and Russians pulled nearly all of the defenders away from the southern side of the city.

The next day, August 16, the allies, finally moving together, occupied the Forbidden City. They met some resistance there, but nothing like Tianjin or even the level of the last several days. When the day ended, the coalition forces found themselves in possession of the heart of the Chinese Empire, empty save for a few hundred eunuchs left behind by the court. There was still a substantial amount of fighting going on as the outer parts of the city were cleared of defenders, but with the taking of the heart of Beijing, the campaign was, for all intents and purposes, ended.

Perhaps the most amazing discovery in this entire liberation came not in the legations themselves but to their north. There, in the giant stone Beitang Cathedral, coalition forces discovered a group that consisted of hundreds of Chinese Christians, a few Catholic nuns and priests, and Bishop Pierre-Marie-Alphonse Favier, who had written the prescient warning letter of May. They were protected by a small force of French soldiers and had been holding out since the start. It had been fifty-five days of attacks and terror, and perhaps the only thing that saved the congregation, besides the valor of the French defenders, was that the stone of the cathedral would not burn. Favier himself was somewhat phlegmatic about the whole thing. "It is almost a pity that we were not all massacred," the bishop said. "We should have died martyrs."[34]

Small-scale engagements continued. On August 19, near Tianjin, a combined force of American, British, and Japanese cavalry, under command of the American lieutenant colonel E. J. Wint, engaged and defeated an entrenched group of Boxers and imperial troops. On August 23, to the southwest of Beijing, Colonel Gartside-Tipping and his lancers fought off a tiny force of Boxers. Gartside-Tipping was not wounded, but the weight of a stressful campaign got to him and he collapsed under a tree. The treatment, frankly, sounded somewhat more worrying than the affliction, as "ether was injected, artificial respiration resorted to, and a teacupful of brandy poured down" his throat. It was the finish of the campaign for Gartside-Tipping, and in fact the "severe overstrain of the heart" ended his military career.[35]

The appointed commander of that campaign, Count von Waldersee, had not yet left Berlin. He spent the day of the sixteenth, even as Beijing was falling to the allies, visiting the American embassy and making a speech to workers in Hannover. In a discussion with reporters that day, von Waldersee tried to assert his relevance, saying: "The general situation for the allies is unfavorable, even if Peking is taken or is about to be taken, since the allies are everywhere on the defensive, except in this advance upon Peking."[36] "Except in this advance upon Peking" seems in retrospect a rather major exception, indeed, but von Waldersee was in a singularly unenviable position, the commander of a war won without him.

## "THE AIR OF THIS TOWN FAIRLY REEKS WITH LOOT"

With the fighting essentially over, the thoughts of the Western commanders turned to the occupation. Beijing was split among the various national parties, with each nation responsible for supervising its particular area. For the first several weeks after the occupation, chaos ruled, as Gaselee remembered:

> The condition in and about the city and along the line of communication was bad. Looting of the city, uncontrolled foraging in surrounding country, and seizure

by soldiers of everything a Chinaman might have, as vegetables, eggs, chickens, sheep, cattle, etc. . . . indiscriminate and generally unprovoked shooting of Chinese . . . It is safe to say that where one real Boxer has been killed since the capture of Pekin, fifty harmless coolies or laborers . . . including not a few women and children, have been slain.[37]

Even in the midst of this chaos, however, there was time for a victory parade. On August 28, units of the assembled foreign armies gathered and marched through the Forbidden City. The march, as Sydney Adamson, the correspondent for the *New York Evening Post*, wrote, was not taken terribly seriously by the troops, though Adamson did highlight one burgeoning rivalry: "When the Russians came through . . . every Japanese, from the generals to the privates, watched every Russian with a serious, critical look; every man was a possible enemy, and with shut mouths they took their measure."[38] The parade had elements of tragedy and farce intertwined. The troops marched in over a bridge that spanned a "ceremonial moat, stagnant and covered with a heavy layer of green scum, only broken by the bloated, blue mass of a dead Chinaman."[39] When they were done, the allied officers and assembled correspondents had tea in the imperial palace, "handed out by real blue-button mandarins."[40]

The main goal of most of the foreign commanders was to restore something resembling order as quickly as possible so that they could go home. With the possible exception of the Germans, no nation wanted to try to hold Beijing permanently; it would simply have been too costly in money and men. They needed to reestablish civil authority as quickly as possible if that were to come true. This need to reestablish order led to violence by the troops against civilians, often in dubious ways. Amar Singh reported that the Russians "thrashed" the Chinese "whenever they could not make them understand." The frequent lack of differentiation between Boxers and civilians could lead to violence. After a Russian report of a Boxer attack, Singh found "among the eight people who were called Boxers, six were women." They might have been Boxers, who had female auxiliaries, but Singh was not convinced. "Probably they had been robbed, raped, and then slain to cover the whole thing."[41]

The rules followed by the Americans came from the military's General Order 100, which had been written during the American Civil War to guide Union occupation of the South. These rules outlined a treatment of occupied territories as brother would treat brother, or parent, child. This was, in fact, quite literally the inspiration, as Francis Lieber, the lawyer who authored General Order 100, had sons fighting for both sides in the Civil War. In Beijing, they brought a sympathetic and efficient American occupation that, while witness to a fair number of individual abuses, for the most part ranked as the best-run occupation. General Chaffee, in writing about the earlier abuses, had been less concerned with the moral implications of the violence than the practical: "All of this [violence] did not tend . . . to gain for the troops the confidence of the masses, with whom . . . we have no quarrel, but whose labor we need."[42]

Chaffee aimed to woo the Chinese residents to cooperation as quickly as he could. He needed to reassure them that cooperation with the occupiers would not cause them problems with the Boxers or whatever Chinese government was reestablished. The Chinese being wooed had a delicate balancing act. They had little choice but to cooperate with the Americans, but doing so would put them at risk from any remaining Boxers, or from the post-occupation Chinese government, who could well look with some suspicion on collaborators. Despite this, the local Chinese elite worked effectively with the American authorities.

Chaffee listened to Chinese feedback, and they listened to him. After the locals had protested the American practice of going house to house searching for weapons, Chaffee ended it. In return, the locals organized a Chinese police force who accompanied American units on their patrols, to translate and act as cultural go-betweens with the populace. The Americans allowed the Chinese legal system to function while handling crimes committed by foreigners themselves. Army doctors drew up rules of sanitation and enforced them, preventing outbreaks of disease, and started a policy of inoculations for the inhabitants. Captain John Tilson, the American liaison with the Chinese, hired a local company to clean up abandoned privies, and set up a program of medical checkups for the area's prostitutes. When winter came, Chaffee encouraged the reestablishment of shelters for the poor and charity food kitchens and put them under American protection.[43]

Not everything went smoothly. There were also issues of communication between the Americans and the Chinese, perhaps most farcically when a group of Buddhist monks came to believe that the American soldiers who had come into their monastery courtyard were planning to burn down the building. The Americans, in turn, could not understand why the monks had reacted with such horror to their request to use the monastery's ovens to bake bread. Some were less than humorous. Attacks on civilians were not uncommon by soldiers of all nationalities, and that included the Americans. The reason might be that they suspected the Chinese person of being a Boxer, that they wanted something from him, or for no reason beyond sport. To take one example, Stephan Dwyer, a private in the U.S. Marine Corps, entered a Chinese dwelling on August 17 and used a club to "brutally assault and strike a Chinese child of tender years . . . driving it from its home and thereby hastening its death." He also forced out the male resident of the house and then raped the two women present. But Chaffee reacted to the cases that came to his attention with vigorous condemnation and prosecution. In Dwyer's case, the private was arrested, found guilty at court-martial, and sentenced to life in prison at Alcatraz in San Francisco.

In any case, the American occupation went well enough that within a month, ordinary Chinese were flocking into the American sector from the other areas of Beijing, and a housing shortage developed. This was not the only indication of progress. In March 1901, as discussions of an American withdrawal from Beijing were mounting, a petition signed by thirteen thousand Chinese was presented to General Chaffee, asking the United States to stay.[44]

Few aspects of the occupation were so benign. Beijing was a treasure trove, and the wealth on display in the Forbidden City beggared the imagination of the Western soldiers. The rest of the city could not match the gilded and royal display there, but had enormous quantities of riches as well. Looting began immediately and continued without much in the way of compunction or mixed feelings. Charles Henry Martin wrote to his wife that he had acquired "three (3) handsome Russian sable cloaks, one cloak of ermine and astrakhan, one great coat of silver fox, four (4) bolts of silk, one hand-painted fan and several other articles of lesser value."[45]

Each country was deeply critical of the others' looting, while only sheepishly admitting its own. Amar Singh, the Indian army officer, wrote that "the Cossacks plunder like devils" and detailed the horrendous nature of Russian abuses, only to admit moments later, in a "rather ashamed" way, that he had ordered his men to loot and then "brought a mare and a mule foal as a plunder."[46]

The "air of this town fairly reeks with loot," wrote one observer.[47] In fact, the British went so far as to organize it, holding daily auctions of looted goods in their sector of the city. The loot made its way out quickly. By September. The New York *Sun* reporter Wilbur Chamberlin, who was making his way to

Beijing, reported from Shanghai, "Everybody who comes from [Beijing] brings a box of stolen goods. Of course they don't say *they* stole the stuff, but that they bought it from the people who did steal it."[48] This "carnival of loot," as *The Sydney Morning Herald* called it, became something of an international scandal, with newspapers reporting on the widespread thievery by Western soldiers and making the obvious comparison to Western claims of superiority. "The great Christian nations of the world are being represented in China by robbing, rapine, [and] looting soldiery."[49] "Civilization," the London *Daily Express* wrote, should "have the grace to blush."[50] It is hard to tell, given the way in which much of the looting was covered up, denied, or minimized, who was the most industrious, but Japanese officers, who "thought nothing of pillaging before breakfast," managed to loot enough silver ingots that the haul was measured in tons rather than pounds when a Japanese newspaper exposed it in 1901.[51]

## VON WALDERSEE

Looming over the administration of the city was the "approach of the much-prepared Waldersee," as one U.S. official viciously put it.[52] He made it to Shanghai on September 19, to be greeted by a crowd of thousands, perhaps interested to see the man responsible for remaking northern China. Wilbur Chamberlin witnessed von Waldersee's arrival and was not impressed:

> The Count isn't a bad-looking fellow, but he wears more gold lace than a Japanese quarantine official . . . The Count was accompanied by his staff, each member of which had a separate and distinct load of gold lace, and, in addition to that, a string of medals a foot long

which he wore across his bosom. Each member of the staff was accompanied by a valet, who vied with the master in the yellowness of his decorations.

Von Waldersee and his retinue stayed at the Astor House hotel in some luxury.[53]

Von Waldersee continued his journey northward, finally reaching Beijing in the middle of October. He found little in the way of a war left to fight. That did not deter either the count or the Germans themselves. "The Germans did not get here until the worst of the fighting was over, and they have been trying to make up for loss of time since."[54] If there wasn't a war left to fight, the Germans would find one, or create one, if necessary. Von Waldersee did not think that the Chinese had been taught enough of a lesson. "One can only command the respect of the Asian through force and its ruthless application." The Chinese, von Waldersee continued, had earned "no outdated clemency."[55]

That attitude percolated down to the common soldiers of the German units, and thus the experience of Chinese in the German section of Beijing was much different from that of the American. Looting was not only commonplace but essentially approved of, and the local Chinese suffered. One (admittedly American) correspondent wrote of the German army as a "band of pirates," with the following result:

> [The German district] is deserted . . . The reason is that the German soldiers, with or without the knowledge of their officers, steal everything they can lay their hands on that can be carried off . . . The moment a Chinaman tries to open his shop in the German section of the city, the German soldier comes around and steals his stock. It's a great game, I tell you. They have no shame about it at all.[56]

Von Waldersee established an aggressive German policy of patrolling the area around Beijing, in addition to the city itself. That patrolling encountered Boxers in August and September, albeit not substantial forces. The British fought a force of Boxers about twelve miles northwest of Beijing in the middle of September. Those Boxers had had a Gatling gun among their weapons but, as ever, were unable to stand up to determined British assaults. A German force later that month encountered Boxers near Huangcun, as Fred Whiting, an American correspondent, wrote:

A party of about thirty Boxers, evidently headed off, were facing the Germans, and going through their dance, or Boxer movements. They were led by a man on a white horse. He wore, like most of these people, bright red sashes and shoulder belts, and bright colored cloth wound around his head. The Boxers were armed with Mannlicher rifles, spears, and swords, but the whole of them in a short time were shot down, while four of our men were wounded.[57]

Von Waldersee decided to increase the aggressiveness by mounting an expedition to Paotingfu, "a noted anti-foreign town, which was practically the center of the Boxer movement."[58] But the thrust was unsatisfying at best. Chinese imperial forces along the way pulled back from the German advance, unwilling to fight. Sometimes the Germans gave them little choice, sending cavalry units on broad sweeps, "ostensibly to get forage," but actually looking for Chinese to attack.[59]

Paotingfu was sadly unrewarding. There were no sizable Boxer forces there, and the chief treasurer of the city, rather than resisting, came out to greet the foreign forces. The Germans satisfied themselves by fining the city a substantial amount of money, executing the chief treasurer for siding with the Boxers, and blowing up a number of temples and the four corners of the city walls. Whether von Waldersee wanted to admit it or not, the conflict was in its last stages, and what remained was that least glorious of military ventures, post-combat reconstruction. By September, "ordinary routine" was prevailing.[60]

## NEGOTIATION

But if von Waldersee was aggressive with the Chinese, he was not so with the other powers. Quite the opposite, in fact, and it is to his credit that he managed the tense imperial relationships with some effectiveness, largely defusing what could have been a combative situation. As one British private wrote early in the occupation, "The [Russians and Germans] would like a slice at our throats at the first opportunity and they can start as soon as they like."[61]

Von Waldersee stopped the squabbles. This is to say not that there were no imperial conflicts but that they never rose to the level of actual conflict, despite some rather severe provocation. The British and the Russians wrangled over the railway lines between Dagu and Tianjin, as well as up to Beijing, with the British at one point claiming that "the only thing that is established beyond doubt & contradiction is that everybody is grabbing our railways."[62] Russia seized towns in Manchuria, and the British took a city just south of the Great Wall, Shanhaiguan, to prevent Russian penetration of that line. The Japanese and the Russians eyed each other warily, foreshadowing the war they would eventually fight. But the alliance that had carried the allied powers through the conflict held reasonably well, at least enough to negotiate a final treaty. "When I left China, what amazed me most," said a British officer, "was that the International Expedition had not turned into the International War."[63]

The treaty was not kind to China, or even particularly fair, but that should not come as a shock in the imperial world of 1900. The first negotiating question that came up was, of course, with whom exactly were the allies going to negotiate? On August 29, Gaselee wrote plaintively to the secretary of state for India: "No government to deal with at present."[64] Sir Ernest Satow, the new British minister (sent to replace MacDonald), found himself cooling his heels in Beijing, without anyone to whom to present his credentials.[65] Both the empress dowager and the emperor were incommunicado, fleeing westward. They were hardly likely to come back to negotiate a treaty, since that would put them under control of the allies. Their negotiating position was weak to start with, and that would not strengthen it. There was some enthusiasm for chasing the throne to its refuge in Xi'an, but no one other than the French and Germans was all that interested.

A possible alternative for the allies was to sideline the dynasty altogether. They could negotiate with the provincial governors who had remained neutral. Those governors were in contact with the powers and could thus be negotiated with directly. But what they could deliver was unclear. They could not really claim to represent the dynasty, and in the absence of a continued occupation of Beijing the terms of anything they signed would be open to abrogation. The allies were reluctant to set up a situation where they might have to intervene again.

In fact, that was the central issue of negotiating a treaty. It had to be with a Chinese representative who could deliver. Given that requirement, the allies had to negotiate with the dynasty. The empress dowager, for all her weakness, was the only one who had any ability to hand over what she promised. It was the odd irony that for all the public and private criticism of Cixi by the allies, they found at last that they needed her. At the end of August both Japan and Russia, with the acquiescence of the other powers, assured the Chinese that the empress dowager would be spared. The allies then spent two somewhat contentious months putting together a Joint Note with preconditions for negotiation to present to the Chinese throne, if it could be found.

Cixi herself had little alternative to negotiating with the allies. The catastrophic loss of the campaign and the capitulation of Beijing put her in a precarious position indeed. Dynasties had fallen in lesser situations, and her coup d'état of 1898 already made her political position somewhat irregular. But the same factors that allowed 1898 to succeed still held. Cixi, as well as the dynasty, was one of the few political forces that most Chinese would accept. There was no one else of sufficient standing and authority to establish legitimate rule, at least not without an extended civil war. Given the disasters of the last decade, few Chinese of any power wished to see such an internal conflict.

It was a mark of how devoid of alternatives the Chinese political class was at this point that a dynasty stumbling through its last days, with only a decade left of life, would nonetheless be the only option. The allied decision to negotiate with Cixi's chosen representative confirmed the dynasty's standing. If the victors of the conflict were willing to deal with the empress dowager in a way that they would not with other Chinese politicians, then the dynasty had another advantage, albeit one flowing from a foreign source. In October, the Chinese told the Marquess of Salisbury that they were "anxious that the peace negotiations should be commenced without further delay."[66]

This is not to say that the court was universally in favor of negotiating with the allies. Some officials, showing an impressively obtuse blindness to their current situation, advocated resuming the war in early November. Given the German provocations, this was an understandable attitude—understandable but insane. Calmer heads prevailed and began easing the way through negotiations by delicately rewriting the history of what had happened. Robert Hart was told, in a meeting with Qing officials, that the empress dowager and the emperor had both actually *opposed* the war but had been held captive by reactionary forces in the court and forced to agree to fight. Prince Duan became something of an official scapegoat for this story. It was, of course, false, and Hart himself knew it, but it gave the Qing a face-saving way to participate in the negotiations.[67] The allies presented the Joint Note to a representative of the Chinese on December 24.

So it was that Li Hongzhang, Cixi's delegate, came to be the lead Chinese negotiator throughout 1900–1901, culminating in the signing of the Boxer Protocol in September 1901. It was not an easy negotiation for the aged diplomat, dealing as he was with an opposite party that was Hydra-like in its different desires, agenda, and approaches. Each power looked to gain from the protocol specific imperial advantages for itself, and all were aggressive in seeking those advantages. Two things eased Li's job. The first was that the template of the treaty was clear from earlier ones. The Chinese would have to pay, and pay dearly, in land, concessions, and, most important, money to get the allied powers out of their capital. That had been the model for decades' worth of treaties, and it was the model now. Second, Li used the competing interests of the powers to help China by playing those powers off against each other. He was limited in how much he could manage this, but the diplomat, familiar with the West from his travels there, had a delicate sense of how to maneuver things to his benefit. Neither advantage was particularly large, it should be noted, and did not change "the deep sea of China's utter helplessness."[68]

From the beginning, the negotiating issue was largely how to deal with Russia and Japan, the only two substantial land powers in Asia that could continue to threaten China. None of the other powers were willing or able to keep sufficiently large numbers of troops in China to threaten the dynasty. Britain was occupied with South Africa, and in any case India always remained its top priority. The United States was fighting in the Philippines and did not have a particular interest in asserting a large territorial claim to China. Germany might have been willing to do so but did not have the imperial infrastructure to support a long-term military commitment to Asia. France's interests were in Indochina and southern China. By contrast, both Russia and Japan were interested in northern China, and took the Boxer crisis as an opportunity to strengthen their presence there.

Li, as he had done after the Sino-Japanese War, looked to the Russians to provide a counterweight to the Japanese. If the Chinese could play the two powers off against each other, some kind of independent movement might be preserved. Even better, Russia was the stronger power, more of a dominating force than the newly arriving Japan. The Russians would make the Japanese behave themselves. Allying with the Russians even informally would mean conceding Manchuria and, indeed, most of northeastern China above the Great Wall to the Russians. Given China's catastrophic position, however, Li perhaps figured that he had no choice.

It was a mistake in the sense that it did not work. The Japanese were not particularly cowed by the Russians, nor, it turned out, were they weaker than the Russians, as the 1904–1905 Russo-Japanese War would demonstrate. So Li allied himself with the wrong side. But neither Li nor the dynasty had a better option. Given Li's, and China's, situation in 1900, he had little choice but to do what he did.

No one paid John Hay's Open Door Policy more than lip service during the negotiations. Joseph Chamberlain, the secretary of state for the colonies, wrote of British support for the Open Door in September 1900, but then, in the same memo, blithely spoke of setting one power against another. Britain, Chamberlain argued, should "endeavor to make use of the present opportunity to emphasize the breach between Russia and Germany, and Russia and Japan."[69] China, the allies felt, had brought this wrath upon itself.

Thus, the Boxer Protocol, as the treaty was called, was a harsh and unforgiving one. It quite literally mortgaged the Qing future to Western powers. The dynasty would pay 450 million silver taels, about $335 million or £67 million, in indemnities. The only thing that ameliorated that penalty even slightly was that the money was payable as a mortgage, over thirty-nine years at 4 percent interest. The thirty-nine-year stretch ended in December 1940, when, it should be noted, the Germans were occupying a much nearer capital city than Beijing. As with a mortgage, interest accrued, and by some estimates the Chinese paid $600–$700 million in the end.[70]

Another section of the treaty aimed to punish those responsible. The Boxers, the allies firmly believed, had been organized and run from the court. If it was a polite fiction that the empress dowager and the emperor had been opposed, then others had to be punished. Prince Duan was sentenced to exile, and a range of more junior courtiers were condemned to committing suicide. Most already had several months before. Some of the pro-Boxer officials had had the bad taste to die during the war, and they received "posthumous degradation." A number of government officials who had "protested against the outrageous breaches of international law" and been executed by the throne in the midst of the conflict had their memories "rehabilitated." Those officials, obviously, were not available to comment on the value of that rehabilitation.[71]

The rest of the treaty set about organizing a structure to prevent something like the siege from ever happening again, or, alternatively, giving allied forces easy access to Beijing. Admiral Seymour's failure, the allies hoped, would not be repeated. The Zongli Yamen was reorganized into a Ministry of Foreign Affairs, with "precedence over the six other Ministries of State."

The Dagu Forts were torn down, and the Chinese promised not to rebuild them. A river-clearing project was resumed on the Hai River to ensure its navigability. While most of the allied troops would leave that September, the Qing agreed to allow the foreign powers to occupy "certain points" along the route from Dagu to Beijing, "for the maintenance of open communication between the capital and the sea." These included Tianjin and stops along the Hai. The legation quarter was put under the "exclusive control" of the foreign powers, Chinese were not allowed to live there, and the allied nations were permitted to make the area "defensible" if they wished. The importation of arms and ammunition into China was banned for two years, with possible renewals.[72]

The final parts of the treaty were aimed at shaming the Chinese for their actions and making the remembrance of that shame permanent. The treaty appointed Chinese ambassadors to Germany and Japan, whose first job was to travel to their assigned countries and convey regrets for the "assassination" of Baron von Ketteler and Chancellor Sugiyama. In addition, the treaty required the Chinese to "erect on the spot of the assassination of [von Ketteler] a commemorative monument, worthy of the rank of the deceased, and bearing an inscription in the Latin, German, and Chinese languages, which shall express the regrets of His Majesty the Emperor of China for the murder committed." The von Ketteler monument was not the only one. The Chinese had to build "an expiatory monument in each of the foreign or international cemeteries which were desecrated." In essence, the atonement for the uprising and siege would be both monetary and memorialized. Both would stretch over years, if not decades. Every time the Chinese government made a payment on the indemnity, every time an ordinary Chinese passed the monuments, they would be reminded of 1900.[73]

The empress dowager was not pleased with the treaty, but she had little choice but to accept it. It was signed on September 7, 1901. Li Hongzhang, after signing for China, retired to his bed and died a month later. The official cause of death was liver failure, but it might as well have been the exhaustion of the Qing dynasty, made personal in one man. With the treaty signed, there was no reason for the Qing court to remain outside of Beijing, and so Cixi and her officials and retainers gathered themselves and began to make the long, slow march back to Beijing from the west, starting in December 1901. Unlike the allied marches of summer 1900, it was not the heat that hit them hardest but the cold. On a raw day in early January 1902, the imperial column finally wended its way into Beijing and back home to the Forbidden City. It had been a disastrous two years, part of a disastrous decade, the end of a disastrous century. The rulers might be back in the capital, but there was no sign that China's flight would stop, or its plight ease. We might think for a minute not of Cixi, the empress dowager, but of Lady Yehenara, the young concubine brought to the emperor in the 1850s, one small pawn in a great household political game. Like China itself, Lady Yehenara had survived another catastrophe—not well, or without consequences, but at least alive.

# CONCLUSION

On the last day of 1900, in a bitterly cold Beijing, the supposed murderer of Baron von Ketteler, a Manchu soldier named En Hai, was led to the spot where the German had died. Whether he was actually guilty, of murder or even self-defense, remains unclear, but on that December 31 it was convenient for everyone that he was the death dealer. He was handed over to the Chinese authorities and, kneeling on the ground in front of a mixed crowd of Chinese and foreigners, decapitated by the executioner's sword. He might have lain there as a symbol of China itself, its guilt perpetually assumed and its punishment always assured.[1]

What is most remarkable about the summer of 1900 in a military sense is how close a thing the fighting actually was. The perception afterward was of an overwhelming triumph by the West, fed by the easy victories of the second expedition. But the situation hung much more in the balance than the casual capture of Beijing might have made it seem. Admiral Seymour's expedition came close to being an utter disaster, and had not the fortuitous capture of the Xigu Arsenal presented itself, the entire column might have been wiped out or captured. The Battle of Tianjin, too, was close, and by the end of the first day an allied defeat seemed likely. The second expedition was, in many ways, as much of a gamble as the first. The lack of cooperation and the ad hoc command structure had made the coalition forces highly disorganized—if only the Chinese could have reacted. At Beicang and Huangcun, the Chinese organized themselves efficiently and well, and simply could not execute their defensive plan well enough to slow down the advancing allies. The imperial aggressiveness of the Western powers got them repeatedly into dire straits, but the Chinese could never fully take advantage of those moments of vulnerability.

The soldiers involved knew how close it had been. As a mark of that closeness, and "being desirous of perpetuating the associations formed during the historic expedition for the relief of their distressed countrymen in China," the officers of the U.S. Army founded the Military Order of the Dragon in Beijing in 1901.[2] It was open to all who had served during the crisis in the army, marines, and navy or had been a diplomatic officer. Honorary membership was extended to foreign officers as well, and "hereditary membership" to male descendants of the members. Annual meetings were planned.

The ultimate global result of that summer was the continued redrawing of the imperial map of Asia. China spent most of the nineteenth century losing its ability to resist the imperial powers. By the end, it found itself unable to resist even the new powers in Asia like the United States and Japan. Within five years, that latter nation showed itself to be not only the strongest of the Asian nations but, after hammering the Russians in 1904–1905, a country worthy of standing with the great powers. This was presaged in 1900, as the Japanese did a substantial amount of the most critical fighting. Their intervention overnight at Tianjin changed the course of that battle and perhaps the campaign. The Japanese learned from the uprising that they held the whip hand in Asia and even the great powers needed their assistance there.[3] They were, more than that, well liked by the other coalition powers for their discipline and stoicism. This was nowhere more ironic than in the solid relations between the Japanese and the Americans, a relationship that would turn sour over the ensuing decades. The culmination of that came on December 8, 1941, when American marines stationed in Beijing, under the terms of the Boxer Protocol, awoke to find themselves under the guns of Japanese soldiers who had taken the walls of the legation overnight.[4]

Many of the actors in the Boxer Uprising did not long outlast the end of that revolt. Queen Victoria of England did not even see the signing of the protocol, dying in January 1901 as her soldiers shivered in wintry China. The service medal for the China campaign would be the last that portrayed her image.[5] President William McKinley of the United States fell to an assassin's bullet in September 1901, barely outliving Li Hongzhang, and was succeeded by the fire-breathing Teddy Roosevelt. The empress dowager and the Guangxu emperor died within days of each other in 1908. The dynasty itself staggered on for only a few more years. The kaiser of Germany outlived them all, but not as kaiser. Germany immolated itself, along with the rest of Europe, in the sanguinary bellicosity of World War I, and Wilhelm II was forced into exile in 1918, living out his life in the Netherlands. He survived long enough to see the Reich rise in Germany and sent Adolf Hitler an admiring message upon the German conquest of France: "Congratulations, you have won using my troops." Wilhelm never did learn either diplomacy or tact.

Even the institutions that fought in China survived only in greatly different forms. Perhaps the only exception to this were the missionary societies, which redoubled their efforts in China. As *The Missionary Herald* put it, when speaking of the slaughter at Paotingfu: "And now, who will be 'baptized for the dead'? Who will enter into their labors by more faithful praying and give, by a more self-sacrificing devotion . . . on the ground made sacred by their blood?"[6] They did not escape criticism in the aftermath, with Mark Twain, among others, criticizing them for being more interested in a "monument" than in truly helping the Chinese.[7] Nonetheless, as one missionary put it, "in spite of everything, siege, massacres, looting, atrocities, newspaper reports, and Mark Twain, I believe the work is going on."[8]

Others changed much more dramatically. Both the British and the American armies would be greatly altered in the first decade of the twentieth century, the former by Richard Haldane, the activist secretary of state for war, and the latter by Elihu Root, the similarly reformist secretary of war. The British navy would find itself locked in a naval race with the Germans, building giant dreadnoughts to wage an apocalyptic battle with the High Seas Fleet in the North Sea instead of the small ships like the *Fame* and the *Whiting* that had carried the day in China. Even the global balance that had driven so much about 1900 disappeared as well. The imperial system dissolved in the fire of total war, and its members, most notably Russia, Austria-Hungary, and Germany, dissolved with it. By 1920, they were all gone, replaced by countries and governments mostly uninterested in the sporting rivalry of empire. Even those that survived, like the British and French Empires, were humbled and weakened, well past ripeness when the horrors of World War II completed the destruction. British India, which had sent so many troops to suppress the Boxers, saw the rise of a new revolutionary movement and a new leader, Mohandas Gandhi. Amar Singh, who helped occupy Beijing, found himself part of a unit suppressing one of Gandhi's protests in 1920.[9] Unlike the Boxers, the Indians would win their conflict. In Beijing itself, the wall that had surrounded the legations was rebuilt, with most of the old fortification scrapped. By 1927, only a few chunks of it remained, incorporated into the new wall. On one of those, a 1927 visitor found, someone had chiseled LEST WE FORGET.[10]

Forget they had, to a great degree. It is an irony of the era that even those who thought themselves civilized and advanced in 1900 found themselves just as quickly obsolete. Modernity was a brutal mistress.

## THE BOXERS

What about the Boxers themselves? If they failed, they did nonetheless serve as both an example and an inspiration to a generation of revolutionaries. The ease with which the Western powers humiliated China led intellectuals and leaders to work on rebuilding China's strength. Reform movements started, at first under the dynasty and then under the revolutionary government that replaced it.[11] What was born was not necessarily agreement on the way to strength but a consensus belief in the Chinese nation. Sun Yixian (Sun Yat-sen) and Mao Zedong (Mao Tse-tung) agreed on little, but they were Chinese patriots, above all.

The very blankness of the movement allowed observers then and after to impose their own visions upon the Boxers, to assimilate them to serve later agendas.[12] Mao Zedong, for example, would hold up the Boxers as a critical early resistance movement. The peasant movements, of which the Boxers were one, were for Mao the historical levers breaking down the structures of Chinese society, "the real motive force of development in China's feudal society."[13] In this rendering, the Boxers, and other peasant movements, did the hard and dirty work of preparing China for a true, Marxist revolution. They were the "great and tragic prologue" for Mao's own revolution, resisting the foreign capitalist interlopers.[14]

As a Chinese scholar in the 1970s wrote: "The worldshaking Yi Ho Tuan Movement is the glory and pride of the Chinese people. It laid a cornerstone for the great victory of their revolution 50 years later. It gave the invaders a taste of the people's heavy fist."[15] Members of the Red Guard during Mao's Cultural Revolution of the 1960s called themselves the "new Boxers," and aged Boxer veterans were brought out to cement the connection.[16]

Other Chinese intellectuals of the twentieth century, eager to make their nation up-to-date in good Western fashion, saw the Boxers as the avatar of savage tradition, a style long obsolescent. Chen Duxiu wrote in 1918 that China could follow the Boxers into "despotism and superstition," or move into the modern world of "republicanism, science, and atheism."[17]

Many Westerners saw in the Boxers a kind of primitiveness that justified the very kind of civilization raising that Kipling had spoken of: "half-devil and half-child," indeed. The Boxers—in this sense—*were* the White Man's Burden, writ large and bloody. Other Westerners saw the Boxer movement almost as an inexplicable disaster, a fire that without rhyme or reason swept over northern China in the summer of 1900, dousing all in its reach. The Boxers were a natural disaster, not really to be understood, but merely to be survived.

There were elements of truth in all of these. The Boxers did, for the most part, abhor the new world that was emerging in China. Modern it might be, but modern was of little use to those whom it displaced in the interests of efficiency, productivity, and progress. The Boxers were a movement of the lower classes, and they were suspicious of both the foreigners and the new Chinese groups who had made their compromises with the fruits of the Industrial Revolution. They were certainly savage, inflicting upon many of their enemies vicious and even devilish executions. The movement did rise up quickly like a forest fire, burning all it touched, and then disappear almost without notice or explanation.

But that does not mean that all those images, Mao's as much as those of the imperialists, were not caricatures. Some of the distortions were obvious. There were several thousand soldiers, sailors, and marines from a range of Western countries who would have a comment about who exactly had the "heavy fist" in the Boxer Rebellion. But some of the distortions were more subtle. Mao's formulation essentially eliminated any consideration of the individuals within the Boxer movement. In his history, they had become a group force, important only for what they represented in Marxist and revolutionary terms. Oddly, Mao was as guilty of imperialism as were the Westerners in 1900, albeit a historical imperialism: conquering the past for his own exploitation.

On the Western side, similar arguments hold true. The Boxers were not the irrational childlike devils of Kipling's formulation. There were good and solid reasons that the Chinese peasants reacted as they did, and good and solid reasons why the Boxers acted as they did. Nor is the natural disaster image particularly useful, abdicating as it does any attempt at explanation. The Boxer movement was mysterious, but that is not the same thing as inexplicable. In this, perhaps we might acknowledge that the danger of imperialism, Western or Maoist, stretches to historians as well, and strive to avoid it.

Above all, the Boxers were human beings reacting to an enormously chaotic situation, a world in which the environment, economy, government, and society seemed to be conspiring against them. The Boxer movement offered for many Chinese a way to control a world that was fracturing around them. The control proved illusory, but that did not make the need any less important. Of all the actors in this story, the Boxers, despite their violence, were perhaps the least sinning.

# NOTES

## INTRODUCTION: A MORNING WALK

1. Roger Keyes, *Adventures Ashore and Afloat* (London: White Lion, 1939), 241.
2. Keyes to Bruce, June 26, 1900, Public Records Office (hereafter PRO) ADM 116/115.
3. Ibid.
4. Bruce to Admiralty, July 11, 1900, PRO ADM 116/115.

## 1: AN IMPERIAL WORLD, AN IMPERIAL CHINA

1. George Steinmetz, "'The Devil's Handwriting': Precolonial Discourse, Ethnographic Acuity, and Cross-Identification in German Colonialism," *Comparative Studies in Society and History* 45, no. 1 (2003): 67.
2. Rudyard Kipling, *Gunga Din and Other Favorite Poems* (New York: Dover, 1990), 27.
3. Ibid., 52.
4. Quoted in Thomas R. Metcalf, *Imperial Connections: India in the Indian Ocean Arena, 1860–1920* (Berkeley: University of California Press, 2007), 88.
5. Tony Ballantyne and Antoinette M. Burton, *Bodies in Contact: Rethinking Colonial Encounters in World History* (Durham, N.C.: Duke University Press, 2005), contains a number of useful discussions of this community.
6. Ibid., 2.
7. Brigadier General Gaussen, "Under a German C-in-C," *Cavalry Journal* (1940): 523–42, describing Colonel Francis Gartside-Tipping of the Indian army.

8. See, for example, the way Theodore Roosevelt had said Mahanian things well before knowing Mahan's works. Henry Hendrix II, "Roosevelt's Naval Thinking Before Mahan," in *Theodore Roosevelt, the U.S. Navy, and the Spanish-American War*, ed. Edward J. Marolda (New York: Palgrave, 2001).

9. For a discussion of one of those thinkers, see Johannes Siemes, "Hermann Roesler's Commentaries on the Meiji Constitution," *Monumenta Nipponica* 17, no. 1 (1962): 1–66.

10. Edward J. Drea, *Japan's Imperial Army: Its Rise and Fall, 1853–1945* (Lawrence: University Press of Kansas, 2009), 83.

11. Quoted in Edward I. Chen, "Japan's Decision to Annex Taiwan: A Study of Itō-Mutsu Diplomacy, 1894–95," *Journal of Asian Studies* 37, no. 1 (1977): 71.

12. Quoted ibid., 64.

13. Frank W. Iklé, "The Triple Intervention: Japan's Lesson in the Diplomacy of Imperialism," *Monumenta Nipponica* 22, no. 1 (1967): 127–28.

14. Hayashi Tadasu and Li Hung-Chang, "Convention Between Japan and China for the Retrocession by Japan to China of the Southern Portion of the Province of Feng-Tien," *American Journal of International Law* 1, no. 4 (1907): 384–86.

15. Iklé, "Triple Intervention," 122.

16. Ibid., 130, quoted in George B. Sansom, *The Western World and Japan* (London: Cresset Press, 1950), 406.

17. Chen, "Japan's Decision," 64.

18. Drea, *Japan's Imperial Army*, 95. See also Yoji Koda, "The Russo-Japanese War: Primary Causes of Japanese Success," *Naval War College Review* 58, no. 2 (2005): 11–44, for Japanese reactions.

19. Allen S. Will, *World-Crisis in China, 1900: A Short Account of the Outbreak of the War with the "Boxers," and Ensuing Foreign Complications* (Baltimore: John Murphy, 1900), 74.

20. Quoted in Charles B. Wordell, *Japan in American Fiction, 1880–1905* (London: Ganesha, 2001), xliv.

21. Quoted in Joseph M. Henning, "White Mongols? The War and American Discourse on Race and Religion," in *The Impact of the Russo-Japanese War*, ed. Rotem Kowner (London: Routledge, 2007), 158.

22. Drea, *Japan's Imperial Army*, 86.

23. A. E. Campbell, "Great Britain and the United States in the Far East, 1895–1903," *Historical Journal* 1, no. 2 (1958): 154–75.

24. Paul John Bailey, *China in the Twentieth Century*, 2nd ed. (Oxford: Blackwell, 2001), 20.

25. R. G. Tiedemann, "The Persistence of Banditry: Incidents in Border Districts of the North China Plain," *Modern China* 8, no. 4 (Oct. 1982): 395–433.

26. Jean Chesneaux, *Peasant Revolts in China, 1840–1949* (London: Thames & Hudson, 1973), 7.

27. G. Thompson Brown, *Earthen Vessels and Transcendent Power: American Presbyterians in China, 1837–1952* (Maryknoll, N.Y.: Orbis Books, 1997), 14.

28. Quoted in J. Y. Wong, "The 'Arrow' Incident: A Reappraisal," *Modern Asian Studies* 8, no. 3 (1974): 373–89.

29. Archibald Forbes, *Chinese Gordon, a Succinct Record of His Life* (New York: Funk & Wagnalls, 1884), 24.

30. Peter Thompson and Robert Macklin, *The Man Who Died Twice: The Life and Adventures of Morrison of Peking* (Crows Nest, N.S.W.: Allen & Unwin, 2004), 163.

31. Heidi Christein, "A Detroit Baroness in Peking," *Michigan History Magazine* 81, no. 1 (1997): 10–15.

32. Ibid.

33. Diana Preston, "An Ohioan in China: Adna Chaffee and the Boxer Rebellion," *Timeline* 19, no. 1 (2002): 32–47.

34. Ralph Powell, *The Rise of Chinese Military Power, 1895–1912* (Princeton, N.J.: Princeton University Press, 1955), 53.

35. Arthur Lewis Rosenbaum, "The Manchuria Bridgehead: Anglo-Russian Rivalry and the Imperial Railways of North China, 1897–1902," *Modern Asian Studies* 10, no. 1 (1976): 43.

36. Ibid.

37. Lanxin Xiang, *The Origins of the Boxer War: A Multinational Study* (London: Routledge, 2003), 1.

38. Sue Fawn Chung, "The Much Maligned Empress Dowager: A Revisionist Study of the Empress Dowager Tz'u-Hsi," *Modern Asian Studies* 13, no. 2 (1979): 177–96.

## 2: A POPULAR ERUPTION

1. Paul John Bailey, *China in the Twentieth Century*, 2nd ed. (Oxford: Blackwell, 2001), 37.

2. Ma Jianzhong, *Strengthen the Country and Enrich the People: The Reform Writings of Ma Jianzhong, 1845–1900*, trans. Paul John Bailey (Richmond, Surrey: Curzon, 1998), 58.

3. A. E. Campbell, "Great Britain and the United States in the Far East, 1895–1903," *Historical Journal* 1, no. 2 (1958): 154–75.

4. Wilbur J. Chamberlin and Georgia Louise Chamberlin, *Ordered to China: Letters of Wilbur J. Chamberlin Written from China While Under Commission from the New York "Sun" During the Boxer Uprising of 1900 and the International Complications Which Followed* (New York: F. A. Stokes, 1903), 43.

5. Lanxin Xiang, *The Origins of the Boxer War: A Multinational Study* (London: Routledge, 2003), 38.
6. G. Thompson Brown, "Through Fire and Sword: Presbyterians and the Boxer Year in North China," *Journal of Presbyterian History* 78, no. 3 (2000): 193–206.
7. Stig Thogersen, *A County of Culture: Twentieth-Century China Seen from the Village Schools of Zouping, Shandong* (Ann Arbor: University of Michigan Press, 2002), 53.
8. G. Thompson Brown, *Earthen Vessels and Transcendent Power: American Presbyterians in China, 1837–1952* (Maryknoll, N.Y.: Orbis Books, 1997), 67.
9. Susanna Ashton, "Compound Walls: Eva Jane Price's Letters from a Chinese Mission, 1890–1900," *Frontiers* 17, no. 3 (1996): 80–94.
10. Quoted in Brown, *Earthen Vessels*, 83.
11. Thogersen, *County of Culture*, 55.
12. Ryan Dunch, "Beyond Cultural Imperialism: Cultural Theory, Christian Missions, and Global Modernity," *History and Theory* 41, no. 3 (2002): 301–25.
13. Robert Hart, *"These from the Land of Sinim": Essays on the Chinese Question* (London: Chapman & Hall, 1901), 136.
14. Brown, *Earthen Vessels*, 83.
15. Joseph Esherick, *The Origins of the Boxer Uprising* (Berkeley: University of California Press, 1987), 83.
16. Brown, "Through Fire and Sword."
17. R. G. Tiedemann, "The Church Militant: Armed Conflicts Between Christians and Boxers in North China," in *The Boxers, China, and the World*, ed. Robert Bickers and R. G. Tiedemann (New York: Rowman & Littlefield, 2007).
18. Xiang, *Origins of the Boxer War*, 59–61.
19. Tiedemann, "Church Militant," 22.
20. Xiang, *Origins of the Boxer War*, 58.
21. Esherick, *Origins of the Boxer Uprising*, 80.
22. George Steinmetz, "'The Devil's Handwriting': Precolonial Discourse, Ethnographic Acuity, and Cross-Identification in German Colonialism," *Comparative Studies in Society and History* 45, no. 1 (2003): 41–95.
23. Quoted in Esherick, *Origins of the Boxer Uprising*, 92.
24. Ibid.
25. Ibid., 99.
26. Ibid., 64–65.
27. Hart, *"These from the Land of Sinim,"* 2.
28. Jerome Ch'en, "The Nature and Characteristics of the Boxer Movement—a Morphological Study," *Bulletin of the School of Oriental and African Studies* 23, no. 2 (1960): 287–308.

## 3: AN INFORMAL WAR

1. John Gould Curtis, *American History Told by Contemporaries* (New York: General Books LLC, 2010), 2:618.
2. *New York Times*, Jan. 26, 29, 1900.
3. *New York Times*, Jan. 26, 1900.
4. *New York Times*, Jan. 17, 1900.
5. Ibid.
6. *New York Times*, Jan. 20, 16, 1900.
7. Arthur Henderson Smith, *Village Life in China* (New York: F. H. Revell, 1899); *New York Times*, Jan. 6, 1900.
8. *New York Times*, Jan. 17, 1900.
9. Jules Davids, ed., *Boxer Uprising*, vol. 5 of *American Diplomatic and Public Papers—the United States and China: Series III, the Sino-Japanese War to the Russo-Japanese War, 1894–1905* (Wilmington, Del.: Scholarly Resources, 1981), 32.
10. *New York Times*, Apr. 2, 1900.
11. Imperial decree, Jan. 11, 1900, PRO FO 233/124.
12. Ibid.
13. Ibid.
14. Davids, *Boxer Uprising*, 33.
15. The story was reported in the *North-China Daily News* and then by *The New York Times*, May 17, 1900.
16. Davids, *Boxer Uprising*, 38.
17. J. Robinson to MacDonald, Jan. 14, 1900, PRO FO 674/79.
18. S. M. Pritchard to Carles, Mar. 8, 1900, PRO FO 674/79.
19. Letter to Carles, Apr. 16, 1900, PRO FO 674/79.
20. Frederic Alan Sharf and Peter Harrington, *China, 1900: The Eyewitnesses Speak: The Experience of Westerners in China During the Boxer Rebellion, as Described by Participants in Letters, Diaries, and Photographs* (Mechanicsburg, Pa.: Stackpole Books, 2000), 26.
21. Quoted in Peter Thompson and Robert Macklin, *The Man Who Died Twice: The Life and Adventures of Morrison of Peking* (Crows Nest, N.S.W.: Allen & Unwin, 2004), 164.
22. Letter to Carles, n.d., PRO FO 674/79.
23. For "vile," see letter to Carles, Mar. 29, 1900, PRO FO 674/79. For "calumnious," see letter to Carles, June 3, 1900, PRO FO 674/79.
24. Jerome Ch'en, "The Nature and Characteristics of the Boxer Movement—a Morphological Study," *Bulletin of the School of Oriental and African Studies* 23, no. 2 (1960): 287–308.
25. Letter to Carles, May 15, 1900, PRO FO 674/79.
26. Davids, *Boxer Uprising*, 36.
27. Letter to Carles, June 3, 1900, PRO FO 674/79.
28. Letter to Carles, May 15, 1900, PRO FO 674/79.

29. Reid to Foreign Office, June 12, 1900, PRO FO 228/1340.

30. Davids, *Boxer Uprising*, 34.

31. Letter to Carles, Apr. 30, 1900, PRO FO 674/79.

32. Sharf and Harrington, *Eyewitnesses*, 26.

33. Reid to Foreign Office, July 30, 1900, PRO FO 228/1340.

34. Jane Elliott, *Some Did It for Civilisation, Some Did It for Their Country: A Revised View of the Boxer War* (Hong Kong: Chinese University Press, 2002), 452. Elliott goes on to say that Yang was an "exemplary figure of leadership qualities," something hard to square with leading his force into an ambush.

35. Ibid., 452.

36. Quotations and information taken from A.A.S. Barnes, *On Active Service with the Chinese Regiment: A Record of the Operations of the First Chinese Regiment in North China from March to October 1900*, 2nd ed. (London: Grant Richards, 1902), 7–12.

37. Lieutenant George Cecil Brooke, Border Regiment, 1900, National Army Museum (NAM) 2004-09-244.

38. Reid to Foreign Office, July 26, 1900, PRO FO 228/1340.

39. House of Commons Debates, Feb. 14, 1900, vol. 78, cc. 1466–520.

40. Thompson and Macklin, *Morrison*, 165.

41. Favier to Pichon, May 19, 1900, NAM 9102-255.

42. Ibid.

43. House of Commons Debates, May 11, 1900, vol. 82, cc. 1369–70.

44. Mary Porter Gamewell, *Mary Porter Gamewell and Her Story of the Siege in Peking*, ed. Alexander Harrison Tuttle (New York: Eaton & Mains, 1907), 189.

45. Ibid., 187.

46. Robert Coltman, *Beleaguered in Peking: The Boxer's War Against the Foreigner* (Philadelphia: F. A. Davis, 1901), 62.

47. Gamewell, *Siege*, 189–90.

48. R. G. Cooper, "A Private's View of the Siege of Peking in 1900," *Journal of the Society for Army Historical Research* (1983): 84.

49. Ibid., 85.

50. Lanxin Xiang, "Who Killed Baron Ketteler?" in *The Origins of the Boxer War: A Multinational Study* (London: Routledge, 2003), 331–52.

51. Ibid., 343; *New York Times*, June 17, 1900.

52. For the first, see the discussion in Henry Keown-Boyd, *The Fists of Righteous Harmony: A History of the Boxer Uprising in China in the Year 1900* (London: Leo Cooper, 1991), 87–89; for the latter, see Xiang, "Who Killed Baron Ketteler?" 343.

53. Mrs. M. S. Woodward, "The Personal Side of the Siege of Peking," *Independent*, no. 52 (2712): 2782.

## 4: EVERY IMPEDIMENT MADE

1. "Report on Total Destruction of Imperial Chinese Railway Head Office, Tientsin," July 4, 1900, PRO FO 674/79.

2. Clive Bigham Mersey, *A Year in China, 1899–1900* (New York: Macmillan, 1901), 164.

3. Extract from letter to be sent by Foreign Office to Admiralty, PRO ADM 116/114.

4. Joseph K. Taussig, "Experiences During the Boxer Rebellion," *United States Naval Institute Proceedings* 53, no. 4 (1927): 403–20.

5. Mersey, *Year in China*, 171.

6. Taussig, "Experiences," 409.

7. Mersey, *Year in China*, 171.

8. Ibid., 170.

9. Lanxin Xiang, *The Origins of the Boxer War: A Multinational Study* (London: Routledge, 2003), 249.

10. Ibid., 256.

11. Ibid., 245; for quotation, see FO 65/1599.

12. Taussig, "Experiences," 410.

13. Frederic Alan Sharf and Peter Harrington, *China, 1900: The Eyewitnesses Speak: The Experience of Westerners in China During the Boxer Rebellion, as Described by Participants in Letters, Diaries, and Photographs* (Mechanicsburg, Pa.: Stackpole Books, 2000).

14. Seymour to H.M. Consul at Tientsin, telegram, June 11, 1900, PRO ADM 116/114.

15. Seymour to H.M. Consul at Tientsin, telegram, June 13, 1900, PRO ADM 116/114.

16. Xiang, *Origins of the Boxer War*, 264.

17. Seymour, report to the Admiralty, June 27, 1900, PRO ADM 116/114.

18. Mersey, *Year in China*, 172.

19. Taussig, "Experiences," 410.

20. Ibid., 411.

21. Richard Brooks, *The Long Arm of Empire: Naval Brigades from the Crimea to the Boxer Rebellion* (London: Constable, 1999), 239.

22. Seymour, report to the Admiralty, June 27, 1900.

23. Taussig, "Experiences," 412.

24. Jane Elliott, *Some Did It for Civilisation, Some Did It for Their Country: A Revised View of the Boxer War* (Hong Kong: Chinese University Press, 2002), 502.

25. "Report on Action at Taku [Dagu] on June 17, 1900, by Lieutenant and Commander MacKenzie of Her Majesty's Ship 'Whiting,'" PRO ADM 116/114.

26. Charles C. Dix, *The World's Navies in the Boxer Rebellion (China 1900)* (London: Digby, Long, 1905), 28.
27. "Report on Action at Taku [Dagu] on June 17, 1900."
28. Ibid.
29. Robert D. Heinl Jr., "Hell in China," *Marine Corps Gazette* 43, no. 11 (1959): 55–68.
30. Bruce, report to the Admiralty, June 25, 1900, PRO ADM 116/114. For reports on the telegraph, see Seymour to Admiralty, July 8, 1900, PRO WO 32/6145.
31. Bruce to Admiralty, June 16, 1900, PRO ADM 116/114.
32. James B. Agnew, "Coalition Warfare—Relieving the Peking Legations, 1900," *Military Review* 56, no. 10 (1976): 58–70.
33. Bruce, report to the Admiralty, June 25, 1900.
34. William Reynolds Braisted, *The United States Navy in the Pacific, 1897–1909* (New York: Greenwood, 1969), 81; quotation from Michael Miller, "Marines in the Boxer Rebellion," *American History Illustrated* 22, no. 9 (1988): 38–47.
35. Dennis L. Noble, *The Eagle and the Dragon: The United States Military in China, 1901–1937* (New York: Greenwood, 1990), 12.
36. Quotation from Hosea Ballou Morse, *The International Relations of the Chinese Empire* (London: Longmans, Green, 1918), 65; see Braisted, *United States Navy in the Pacific*, 81–87, for a discussion of Kempff.
37. Dix, *World's Navies*, 35.
38. Cradock to Rear Admiral Bruce, dispatch, June 20, 1900, PRO ADM 116/115.
39. Major E.W.M. Norie, *Official Account of Military Operations in China 1900–01* (London: War Office, 1903), in PRO WO 33/285.
40. "Account of Mrs. James Jones, American Visitor," in Sharf and Harrington, *Eyewitnesses*, 91.
41. "China 1900: Officers and Men Recommended for Service," PRO ADM 1/7456.
42. British account of military operations in China, WO 33/285.
43. "Report of Captain M. Nagamine, Japanese Naval Officer," in Sharf and Harrington, *Eyewitnesses*, 96.
44. "Report on Action at Taku [Dagu] on June 17, 1900."
45. Dix, *World's Navies*, 40–41.
46. Cradock to Bruce, dispatch, June 20, 1900.
47. Bruce, report to the Admiralty, June 25, 1900.
48. "Account of Chief Officer J. Gordon, Steamship Officer," in Sharf and Harrington, *Eyewitnesses*, 94.
49. "Account of Mrs. James Jones, American Visitor," 92.
50. Roger Keyes, *Adventures Ashore and Afloat* (London: White Lion, 1939), 217.

51. Ibid., 218.
52. "Report on Action at Taku [Dagu] on June 17, 1900."
53. Keyes, *Ashore and Afloat*, 218.
54. Keyes to Bruce, June 17, 1900, PRO ADM 116/115.
55. Bruce, report to the Admiralty, June 25, 1900.
56. "Account of Mrs. James Jones, American Visitor," 92.
57. Copy of a telegram received from the governor of Shantung, n.d., PRO ADM 125/109.
58. Jerome Ch'en, "The Nature and Characteristics of the Boxer Movement—a Morphological Study," *Bulletin of the School of Oriental and African Studies* 23, no. 2 (1960): 287–308.
59. Seymour, report to the Admiralty, June 27, 1900.
60. Taussig, "Experiences," 415.
61. Ibid.
62. Seymour, report to the Admiralty, June 27, 1900.
63. Ibid.
64. Mersey, *Year in China*, 177.
65. Seymour, report to the Admiralty, June 27, 1900.
66. Ibid.
67. Mersey, *Year in China*, 180.
68. Seymour, report to the Admiralty, June 27, 1900.
69. Mersey, *Year in China*, 180–81.
70. Quoted in Donald F. Bittner, "Bored in Bermuda, Died in China: The Military Career (1890–1900) of Captain H.T.R. Lloyd, Royal Marine Light Infantry," *Mariner's Mirror* (2004): 410–26.

## 5: "THE FAULT OF NATURE"

1. Joseph K. Taussig, "Experiences During the Boxer Rebellion," *United States Naval Institute Proceedings* 53, no. 4 (1927): 419.
2. Seymour, report to the Admiralty, June 27, 1900, PRO ADM 116/114.
3. Taussig, "Experiences," 419.
4. Clive Bigham Mersey, *A Year in China, 1899–1900* (New York: Macmillan, 1901), 181–84.
5. Quoted in Donald F. Bittner, "Bored in Bermuda, Died in China: The Military Career (1890–1900) of Captain H.T.R. Lloyd, Royal Marine Light Infantry," *Mariner's Mirror* (2004): 410–26.
6. Ibid.
7. Mersey, *Year in China*, 186–87.
8. Seymour, report to the Admiralty, June 27, 1900.
9. Carles to Bruce, June 18, 1900, FO 674/84.
10. Tom Walsh, "Herbert Hoover and the Boxer Rebellion," *Prologue* 19, no. 1 (1987): 34–40.

11. Colonel Dorward to Secretary of State for War, June 17, 1900, WO 28/302.
12. WO 33/285, Major E.W.M. Norie, *Official Account of Military Operations in China, 1900–1901*, 14.
13. Bruce to Admiralty nos. 2 & 3, telegrams, June 21, 1900, PRO ADM 116/114.
14. Harry Alanson Ellsworth, *One Hundred Eighty Landings of United States Marines, 1800–1934* (Washington, D.C.: History and Museums Division, Headquarters, U.S. Marine Corps, 1974), 35.
15. *Annual Reports of the Navy Department* (1900), 1151.
16. James J. Sullivan, "The Diary of Pvt. Sullivan," *Marine Corps Gazette* 52, no. 11 (1968): 68–74.
17. U.S. Infantry School, *Monographs of the World War* (Fort Benning, Ga.: Infantry School, 1923), 658; see also Francis X. Holbrook, "Brave Hearts and Bright Weapons," *Marine Corps Gazette* 57, no. 11 (1973): 56–65.
18. Ellsworth, *One Hundred Eighty Landings*, 36.
19. *Annual Reports of the Navy Department* (1900), 1151.
20. Ibid.
21. Alfred Temple Patterson, "A Midshipman in the Boxer Rebellion," *Mariner's Mirror* (1977): 351–58.
22. Quotations from Sullivan, "Diary of Pvt. Sullivan."
23. Michael Miller, "Marines in the Boxer Rebellion," *American History Illustrated* 22, no. 9 (1988): 38–47.
24. Robert D. Heinl Jr., "Hell in China," *Marine Corps Gazette* 43, no. 11 (1959): 55–68.
25. Ibid.
26. Taku [Dagu] Commissioner to Secretary of State for War, June 26, 1900, PRO WO 106/6265.
27. Frederick Brown, *From Tientsin to Peking with the Allied Forces* (New York: Arno, 1970), 31.
28. Charles C. Dix, *The World's Navies in the Boxer Rebellion (China 1900)* (London: Digby, Long, 1905), 69.
29. Norie, *Military Operations* (1903), in WO 33/285.
30. Ibid.
31. Mersey, *Year in China*, 188.
32. WO 33/285.
33. Bruce, report to the Admiralty, June 25, 1900, PRO ADM 116/114.
34. Graham Henry Stuart, *French Foreign Policy from Fashoda to Serajevo (1898–1914)* (New York: Century, 1920), 53.
35. Midleton [William Brodrick] to Salisbury, June 12, 1900, PRO 30/67/5.
36. See, for example, "List of Foreign Vessels at Taku [Dagu]," June 2, 1900, in PRO ADM 116/114.
37. Salisbury to Whitehead, June 12, 1900, PRO 30/67/5.

38. Midleton Papers, n.d. 1900, PRO 30/67/5.
39. Salisbury to Brodrich, June 15, 1900, PRO 30/67/5.
40. Ariane Knüsel, "'Western Civilization' Against 'Hordes of Yellow Savages': British Perceptions of the Boxer Rebellion," *Asiatische Studien* (2008): 69.
41. Salisbury, "Memo as to Position at Taku [Dagu]," June 25, 1900, PRO 30/67/5.
42. Secretary of State for India to Viceroy of India, June 18, 1900, WO 28/302.
43. Viceroy of India to Secretary of State for India, June 22, 1900, PRO WO 106/6265.
44. C. A. Bayly, "The Boxer Uprising and India: Globalizing Myths," in *The Boxers, China, and the World*, ed. Robert Bickers and R. G. Tiedemann (New York: Rowman & Littlefield, 2007), 147–55.
45. Thomas R. Metcalf, *Imperial Connections: India in the Indian Ocean Arena, 1860–1920* (Berkeley: University of California Press, 2007), 88.
46. "Reports on the Working of the Intelligence Branch in Some Recent Campaigns (1895–1901)," PRO WO 106/290.
47. Secretary of State for India to Viceroy of India, June 29, 1900, PRO WO 32/6144.
48. House of Commons Debates, July 26, 1900, vol. 86, 1299.
49. House of Commons Debates, July 23, 1900, vol. 86, 853–54.
50. Dorward to Secretary of State for War, June 18, 1900, Bruce to Adjutant General, June 19, 1900, PRO WO 106/6265.
51. MacArthur to Adjutant General, telegram, June 16, 1900, in *Military Operations in China* (Washington, D.C.: War Office, 1900), 7:142.
52. Adjutant General to MacArthur, June 16, 1900, ibid.
53. Charles Dana Gibson and E. Kay Gibson, *Over Seas: U.S. Army Maritime Operations 1898 Through the Fall of the Philippines* (Camden, Maine: Ensign, 2002), 85.
54. Preceding account and quotations taken from Fred R. Brown, *History of the Ninth U.S. Infantry, 1799–1909* (Chicago: R. R. Donnelley & Sons, 1909), 430–50.
55. William Patchin (Ninth U.S. Infantry), Spanish-American War Veterans Survey 51/25, Military History Institute.
56. Diana Preston, "An Ohioan in China: Adna Chaffee and the Boxer Rebellion," *Timeline* 19, no. 1 (2002): 32–47.
57. Adjutant General to Chaffee, telegram, June 30, 1900, in WO 33/285, 145.
58. Figures for table from WO 33/285, 32.
59. Quotations from Gordon Casserly, *The Land of the Boxers* (London: Longmans, Green, 1903), 8–21.
60. R. G. Cooper, "A Private's View of the Siege of Peking in 1900," *Journal of the Society for Army Historical Research* (1983): 81–91.
61. Huanwen Cheng and Donald G. Davis, "Loss of a Recorded Heritage:

Destruction of Chinese Books in the Peking Siege of 1900," *Library Trends* 55, no. 3 (2007): 431–41.

62. "China, 1900: Officers and Men Recommended for Services," PRO ADM 1/7456.

63. Ibid.

64. Heinl, "Hell in China."

65. Sam S. Richardson, *The Royal Marines and Hong Kong* (Hong Kong: Royal Marines Historical Society, 1997), 17.

66. John T. Myers, "Military Operations and Defenses of the Siege of Peking," *Proceedings of the United States Naval Institute* 28, no. 3 (1902): 549, 551.

67. For the former, see Diana Preston, *The Boxer Rebellion: The Dramatic Story of China's War on Foreigners That Shook the World in the Summer of 1900* (New York: Berkley, 2001), 279; for the latter, see Roger Thompson, "Reporting the Taiyuan Massacre: Culture and Politics in the China War of 1900," in *Boxers, China, and the World*, ed. Bickers and Tiedemann, 65–93.

68. Edward Hobart Seymour, *My Naval Career and Travels* (London: Smith, Elder, 1911), 184.

69. Richard Brooks, *The Long Arm of Empire: Naval Brigades from the Crimea to the Boxer Rebellion* (London: Constable, 1999), 241.

## 6: THE BATTLE OF TIANJIN

1. "China Medal 1900," PRO MINT 20/34.

2. Seymour to Admiralty, July 12, 1900, PRO ADM 116/114.

3. General Dorward to War Office, July 19, 1900, PRO ADM 116/114.

4. WO 33/285, 28–31.

5. Salisbury to Sir E. Monson, July 3, 1900, PRO ADM 116/116.

6. See, for example, the exchange at House of Commons Debates, July 12, 1900, vol. 85, c. 1305.

7. Brigadier General Gaussen, "Under a German C-in-C," *Cavalry Journal* (1940): 523–42.

8. "General Alexander Rittich's pamphlet on railways," in FO 65/1599.

9. Quoted in Graham Henry Stuart, *French Foreign Policy from Fashoda to Serajevo (1898–1914)* (New York: Century, 1920), 63.

10. Ibid., 61.

11. Alfred Temple Patterson, "A Midshipman in the Boxer Rebellion," *Mariner's Mirror* (1977): 351–58.

12. A.A.S. Barnes, *On Active Service with the Chinese Regiment: A Record of the Operations of the First Chinese Regiment in North China from March to October 1900*, 2nd ed. (London: Grant Richards, 1902), 51.

13. James Ricalton, *China Through the Stereoscope* (New York: Underwood & Underwood, 1901), 198.
14. Frederick Brown, *From Tientsin to Peking with the Allied Forces* (New York: Arno, 1970), 35.
15. Ibid.
16. Charles C. Dix, *The World's Navies in the Boxer Rebellion (China 1900)* (London: Digby, Long, 1905), 64.
17. *The Boxer Rising: A History of the Boxer Trouble in China* ([Shanghai]: Shanghai Mercury, 1900), 15.
18. Barnes, *Active Service*, 84.
19. Dix, *World's Navies*, 72.
20. Ricalton, *Stereoscope*, 206.
21. Barnes, *Active Service*, 48.
22. Norie, *Official Account of Military Operations in China 1900–01*, PRO WO 33/285.
23. Seymour to Admiralty, July 12, 1900, PRO ADM 116/114.
24. Anne Skelly, "The Eagle and the Dragon," *American History Illustrated* 22, no. 9 (1988): 34–37.
25. Barnes, *Active Service*, 84.
26. Seymour to Admiralty, July 12, 1900, PRO ADM 116/114.
27. Ricalton, *Stereoscope*, 191.
28. James Harrison Wilson, *China: Travels and Investigations in the "Middle Kingdom"—a Study of Its Civilization and Possibilities, Together with an Account of the Boxer War, the Relief of the Legations, and the Re-establishment of Peace*, 3rd ed. (New York: D. Appleton, 1901), 377–78.
29. Both quotations from Fred R. Brown, *History of the Ninth U.S. Infantry, 1799–1909* (Chicago: R. R. Donnelley & Sons, 1909).
30. L.W.C. Davidson and U.S. Navy, "Operations in North China," *Proceedings of the United States Naval Institute* 26, no. 4 (1900): 637–46.
31. "China 1900: Officers and Men Recommended for Services," PRO ADM 1/7456.
32. Frederic Alan Sharf and Peter Harrington, *China, 1900: The Eyewitnesses Speak: The Experience of Westerners in China During the Boxer Rebellion, as Described by Participants in Letters, Diaries, and Photographs* (Mechanicsburg, Pa.: Stackpole Books, 2000), 117.
33. Bayly quoted ibid.
34. Barnes, *Active Service*, 78.
35. Ricalton, *Stereoscope*, 218.
36. Davidson and U.S. Navy, "Operations in North China."
37. Henry Leonard, "The Visit of the Allies to China in 1900," in *Civil War and Miscellaneous Papers* (Boston: Military Historical Society of Massachusetts, 1918), 313.

38. Quoted in Sharf and Harrington, *Eyewitnesses*, 147.
39. Brown, *From Tientsin to Peking*, 38.
40. Dix, *World's Navies*, 177.
41. Pope, "The Battle of Tientsin," in *Monographs of the World War.*
42. Davidson and U.S. Navy, "Operations in North China," 644.
43. Quoted in Sharf and Harrington, *Eyewitnesses*, 147.
44. Dix, *World's Navies*, 177.
45. Quoted in Sharf and Harrington, *Eyewitnesses*, 148.
46. Ricalton, *Stereoscope*, 235.
47. Quoted in Robert D. Heinl Jr., "Hell in China," *Marine Corps Gazette* 43, no. 11 (1959): 55–68.
48. Quoted in William J. Duiker, *Cultures in Collision: The Boxer Rebellion* (San Rafael, Calif.: Presidio, 1978), 142.
49. Barnes, *Active Service*, 94.
50. Ricalton, *Stereoscope*, 231.
51. Dix, *World's Navies*, 186.
52. Barnes, *Active Service*, 102.
53. Quoted in Edith W. Newell, "Manila to Peking: Letters Home, 1898–1901," *Oregon Historical Quarterly* 80, no. 2 (1979): 171–96.
54. Leonard, "Visit of the Allies to China, 1900," 313.
55. Lewis Bernstein, "After the Fall: Tianjin Under Foreign Occupation, 1900–1902," in *The Boxers, China, and the World*, ed. Robert Bickers and R. G. Tiedemann (New York: Rowman & Littlefield, 2007), 133–46.
56. Ricalton, *Stereoscope*, 225.
57. Bound scrapbook of newspaper cuttings concerning Boxer Rebellion, 1900, National Army Museum 1986-01-73-1.
58. Ibid.

## 7: THE SECOND EXPEDITION

1. Allen S. Will, *World-Crisis in China, 1900: A Short Account of the Outbreak of the War with the "Boxers," and Ensuing Foreign Complications* (Baltimore: John Murphy, 1900), 7.
2. Michael Chanan, *The Dream That Kicks: The Prehistory and Early Years of Cinema in Britain*, 2nd ed. (London: Routledge, 1995), 240.
3. *Annual Reports of the War Department* (1900), 11.
4. Quoted ibid.
5. July 13, for example, had seen the highest day's casualties of the entire siege. See, for example, Reginald Hargreaves, "Comrades in Arms," *Marine Corps Gazette* 48, no. 10 (1964): 50–55.
6. Wray to Admiralty, Aug. 26, 1900, PRO ADM 116/114.
7. Jack W. Jaunal, "Bill Horton and the Boxer Rebellion," *Marine Corps Gazette* 55, no. 11 (1971): 29–32.

8. Robert Coltman, *Beleaguered in Peking: The Boxer's War Against the Foreigner* (Philadelphia: F. A. Davis, 1901), 119.

9. Hans Van de Ven, "Robert Hart and Gustav Detring During the Boxer Rebellion," *Modern Asian Studies* 40, no. 3 (2006): 631–62.

10. MacDonald to Salisbury, Sept. 20, 1900, PRO ADM 116/114.

11. Manfred Görtemaker, *Deutschland im 19. Jahrhundert: Entwicklungslinien* (Opladen: Leske + Budrich, 1996), 357.

12. The Russian poet Vladimir Soloviov wrote a poem, "The Dragon," that emphasized those feelings and dedicated it to the kaiser. Quoted in E. Sarkisyanz, "Russian Attitudes Toward Asia," *Russian Review* 13, no. 4 (1954): 245–54.

13. Coltman, *Beleaguered in Peking*, 125–26.

14. Dorward to Secretary of State for War, Aug. 4, 1900, PRO WO 106/6265.

15. Salisbury to Sir E. Monson, July 31, 1900, PRO ADM 116/117.

16. Secretary of State for India to Gaselee, Aug. 9, 1900, PRO WO 106/6265.

17. *Annual Reports of the War Department* (1900), p. 6.

18. Operations of the Japanese Contingent, Intelligence Division, War Office, Mar. 1901, National Army Museum 9007-79.

19. "Half-Yearly List of Foreign War Vessels of Which Photographs Are Required," July 1900, PRO FO 228/1340.

20. Paul Henry Clements, *The Boxer Rebellion: A Political and Diplomatic Review* (1915; New York: AMS, 1979), 135.

21. Frederick Brown, *From Tientsin to Peking with the Allied Forces* (New York: Arno, 1970), 1.

22. Major General Sir John Ardagh, "The Position in China," Aug. 8, 1900, PRO 30/42/22.

23. See also House of Commons Debates, July 31, 1900, vol. 87, c. 162.

24. Robert Francis Gartside-Tipping, letters and memoir, NAM 1969-02-3.

25. Howell to Admiralty, Aug. 2, 1900, PRO ADM 116/115.

26. See account of Major Jesse Lee of the Ninth Infantry, Spanish-American War Veterans Survey 51/20, Military History Institute.

27. Carleton Frederick Waite, *Some Elements of International Military Co-operation in the Suppression of the 1900 Antiforeign Rising in China with Special Reference to the Forces of the United States* (Los Angeles: University of Southern California Press, 1935), 9.

28. Fred R. Brown, *History of the Ninth U.S. Infantry, 1799–1909* (Chicago: R. R. Donnelley & Sons, 1909).

29. Charles C. Dix, *The World's Navies in the Boxer Rebellion (China 1900)* (London: Digby, Long, 1905), 197.

30. William C. Harlow, *Logistical Support of the China Relief Expedition* (Fort Leavenworth, Kans.: U.S. Army Command and General Staff College, 1991), 139.

31. Charles Henry Martin Papers, Military History Institute.
32. Gartside-Tipping, Aug. 3, 1900, entry, letters and memoir.
33. Edith W. Newell, "Manila to Peking: Letters Home, 1898–1901," *Oregon Historical Quarterly* 80, no. 2 (1979): 171–96.
34. China Expeditionary Force Orders, 1900, for a list, NAM 2008-06-7.
35. Quoted in Diana Preston, "An Ohioan in China: Adna Chaffee and the Boxer Rebellion," *Timeline* 19, no. 1 (2002): 32–47.
36. Account of Lee.
37. H. B. Vaughan, *St. George and the Chinese Dragon* (London: C. A. Pearson, 1902), 42.
38. "The March to Pekin, 1900—with Comments by an Officer Who Served with the China Relief Expedition," *Quartermaster Review* 11, no. 5 (1932): 36–41.
39. Both quotations from A.A.S. Barnes, *On Active Service with the Chinese Regiment: A Record of the Operations of the First Chinese Regiment in North China from March to October 1900*, 2nd ed. (London: Grant Richards, 1902), 113.
40. PRO WO 106/73, *Report on the Engineer Operations of the British Contingent, China Field Force, July to October, 1900.*
41. The shift in the court's thinking is discussed in Sterling Seagrave and Peggy Seagrave, *Dragon Lady: The Life and Legend of the Last Empress of China* (New York: Vintage, 1993), 354–55.
42. Gartside-Tipping, Aug. 2, 1900, entry, letters and memoir.
43. Martin Papers.
44. Vaughan, *St. George and the Chinese Dragon*, 54.
45. Lieutenant A. G. Churchill, "Japanese Diary of the Tientsin-Beijing Operation," Dec. 26, 1900, PRO WO 32/6145.
46. Ibid.
47. PRO WO 106/73.
48. Gartside-Tipping, Aug. 5, 1900, entry, letters and memoir.
49. Vaughan, *St. George and the Chinese Dragon*, 51.
50. Ibid., 65.
51. Account of Lee.
52. Gaselee, account of the march, Aug. 1900, WO 28/302.
53. Gartside-Tipping, Aug. 5, 1900, entry, letters and memoir.
54. Brown, *From Tientsin to Peking*, 71.
55. Quotations from Frederic May Wise and Meigs Oliver Frost, *A Marine Tells It to You* (New York: J. H. Sears, 1929), 50–51.
56. Colonel Aaron Simon Daggett, report on the Battle of Yang Tsun [Huang-cun], Aug. 7, 1900, in *America in the China Relief Expedition* (Kansas City, Mo.: Hudson-Kimberly, 1903), 177.
57. Ibid.

58. Captain C. H. Martin, report of Aug. 7, 1900, in *Military Operations in China* (Washington, D.C.: War Office, 1900), 7:50.
59. All quotations in Daggett, *China Relief Expedition*, 177–78.
60. Ibid., 178.
61. Ibid., 64.
62. Martin Papers.
63. Gary Murrell, "Perfection of Means, Confusion of Goals: The Military Career of Charles Henry Martin" (Ph.D. diss., University of Oregon, 1995).
64. "Report of Maj. Gen. Adna R. Chaffee, Commanding China Relief Expedition, Battle of Yangtsun [Huangcun], August 6, 1900," in *Military Operations in China*, 31.
65. *Annual Reports of the War Department* 1, no. 9 (1900), 12.
66. Gartside-Tipping, Aug. 6, 1900, entry, letters and memoir.
67. Brigadier General Gaussen, "Under a German C-in-C," *Cavalry Journal* (1940): 536.
68. Quoted in Amar Singh et al., *Reversing the Gaze: Amar Singh's Diary, a Colonial Subject's Narrative of Imperial India* (Boulder, Colo.: Westview, 2002), 131.
69. Jane Elliott, *Some Did It for Civilisation, Some Did It for Their Country: A Revised View of the Boxer War* (Hong Kong: Chinese University Press, 2002), 471.
70. Seagrave and Seagrave, *Dragon Lady*, 360.
71. Elliott, *Some Did It for Civilisation*, 472.
72. Quoted in Clements, *Boxer Rebellion*, 145.
73. Wray to Admiralty, Aug. 26, 1900.
74. Lanxin Xiang, *The Origins of the Boxer War: A Multinational Study* (London: Routledge, 2003), 172.
75. James Bevan, "With the U.S. Marines on the March to Peking, China—1900," *Leatherneck* 18, no. 6 (1935): 5–7, 55–56; for rainfall, see climate series at http://ncdc.noaa.gov.
76. Robert S. Rush and William W. Epley, *Multinational Operations, Alliances, and International Military Cooperation: Past and Future: Proceedings of the Fifth Workshop of the Partnership for Peace Consortium's Military History Working Group*, Vienna, Austria, Apr. 4–8, 2005 (Washington, D.C.: Center for Military History, U.S. Army, 2006), 55.
77. Churchill, "Japanese Diary."
78. Gartside-Tipping, Aug. 8, 1900, entry, letters and memoir.
79. Churchill, "Japanese Diary."
80. Gartside-Tipping, Aug. 9, 1900, entry, letters and memoir.
81. Letter by J. W. Mitchell, Oct. 13, 1900, NAM 8102-31.
82. Robert D. Heinl Jr., "Hell in China," *Marine Corps Gazette* 43, no. 11 (1959): 55–68.

83. Vaughan, *St. George and the Chinese Dragon*, 66.
84. Ibid.
85. Richard Brooks, *The Long Arm of Empire: Naval Brigades from the Crimea to the Boxer Rebellion* (London: Constable, 1999), 245.
86. Ibid.
87. Francis X. Holbrook, "Brave Hearts and Bright Weapons," *Marine Corps Gazette* 57, no. 11 (1973): 56–65.
88. "March to Pekin."
89. Henry Savage Landor, *China and the Allies* (New York: Scribner's, 1901), 364–65.
90. Wilbur J. Chamberlin and Georgia Louise Chamberlin, *Ordered to China: Letters of Wilbur J. Chamberlin Written from China While Under Commission from the New York "Sun" During the Boxer Uprising of 1900 and the International Complications Which Followed* (New York: F. A. Stokes, 1903), 128.
91. Frederic Alan Sharf and Peter Harrington, *The Boxer Rebellion, China, 1900: The Artists' Perspective* (London: Greenhill Books, 2000), 28.
92. James Harrison Wilson, *China: Travels and Investigations in the "Middle Kingdom"—a Study of Its Civilization and Possibilities, Together with an Account of the Boxer War, the Relief of the Legations, and the Re-establishment of Peace*, 3rd ed. (New York: D. Appleton, 1901), 390.
93. Chamberlin and Chamberlin, *Ordered to China*, 128.
94. Barnes, *Active Service*, 122.
95. Coded message from MacDonald to Gaselee, Aug. 5, 1900, NAM 6807-475, has both the message and the scribbled numbers.
96. Wray to Admiralty, Aug. 26, 1900.
97. Edward A. Dieckmann Sr., "Dan Daly: Reluctant Hero," *Marine Corps Gazette* 44, no. 11 (1960): 22–27.
98. Preston, "Ohioan in China."

## 8: "WITH SHUT MOUTHS, THEY TOOK THEIR MEASURE"

1. Lieutenant A. G. Churchill, "Japanese Diary of the Tientsin-Beijing Operation," Dec. 26, 1900, PRO WO 32/6145.
2. Robert Francis Gartside-Tipping, letters and memoir, NAM 1969-02-3.
3. *New York Times*, Aug. 15, 1900.
4. Gartside-Tipping, Aug. 14, 1900, entry, letters and memoir.
5. Ibid.
6. Gaselee, account of the march, Aug. 1900, WO 28/302; and Gaselee to Secretary of State for India, Jan. 17, 1901, WO 28/302.
7. James Bevan, "With the U.S. Marines on the March to Peking, China—1900," *Leatherneck* 18, no. 6 (1935): 5–7, 55–56.

8. Ibid., 56. Titus account here and following drawn from Military History Institute, SAW Veteran's Survey, Titus, Calvin.

9. Daggett, report of Aug. 19, 1900, in *Annual Reports of the War Department* 1, no. 9 (1900): 60.

10. Charles Pelot Summerall, "The Way of Duty, Honor, Country," unpublished manuscript, courtesy of Tim Nenninger.

11. Both quotations from telegram from General Gaselee, Aug. 15, 1900, PRO ADM 125/109.

12. Daggett, report of Aug. 19, 1900, 60.

13. Gartside-Tipping, Aug. 14, 1900, entry, letters and memoir.

14. Roger Keyes, letter of Sept. 6, 1900, in Frederic Alan Sharf and Peter Harrington, *China, 1900: The Eyewitnesses Speak: The Experience of Westerners in China During the Boxer Rebellion, as Described by Participants in Letters, Diaries, and Photographs* (Mechanicsburg, Pa.: Stackpole Books, 2000), 205.

15. Frederick Brown, *From Tientsin to Peking with the Allied Forces* (New York: Arno, 1970), 109.

16. Gartside-Tipping, Aug. 14, 1900, entry, letters and memoir.

17. Churchill, "Japanese Diary."

18. Ibid.

19. Telegram to Japanese Consul at Tianjin, enclosure from W. R. Carles to Salisbury, Aug. 20, 1900, PRO ADM 116/116.

20. Mingzheng Shi, "From Imperial Gardens to Public Parks: The Transformation of Urban Space in Early Twentieth-Century Beijing," *Modern China* 24, no. 3 (1998): 219-54.

21. Quoted in PRO WO 106/6247, entry of Aug. 15, 1900.

22. Frederic May Wise and Meigs Oliver Frost, *A Marine Tells It to You* (New York: J. H. Sears, 1929), 60.

23. Summerall, "Way of Duty."

24. Wise and Frost, *Marine Tells It to You*, 61.

25. Ibid.

26. Ibid.

27. Daggett, report of Aug. 19, 1900, 60.

28. Ibid. and Littleton Waller, "Report," *Annual Reports of the War Department* 1, no. 9 (1900): 82.

29. *Annual Reports of the War Department* 1, no. 9 (1900): 66.

30. Daggett, report of Aug. 19, 1900, 60.

31. Gaselee to Secretary of State for India, Jan. 17, 1901, WO 28/302.

32. Daggett, report of Aug. 19, 1900, 60.

33. Leslie R. Groves Sr. Papers, 1891-1901, Military History Institute.

34. William J. Duiker, *Cultures in Collision: The Boxer Rebellion* (San Rafael, Calif.: Presidio, 1978), 175.

35. Gartside-Tipping, Editor's Note, undated, letters and memoir.

36. *New York Times*, Aug. 17, 1900.
37. Roger Thomson, "Military Dimensions of the 'Boxer Uprising' in Shanxi Province," in *Warfare in Chinese History*, ed. Hans J. Van de Ven (Leiden: Brill, 2000), 313.
38. Frederic Alan Sharf and Peter Harrington, *The Boxer Rebellion, China, 1900: The Artists' Perspective* (London: Greenhill Books, 2000), 26.
39. Ibid., 25.
40. Ibid.
41. Amar Singh et al., *Reversing the Gaze: Amar Singh's Diary, a Colonial Subject's Narrative of Imperial India* (Boulder, Colo.: Westview, 2002), 130.
42. *Philadelphia City and State*, Jan. 10, 1901, 409.
43. Michael H. Hunt, "The Forgotten Occupation: Peking, 1900–1901," *Pacific Historical Review* 48, no. 4 (1979): 501–29.
44. Ibid.
45. Charles Henry Martin Papers, Aug. 20, 1900, Military History Institute.
46. Singh et al., *Reversing the Gaze*, 129–30.
47. Wilbur J. Chamberlin and Georgia Louise Chamberlin, *Ordered to China: Letters of Wilbur J. Chamberlin Written from China While Under Commission from the New York "Sun" During the Boxer Uprising of 1900 and the International Complications Which Followed* (New York: F. A. Stokes, 1903), 99.
48. Ibid., 73.
49. James Hevia, "Looting and Its Discontents: Moral Discourse and the Plunder of Beijing, 1900–1901," in *The Boxers, China, and the World*, ed. Robert Bickers and R. G. Tiedemann (New York: Rowman & Littlefield, 2007), 93; G. Thompson Brown, "Through Fire and Sword: Presbyterians and the Boxer Year in North China," *Journal of Presbyterian History* 78, no. 3 (2000): 193–206.
50. Hevia, "Looting," 102.
51. Ben Middleton, "Scandals of Empire: The Looting of North China and the Japanese Public Sphere," in *Boxers, China, and the World*, ed. Bickers and Tiedemann, 115–32.
52. Unnamed, quoted in William Roscoe Thayer, *The Life and Letters of John Hay* (Boston: Houghton Mifflin, 1915), 244.
53. Quotations from Chamberlin and Chamberlin, *Ordered to China*, 67.
54. Ibid., 129.
55. Hans Van de Ven, "Robert Hart and Gustav Detring During the Boxer Rebellion," *Modern Asian Studies* (2006): 631–62.
56. Chamberlin and Chamberlin, *Ordered to China*, 118–19.
57. Quoted in Sharf and Harrington, *Artists' Perspective*, 30.
58. Ibid.
59. Ibid., 31.
60. Photograph album and diary kept by S. H. Climo, Twenty-fourth Punjabis, 1900–1901, NAM 1974-03-102-1.

61. Letter by J. W. Mitchell, Oct. 13, 1900, NAM 8102-31.
62. T. G. Otte, "'Not Proficient in Table-Thumping': Sir Ernest Satow at Peking, 1900–1906," *Diplomacy & Statecraft* 13, no. 2 (2002): 167.
63. Brigadier General Gaussen, "Under a German C-in-C," *Cavalry Journal* (1940): 523–42.
64. Gaselee to Secretary of State for India, Aug. 29, 1900, PRO WO 106/6265.
65. Otte, "Table-Thumping," 167.
66. Salisbury to Claude MacDonald, Oct. 8, 1900, PRO ADM 116/116.
67. Van de Ven, "Robert Hart and Gustav Detring," 641.
68. J.O.P. Bland, *Li Hung-chang* (London: Constable, 1917), 209.
69. "Diary of the Principal Events in China During the Boxer Rebellion, 1900," in PRO CAB 37/53.
70. Paul Henry Clements, *The Boxer Rebellion: A Political and Diplomatic Review* (1915; New York: AMS, 1979), 202.
71. Quoted ibid., 200–201.
72. Quotations from Theodore McNelly, *Sources in Modern East Asian History and Politics* (New York: Appleton-Century-Crofts, 1967), 13–22.
73. Ibid.

## CONCLUSION

1. *New York Times*, Jan. 2, 1901.
2. Charles Henry Martin Papers, n.d., Military History Institute.
3. Shumpei Okamoto, "A Phase of Meiji Japan's Attitude Toward China: The Case of Komura Jutaro," *Modern Asian Studies* 13, no. 3 (1979): 431–57.
4. Fred Greguras, "Revisiting the Fifty-five Days at Peking," *Journal of America's Military Past* 32, no. 2 (2006): 37–49.
5. PRO MINT 20/34, *China Medal 1900*, September 1901.
6. *Missionary Herald at Home and Abroad* 97, no. 5 (May 1901): 212.
7. Mark Twain, "Editorial Notes," *Messenger and Visitor*, Mar. 6, 1901. Oddly, it is Chinese historians who have been much kinder to the missionaries in recent years. Ryan Dunch, "Beyond Cultural Imperialism: Cultural Theory, Christian Missions, and Global Modernity," *History and Theory* 41, no. 3 (2002): 301–25.
8. G. Thompson Brown, "Through Fire and Sword: Presbyterians and the Boxer Year in North China," *Journal of Presbyterian History* 78, no. 3 (2000): 193–206.
9. Amar Singh et al., *Reversing the Gaze: Amar Singh's Diary, a Colonial Subject's Narrative of Imperial India* (Boulder, Colo.: Westview, 2002), 205–206.
10. "British Memorials in Peking and Tientsin by a British Resident in Peking, 1927," in *The Peking and Tientsin Times* (Tianjin: Tientsin Press, 1927).

11. Mary Backus Rankin, "Nationalistic Contestation and Mobilization Politics: Practice and Rhetoric of Railway-Rights," *Modern China* 28, no. 3 (2002): 315–61.

12. Elizabeth J. Perry, "When Peasants Speak: Sources for the Study of Chinese Rebellions," *Modern China* 6, no. 1 (1980): 72–85.

13. Quoted ibid.

14. Quoted in Stuart Schram, "Some Recent Studies of Revolutionary Movements in China in the Early Twentieth Century," *Bulletin of the School of Oriental and African Studies* 35, no. 3 (1972): 588–605.

15. *The Yi Ho Tuan Movement of 1900* (Beijing: Foreign Languages Press, 1976), 124.

16. Quotation from Jeffrey Wasserstrom, " 'Civilization' and Its Discontents," *Theory and Society* 16, no. 5 (1987): 688.

17. Quoted ibid., 684.

# ACKNOWLEDGMENTS

Writing a book is really a group effort. I get the reward of having my name on the cover, but all the people to whom I owe debts of gratitude will get only this small but heartfelt acknowledgment.

The idea for the book was first suggested by Bongrae Seok in a hallway conversation. Such is the value of having a kind and generous colleague next door. My colleagues at Alvernia University were all that way, and I am particularly grateful to Tom Flynn, Doug Smith, Tim Blessing, Jerry Vigna, Janae Sholtz, Rick Stichler, and Kevin Godfrey. Donna Yarri was my scholarly companion, as was Marc DiPaolo. Victoria Williams was my friend in all things. My new Cornell University colleagues have been just as welcoming. Carol Hagen, Kim Niefer, Nicole Pfeifer, Jack Moran, Jess Matthews, Desmond Jagmohan, Sudeshna Mitra, and Simon Cotton have all been enormously supportive. Barry Strauss and Ed Baptist in the Cornell Department of History are friends.

Researching and writing the book has been supported by a range of people. The Military History Institute at the U.S. Army Heritage and Education Center was a wonderful source of information and was kind enough to give me the General and Mrs. Matthew B. Ridgway Military History Research Grant to help with the project. Richard Sommers was a constant font of good ideas. I hope I have treated Michael Lynch's beloved Manchus fairly and well. The folks at the National Army Museum in London were similarly helpful and highly professional, a pleasure in the ordinary course of things but even more remarkable the day an elderly veteran of World War II brought in a live grenade from that war to donate. "It hasn't gone off yet" was not the most reassuring comment from the gentleman, but the staff of the NAM handled it with aplomb. The folks at Hill and Wang should be noted as well. Thomas LeBien, Liz Maples, Dan Crissman, Dan Gerstle, and Stephen Weil all patiently encouraged me as I waded through the writing and editing. Needless to say, any and all mistakes are mine and mine alone.

My family, as always, has been immensely supportive. My parents, Joel and Rosemary, are getting older but never less vibrant. Madeline Silbey, who arrived in this world just as I was finishing my previous book, is slightly older than this current project, but not by much. She is smarter than us all. I have never asked my wife, Mari, to type my manuscripts, as is a hoary tradition for (male) history professors. She has nonetheless had to deal with a sometimes grumpy and often distracted husband and has done so with grace and love. This book is for her.

# INDEX